Vegetarian Judaism—

A Guide for Everyone

by Roberta Kalechofsky, Ph.D.

 Address inquiries to Micah Publications, 255 Humphrey St., Marblehead, MA 01945.
Fax: 781-639-0772. e-mail: micah@micahbooks.com
Website http://www.micahbooks.com

No part of this book purports to give medical advice or is intended to be used for medical purposes, or as replacement for professional medical attention.

Acknowledgements: Quotations from *The Hungry Soul* by Leon Kass, and from *Prisoned Chickens, Poisoned Eggs,* by Karen Davis, are reproduced by permission of the authors. Quotations from *Beyond Beef*, by Jeremy Rifkin are reproduced by permssion of Penquin, USA.

Book cover, "Tree of Life," by Sara Feldman

Printed by McNaughton & Gunn

Kalechofsky, Roberta.
Vegetarian Judaism : a guide for everyone / by Roberta Kalechofsky, Ph.D.
p. cm.
Includes bibliographical references and index.
ISBN 0-916288-45-5
1. Vegetarianism--Religious aspects--Judaism. 2. Ethics. Jewish.
I. Title.
BM538.V43K35 1998 97-48462
296.3'693--DC21 CIP

MICAH PUBLICATIONS, INC.

fear not, beasts of the field
for the pastures in the wilderness
are clothed with grass
the fig tree bears her fruit
and fig tree and vine yield their strength

Joel 2:22

Other Books by Roberta Kalechofsky

Fiction

K'tia, A Savior of the Jewish People

Bodmin: 1349---
An Epic Novel of Christians and Jews in the Plague Years

Solomon's Wisdon

Orestes in Progress

Justice, My Brother, My Sister

Poetry

The 6th Day of Creation

Haggadah For the Liberated Lamb

Non-Fiction

Autobiography of A Revolutionary:
Essays on Animal and Human Rights

George Orwell: A Monograph

Table of Contents

Chapters

Appendix

Foreword

The impressive growth of vegetarian practice and interest in recent times is primarily the result of growing preoccupation in our societies with our own human health. However, it is also a result of greater awareness of the lives and treatment of animals, as well as greater ecological consciousness.

As this book eloquently clarifies, these matters are of fundamental concern for Judaism, and thus vegetarianism in our time should be an imperative for Jews who seek to live in accordance with the values and responsibilities of the Jewish tradition.

Furthermore, central to these are our obligations toward other people, all created in the Divine Image. This book also demonstrates conclusively that if society at large maintained a vegetarian diet, there would be far more substantial resources available to obviate a great deal of the hunger, starvation, and distress that still prevail in much of the world.

In addition to these powerful arguments for Jewish vegetarianism, there is that Rabbinic tradition which views this lifestyle as the original, Divinely intended dietary ideal, to which we should aspire.

In providing public access to these principles, sources, and more, Roberta Kalechofsky has not only made a singular contribution to the promotion of the sublime ideals of Judaism, but has also facilitated the greater appreciation of the relevance of the Jewish tradition to the contemporary zeitgeist and modern-day challenges.

Thereby, she has helped advance the Jewish goal of "*tikkun olam* ," making our world a better place, and performed the Jewish ideal of *Kiddush Hashem*, sanctification of the Divine Name. Indeed the ultimate fulfillment of the latter depends upon our growing awareness of the Divine Presence in the whole of Creation, as the Prophet Zechariah states, "On that day the Lord shall be one and His name shall be one" (Zech.: 14:9).

Rabbi David Rosen
Israeli Delegate on Permanent Bi-Lateral Commission
With the Vatican
Director, Anti-Defamation League, Israel Office
President, World Conference on Religion and Peace

Acknowledgements

I am indebted to many people who took time out from their busy lives to read this book in manuscript form, and enrich it with their comments. For this task, which required religious and medical knowledge, I was blessed with a committee of readers with backgrounds in Judaica, medicine and science.

Richard Schwartz, as the author of *Judaism and Vegetarianism* and *Judaism and Global Survival*, needs no introduction. He has been an assiduous worker in this cause, with more than seventy articles on Judaism and vegetarianism, which can be found on the Virtual Yeshiva, at www.rasheit.org. I owe my own vegetarianism and, indeed, this book to his book, *Judaism and Vegetarianism,* which I read in manuscript form in 1982, and later published. His influence on a generation of Jewish vegetarians cannot be doubted.

In addition to Richard Schwartz, I have had the benefit of the most varied and conscientious of readers, such as Emanuel Goldman, Professor of Microbiology and Molecular Genetics at New Jersey Medical School in Newark, who also entertains us with his column, "The Vegetarian Cinophile," reviews of films with special interest from a vegetarian perspective; Charles Patterson, with a doctorate in religion from Columbia University and interest in civil and animal rights issue, reflected in books, such as *The Civil Rights Movement*, *Anti-semitism*, *The Road To the Holocaust and Beyond*, was able to relate the issue of animal cruelty to broader social questions. He is currently at work on a book about the common roots of violence against humans and animals. The hands-on experience of Israel Mossman who worked on a dairy farm in his younger days helped my understanding of how farmers make their decisions. A retired businessman with practical knowledge of the dairy and egg farming worlds, he is now the co-ordinator of

"Jewish Vegetarians of North America," and Associate Editor of "The Jewish Vegetarian Newsletter"; Susan Kalev, social worker, psychotherapist and former administrator of Vegetarian Vision, Inc., brought ten years of experience in the health care field in nutrition and holistic medicine; and Dovid Sears, author of books such as *Compassion for Humanity In the Jewish Tradition* , brought his perspective as a Breslav Chassid.

The study of the relationship of nutrition to health is both old and new. Generations of people have known that food is medicine, but the modern world is discovering this anew, under the aegis of science. Much of the information on this subject is fluid. Hence, the confusion which the public often feels. Much traditional knowledge about food has been destroyed; food itself in the modern world, subject to so much technological transformation, is constantly changing. Nutrition cannot be easily studied, for many of the effects of food are cumulative and can take years to understand. Dr. Jay Lavine sharpened my statements about vitamins, food benefits, and diseases related to meat products. As an ophthalmologist, with a specialty in preventive nutrition, and articles in the *Annals of Ophthalmology, Lancet, American Journal of Clinical Nutrition*, and elsewhere, his background was well suited for the task.

Karen Davis, Founder of United Poultry Concerns, did not read the manuscript, but as always, was generous with time on the telephone, when points needed clarification. Much thanks to Sara Feldman who was patient with cover designs to produce the symbolically rich "Tree of Life."

I am mindful of the fact that the laborious work of commenting on this book in manuscript form was a labor of conscience for all. For my husband, who brought his philosophical and scientific talents to this task, it was also a labor of love for me and patience with me. A thousand devils were in the details. He is my constant committee of one in all things I do, from the beginning to the end.

Introduction

"I give you every herb, seed and green thing. These shall be yours for food." *(Genesis 1:29)*

Richard Schwartz' book, *Judaism and Vegetarianism,* and Louis Berman's *Vegetarianism and The Jewish Tradition,* both published in 1982, brought to the attention of the Jewish people the values of vegetarianism and their place in traditional Judaism. Since the publication of these two books, the arguments, indeed the urgency, for vegetarianism have increased. Hence this book. Genetic engineering, cloning, the irradiation of food, the patenting of new life forms, the usurpation of seeds by the chemical industries are changing the nature of farming, and make it imperative for Jews to evaluate the food we eat in the light of our traditional concerns with diet. The increasing presence of pathogens, such as E.coli and salmonella make older inspection systems of meat and chicken obsolete. We now know more about the health hazards of meat *and* the cruelty involved in the production of animal-related foods, such as dairy and eggs, produced under modern methods. In the widest context, a revolution has taken place throughout all food production, from seeds to cows and chickens which should place the issue of food on the top of social action agendas. Genetic engineering may change the cultivation of fruits and vegetables as much as factory farming methods changed the rearing of animals.

Our focus is with the problem of animal husbandry and animal food, with how basic Jewish values are violated by the modern methods of producing animal food, and by the consumption of these foods. In the last century there was a dramatic shift in the diet of the populations in the Western, industrialized nations from a carbohydrate-based diet to a meat-protein-based diet. This shift had enormous consequences for our health and the health care system, for the environment, and for the tradition of husbandry. For Jews, the shift also affected traditional understanding of kashrut to the extent that it changed the breeding and feeding habits of animals.

All commercial meat, whether for the kosher market or the non-kosher market, is raised the same way. Cows and chickens are raised and fed on similar diets of grains, hormones, antibiotics, and chicken litter (a combination of sawdust and chicken manure which, in many cases, makes up 40% of a cow's diet.) The dairy and eggs of these animals come from the same animals, whether sold in a kosher market or a non-kosher market. (Hence, when we use the term "vegetarian" in this book, we refer to *all* animal products.) We call the new system of raising animals that came into place after the second world war, "factory farming," or "intensive rearing," because the animals are kept in close confinement, often in buildings that look like factories. The animals bred under this new system are sometimes called animal machines, or biomachines, for reasons which will become clear. The major distinction in kashrut today, concerning food animals, is salting the meat to remove as much blood as possible, and in the method of killing. Even the meat of castrated animals, forbidden in Leviticus, are accepted in the kosher market. The distinction between kosher and non-kosher meat is made at the ramp to the slaughtering house.

Both shechitah and hallal (Jewish and Muslim ritual slaughter) were exempt from the Humane Slaughter Act of 1958, which requires that animals be rendered unconscious before they are shackled and hoisted into the air. There is a great deal of confusion about this: many people believe that shackling and hoisting are part of the historic religious requirements. They are not. The traditional Jewish way of slaughter was to cast the animal to the ground and cut his jugular as skillfully as possible with a knife that was as sharp as possible, so that the animal could be rendered unconscious in under a minute. During centuries when most Europeans bludgeoned their animals to death or allowed them to bleed to death slowly, shechitah was the most merciful way of slaughtering an animal. Other methods, until recently, were unspeakably grotesque. Diane Ackerman records the myth that inspired European gourmets to first torture their animals before killing them:

> The idea arose that torturing an animal made its meat healthier and better tasting and even though Pope, Lamb, and others wrote about the practice with disgust, people indulged in ghoulish preparations that turned their ktichens into charnel houses. They chopped up live fish which they claimed made the flesh firmer; they tortured bulls before killing them, because they said the meat would otherwise be unhealthy; they tenderized pigs and calves by whipping them to death with knotted ropes; they hung poultry upside down and slowly bled them to death; they skinned living animals.[1]

Such methods and worse were practised into the 19th century. If we go back to Roman times, the lust to indulge the taste buds caused the Roman writer, Plutarch, to cry out, "Oh, what a world of pain we create for a little taste upon the tongue." The Jewish way of slaughtering animals never involved such behavior. Jews rightly regarded shechitah as the sign of commitment to mercy for animal life. Granted the permission to eat meat, shechitah accomplished what it was intended to accomplish--to spare the animal as much pain as possible. The shochet (Jewish ritual slaughterer) was and is not simply a butcher. Contrary to the practice of most societies, where butchers often come from the uneducated, impoverished and desperate levels of society and are often regarded as pariahs, the shochet was expected to be a man of exemplary piety. He was, in the poet Jerome Rothenberg's phrase, "a technician of the sacred."

However, our modern methods of rearing animals for meat, such as the crated veal and the battery hen, are little improvement over the grotesque practices of past centuries. They are simply more hidden. Because most Jewish meat today comes through the same system of factory farming it transforms vegetarianism for the concerned Jew into an imperative that is more than a lifestyle diet. Vegetarianism for such a Jew reaches back into the fundamentals of the Jewish religion.

Louis Berman, in his book, *Vegetarianism and the Jewish Tradition*, [2] traces the origins of shechitah to the downfall of the sacrificial system, which had provided a religious format for the killing of animals for food. Animal sacrifice was widespread throughout the world for millennia. The origins and significance of that practise are fascinating, but beyond the scope of this book. Berman traces the evolution of the shochet from that of the temple priest, who had had responsibility for the animal sacrifice, through shechitah as we know it; but the rules regarding the shochet's profession are post-biblical. It was the job of the shochet not only to kill the animal as mercifully as possible, but to examine the animal for blemishes and evidence of disease which would make it unfit for consumption. The list of damages to limbs, genitals, membranes, etc. are quite specific, but today the causes of meat contamination are more complex. Most chicken livers and lungs are diseased, yet only a diseased crop or craw would invalidate a chicken as non-kosher.

It is more than fair to state that for centuries no other method of slaughtering animals for food was comparable both in the intent and in the practice of sparing the animal unnecessary pain. This lofty sentiment is routinely disregarded today in shackling and hoisting, in the castration of steer (usually without pain killers), in disregarding the commandment that a new born animal must be kept with its mother for eight days, and in the modern method of raising chickens.[3] One may argue that there is no such thing as "humane slaughter"--which we argue in this book--but within the parameters of slaughter there is better and there is worse. Shechitah served the Jewish people well for centuries. It was the sign, the guarantee to the community, that animal life was not to be taken cheaply and that the taking of it carried with it religious obligations. In contrast to the centuries of other peoples' hunting and maiming animals for food, skinning them alive, trapping them, crushing them, and the myriad other dreadful forms of turning a cow into food, the historical record of Jewish slaughter is remarkable.

But change came to the tradition with so-called progress. As veterinarians and doctors came to understand that disease could be contacted through spilt blood, industrialized nations required that animals in the slaughtering plants be shackled and hoisted into the air so that their blood could be cleaned away from the killing area before the next animal was killed. This procedure is extremely painful for the animal. In panic and terror a fifteen hundred pound bull is hoisted upside down by one leg and left dangling above the floor to wait for his throat to be cut. More hygienic the method might be, but it is exceptionally cruel, often wrenching, twisting and breaking the animal's leg as he swings overhead. The barbarity was alien to the spirit of shechitah, and the Jewish community first fought it. *All* animals raised for commercial food, whether for the kosher or non-kosher market, were shackled and hoisted as fully conscious animals until the Humane Act of 1958 was passed, which intended to make this barbarism "humane." This law required that the animal be stunned by a captive bolt shot into its forehead before being shackled and hoisted.[4] Since Jewish and Muslim law require that the animal be conscious before slaughter, as evidence of the animal's health, the Jewish and Muslim communities were exempt from this requirement under the Freedom of Religion Act. This exemption resulted in a misunderstanding about what religious slaughter is. Religious slaughter, as developed by Jewish tradition, did not involve shackling and hoisting. That was a modern imposition, but one which the Jewish community has been slow to correct.

The fate of animals killed according to "humane slaughter" law is only slightly better, and their lives are not at all better. The stunning method itself is not always successful. If the bolt is not administered properly the animal may be semi-conscious and be in pain for some time. Animals have been observed to regain consciousness while swinging in the air. (This is particularly true of pigs, which does not concern Jewish law; nevertheless, the slaughter of pigs, as described in Gail Eisnitz' book, *Slaughterhouse,* [5] is exceptionally brutal.) Laws cannot cover all situations. Much depends on the skill and the sympathy of the slaughterers. Furthermore, in many kosher slaughtering houses (as in all large slaughter houses) the slaughterers work at a merciless pace (owing to the vast quantities of meat now produced). A century ago, in a small shtetl, the shochet may have killed one or two cows a week, and a few chickens, and his behavior could be observed by the community. Today, a kosher slaughtering house may handle two thousand cows a day, and shochets work in shifts around the clock. Today, most rabbis do not go into the slaughter houses, and most Jewish communities do not know where the slaughter houses are, or would wish to go there if they knew. But the slaughtering problem is the final problem in a long tale of torture. The contemporary way of raising animals by the factory farm method has changed the scale of the argument. It is not solely a problem of *how* the animal is killed, and death is often a merciful release from the dreadful conditions under which most animals are confined. Meat today is a violation of every aspect of shechitah. It violates the most fundamental of Jewish concepts: concern for health, for the environment, for the animal, for the Jewish community, for the human race.

These are complicated matters. To deal with them, we have divided the issues into separate chapters, though in reality you cannot separate the problem of environmental pollution from the problem of human health, or the moral problem of factory farming from the problem of environmental pollution. As Andrea Cohen-Kiener comments in her article, "The Shema and Ecology": "The first lesson is that God is One. This powerful simple *sui generis* of yiddishkeit teaches us that all of our actions, interactions and reactions are part of a single reality field." The single reality field is *ha makom,* the name for God, the place; the place is the earth and the earth is holy. *Ha makom* expresses a fundamental Jewish understanding of the relationship of Creator to the creation. The goal is *tikkun olam*, the repair of the world. The undertaking is enormous. It cannot be over-estimated. Our weapons are ourselves, our Jewish values, our understanding of the holiness of creation, and what we eat. The issues are inter-woven; they are separated in this book as a device for clarification. In some instances, some material which is pertinent to several arguments may be repeated if this material can gain cogency when seen from several points of view.

The first two chapters, "Kashrut and Modernity," and "From Living Soul to Animal Machine," are historical, for without an historical perspective, one cannot understand how we got into the situation we are in, nor how the brutish treatment of farm animals today is part of the Enlightenment spirit of progress and industrialization. Other chapters deal with the specific impact of the meat industry upon our health, our environment, the degradation of animal life, and the hidden cost to the hungry. Articles in the appendix are action-oriented, with lists of organizations, books, and suggestions on how to get involved in solving the problem.

Our purpose in the first chapter is not to give an exhaustive history of kashrut, but to indicate the difficulty of practising traditional kashrut with modern food habits. The second chapter, "From Living Soul to Animal Machine," traces the concept of the animal machine and how this concept is related to the present relentless exploitation of farm animals. We can give only an historical sketch here, for the relationship between humans and animals is complicated. It is as long as the history of the human race. Every society has had its philosophy, mythology, and morality concerning this relationship. For the most part, our discussion is confined to Western civilization. The third chapter deals with the relationship between diet and health. In the fourth chapter we explore Jewish views of animal life and how they are violated by modern livestock agriculture, while the fifth chapter relates the traditional Jewish ecological concepts and describes how a meat-centered diet violates them. In the sixth chapter we examine why "cheap meat" is not help for the poor. The final chapter examines ways in which diet divides or can unify Jewish community life.

A theme which runs through this book is the relationship between diet and community welfare or health.With the advent of AIDS and the increasing knowledge of the connection between smoking and lung cancer, the public became aware that lifestyle was related to disease. Consequently, in 1986 the John D. and Catherine T. MacArthur Foundation instituted a study into the relationship between morality ("lifestyle," broadly speaking) and health. The book, *Morality and Medicine*, is an anthology of articles which issued from that study, and which sought to bridge the gulf which divided older views of morality from the contemporary view of medicine:

> We often see medicine and morals posed as if they were categorically alternative ways of viewing health and disease, the medical versus moral explanatory frameworks. Nonetheless...medicine and morals are deeply and fundamentally entangled....the history of health and disease reveals their fundamental attachments. Debates about the relationship between moral behaviors and health date to antiquity. [6]

AIDS and drugs have become turning points in discussions about public health and lifestyle. Nicols Fox, in her book, *Spoiled*, states that AIDS brought to an end the illusion we had of mastery over disease. She also makes the comparison between AIDS and the emergence of pathogens in food, both of which date from the 1980s: AIDS called "into question our basic assumptions about a basic human act: sex. The emerging foodborne pathogens would call into question another basic and essential human behavior: eating."[7]

The relationship between morality and disease was voiced in Exodus 15:26:

> If you will diligently hearken to the voice of the Lord, your God, and will do that which is right in His sight, and will give ear to His commandments, and keep all His statutes, I will put none of these diseases upon you which I put on the Egyptians; for I am the Lord, your healer.

In a culture such as ours, it is distasteful to question lifestyle, but the issue should be faced before a health crisis compells us to make decisions in the panic of epidemics. Moreover, discussions about the relationship between lifestyle and disease should include the fact that the choice to eat meat is a lifestyle choice; the choice of governments to raise animals and chickens by contemporary factory farming methods is a lifestyle choice; the decision of governments to subsidize ranchers and the meat industry is a lifestyle choice, as are subsidies for tobacco farmers. No religion or deity demands these choices. The irresponsibility of citizens in not educating themselves and demanding change is a lifestyle choice; the neglect of Jews to question the meaning of "kosher" today is a lifestyle choice.

Arguments and rhetoric in *Vegetarian Judaism* are both secular and religious because we deal with materials and concepts which are both secular and Jewish. This book was written for the secular Jew who buys meat in a supermarket, and for the observant Jew who buys meat in a kosher market. The problems with meat products embrace the eating and shopping habits of religious and non-religious Jews, as well as everyone else who eats meat products.

As in the book, *Morality and Medicine*, we posit the idea that there is a relationship between morality (in this case diet) and disease without wish to blame victims, or to claim that diet is relevant to every disease. Of course there are diseases which are individual, which are hereditary, which are due to bad luck; however, the significant chronic diseases in our civilization are related to environment and diet; and within diet, specifically to the consumption of animal food.

Our search for new Jewish dietary guidelines rests on five well-known Jewish principles: *pikuach nefesh* (guard your health), *tsa'ar ba'alei chaim* (do not cause pain to living creatures), *bal tashchit* (do not wantonly waste resources, or concern for the environment), *tzeddakah* (behave with charity towards the poor), and *klal Israel* (concern for the community). These are good, moral principles which should inform the diet and behavior of every society.

In criticizing contemporary farming practice, the term "farmer" is inevitably used, but 98% of the production of animal food today is in the hands of agribusinesses and corporations, not in the hands of the small farmer. Only 2% of farms are family farms. Farmers have been victimized by corporate farming as well as the animals. The reality of much farming is far from the bucolic picture the public still indulges itself in. An article by David Ehrenfeld, "A Techno-Pox Upon the Land," in *Harper's* magazine, portrays the debacle in modern farming: [8]

> The modern history of agriculture has two faces. The first, a happy face, is turned toward nonfarmers who live in the developed world. It speaks brightly of technological miracles, such as the 'Green Revolution' and, more recently, genetic engineering, that have resulted in the increased production of food for the world's hungry. The second face is turned toward the few remaining farmers who have survived these miracles. It is downcast and silent, like a mourner at a funeral.

Jim Mason, the co-author of *Animal Factories*, grew up on a farm in Missouri and experienced the shock of the transition from the farm he remembered from his youth to the modern-day reality: [9]

> The reality of a modern animal factory stands in sharp contrast to the farm of our fantasies....I remember this kind of farm. I was raised on one in Missouri in the forties and fifties. The animals on farms then were truly domestic; that is, they were part of the farm household. Families lived from and cared for their animals....Farms like the one of my childhood are rapidly being replaced by animal factories. Animals are reared in huge buildings, crowded in cages stacked up like so many shipping crates. On the factory farms there are no pastures, no streams, no seasons, not even day and night. Animal-wise herdsmen and milkmaids have been replaced by automated feeders, computers, closed-circuit television, and vacuum pumps.....The real nature of factory farming was indeed hard to believe. The contrast to my own farm experience was too strong....I was overwhelmed by the awesome scale and pervasiveness of this new way of animal rearing. I was amazed how little the public knew about these drastic changes in the production of their food.

Descriptions of factory farming are disturbing because they involve so much animal suffering. It is not possible to convey the misery of the contemporary farming system and the case against animal food, without descriptions of this material. They are implicit in the argument for moral order and for a vegetarian Judaism. To turn away, to flip the pages past distressful passages, to concentrate on those passages which console with the splendors of past Jewish thinking on animal life, is what Dr. Dallas Pratt would call "moral sloth." [10]

Occasionally, passages are quoted which use "He" for "God," and "Old Testament" for the Jewish Bible, which may be offensive. It is difficult to excise terms and words we regard as insensitive without distorting the meaning of the passage in which they occur. In treating material from the Bible, translation and interpretation become crucial, more so between Bibles used by Jews and Bibles used by Christians. For example, a pivotal passage in Genesis, which gives Jewish vegetarians their mandate is Genesis 1:29. The following is based on Everett Fox' recent translation (authors' italics):

> God said I give you all plants that bear seeds that are upon the earth, and all the trees in which there is fruit which bears seeds. These shall be yours for *eating*.

The King James version translates the word "food" as *"meat."* (We should note that the word "meat" was and is often used as a synonym for food.) This word is important because it occurs in the same passage in which God gives the human race "dominion over the fish of the sea, the fowl of the heavens, and all living things that crawl upon the earth"--but implicitly excludes eating animals. Jews do not accept the interpretation of "dominion" as "tyrannical" which is a post-Francis Bacon interpretation of the word. Jews are taught that God has dominion over us, but we do not conclude from that that God is cruel or unjust. Neither should we conclude that human dominion over animals was a charter to human beings to torture and destroy animals. There is a tradition of commentary in Jewish writing on the word, "dominion," and on the Jewish use of animals, which is summed up by the biblical scholar, Moses Cassuto: [11]

> You are permitted to use the animals and employ them for work, have dominion over them in order to utilize their services for your subsistence, but must not hold their life cheap nor slaughter them for food. Your natural diet is vegetarian....

Factory farming, the modern method of rearing animals for food, has strained the defense of "kosher" meat, but most Jews are not informed about what is happening, as most urban people are not. Nor is the public, Jewish and non-Jewish, informed about what is happening to farming in general, and to its take-over by chemical companies. While we examine only the issue of meat in this book, the problems go beyond meat. The problems extend to the production of all food, which is now a social and political issue of paramount importance. David Ehrenfeld laments:

> Somehow, in the chaos of technological change, we have lost the distinction between a person and a corporation, inexplicably valuing profit at any cost over basic human needs. In doing so we have forsaken our farmers, the spiritual descendants of those early Hebrew and Greek farmers and pastoralists who first gave us our understanding of social justice, democracy, and the existence of a power greater than our own. [12]

There is an urgent need for all communities to establish dialogue with their leaders, to establish workshops and outreach programs about meat, genetic engineering in crops and animals, and the need for dietary changes which will respond to these problems. As Jews, concerned with the continuity of our traditions as well as with our ability to rise to the command of the hour--for we have always done so--we seek a new definition of kashrut, one which addresses the question of the production of food. Movements such as "eco-kashrut" have begun this work. Rabbi Samuel Weintraub has meditated on the need for a renewed spiritual value in kashrut which would be responsive to our specific contemporary problems: [13]

> ...a renewed attention to *kashrut* should creatively engage our society's concern with health and ecology. Since *kashrut* is, originally, a meditation on the world as 'fresh, pure and strong,' Jewish educators should develop serious, adult classes in ecological *kashrut.*

He questions whether a Jew should "eat lettuce picked by California migrant workers with canisters of toxic organophosphates strung from their shoulders," whether Jews should eat the products of oppressed labor, or the products of "the causes of natural perdition, as is much of cash-cropping and cattle overgrazing." Food production involves us in social issues. Much of the rainforest in Brazil which is being cleared for cattle grazing is done by slave labor.[14] There is a movement in Judaism to re-evaluate kashrut in the light of such modern dilemmas. Among the options for consideration, none is so thorough at once and for all times as the embrace of vegetarianism. It is the only complete moral response to the cruelty and danger in modern meat. Rabbi Samuel Dresner observed that "Philosophy and diet go hand in hand." [15] For the Jew, philosophy, diet, religion and history go hand in hand. A vegetarian Judaism is the historical fulfillment of our dietary commandments and of our ethos, because it restores respect for non-human creatures and for the holiness of all creation.

Vegetarian Judaism is also an inquiry into the relationship between animals and humans, for the question of meat is embedded into our philosophy about nature and the human role in it. This book is an effort to re-establish the biblical view of that relationship as a rebuke to modernism.

1

Kashrut and Modernity

Vegetarian Judaism rests on five important Jewish mandates which are rooted in Torah and which were expanded by Talmudic and rabbinic commentary: pikuach nefesh (the commandment to guard your health and life); tsa'ar ba'alei chaim (avoid causing pain to any living creature); bal tashchit (the commandment not to waste or destroy anything of value); tzedakkah (to help the needy and work for a more just society); and klal Israel (to work for the welfare of the Jewish people). These mandates have been developed over millennia in the Talmud and rabbinic responsa, and have guided the Jewish people throughout centuries. But knowledge and implementation of these mandates have declined since the advent of industrial society. Meat and our attitude towards food animals is at the heart of that decline.

The modern meat-based diet has seriously eroded these principles which are now largely and, particularly for most urban Jews, honored merely in sentiment as nostalgic emblems of the Jewish tradition. Rabbis and many knowledgeable Jews can recite the laws concerning Jewish regard for animal life, but in reality these laws have no more application to much of contemporary Jewish life than sitting in the gate of a wall to render judgment. Even worse, the tradition is too often used as a shield against responsibility for contemporary problems concerning animals.

Meat-eating today violates the intentions of historical kashrut which, as the rabbis traditionally interpreted the tradition, has two purposes. One purpose was to curb the appetite for meat. In this, kashrut has observably failed. Western Jews historically have eaten and eat as much meat as their non-Jewish neighbors. With respect to the *quantity* of meat, Western Jews show no distinction. Indeed, European Jews, as they have become prosperous in the last century, became so identified with a meat-based diet, in spite of the fact that there is no historic or religious reason for it--that the vegetarian option sometimes seems quaint to them. In this respect they are like those Hindus and Japanese who surrender their historic diets to Western carnivorism, and whose children no longer know the dietary traditions of their forebears. Diet becomes a major force for assimilation. Why has kashrut, which was supposed to guard us against over-consumption of meat, failed in this respect?

The second purpose of kashrut, as the rabbis interpreted the tradition, was to refine our sensibilities with respect to animal life and to make us aware of animal pain. Even such an arcane and mysterious commandment that one must not seethe a kid in its mother's milk, was given this interpretation in the first century by the Jewish philosopher, Philo of Alexandria. He gave the commandment its definitive Jewish cast when he declared that to seethe a kid in its mother's milk was morally repulsive because it is "improper that the matter which sustained the living animal should be used to flavour its meat after its death." Rabbinic commentary declared that the prohibition was intended to refine our appetites with respect to meat, and the commandment became applicable to all meat, as the prohibition underwent expansion from 200-420 C.E. The interpretation of this law, as well as of other laws concerning kashrut, became ethical and moral: concern for the animal and concern to refine human sensibility with respect to *all* life. Rabbi Samuel Dresner expressed the sentiment succinctly: "Reverence for Life...is the constant lesson of the laws of Kashrut."[16] Yet kashrut, for most contemporary Jews, has failed in this purpose as well.

Rabbi Dresner complains that kashrut today has practically no significance for the majority of Jews because it lacks connection to the food they eat, particularly meat. How could it have connection, when our meat comes wrapped in cellophane with no resemblance to what was once a living creature? As Rabbi Schachter writes in his introduction to Louis Berman's book, *Vegetarianism &The Jewish Tradition:* [17]

> Modern life separates man not only from the seasons of the year, but from the sick (who are sent off to medical centers), from the old (who are hidden away in nursing homes), from the mentally incompetent (who are likewise 'put away'), and also from the suffering of slaughtered animals, which is now likely to occur thousands of miles away from where a chicken or a pound of hamburger is purchased at the supermarket, pre-wrapped in the same clear plastic and white tray as an eggplant or bunch of broccoli....Today a kosher poultry-processing plant may hire, perhaps, a hundred *shochtim*. Not one customer ever sees their ceremonial acts or functional skills. The screeching, squawking chickens are herded into the plant, and leave as frozen 'food products,' attractively wrapped in plastic bags for display at supermarket counters throughout the country.

Rabbi Schachter relates the complaint of a *ba'al teshuvah* (one who has returned to Judaism) who was disappointed that the religious community he joined showed no awareness of the modern difficulties with food. "Why can't Torah help me reach a high level of food consciousness?" he asked. It can if the methods of how food is produced today is understood and incorporated into a new concept of kashrut. The historical moment has forced the issue. Food, crucially and particularly meat, is a major problem of industrialized societies. Food arrives at supermarkets processed, possibly genetically altered, irradiated, sprayed with pesticides, depleted of natural vitamins, bred to adjust to the difficulties of transportation, packaged, warehoused, stored, shelved, and wrapped with complex labels most of us don't understand. A slab of meat arrives the same way a box of tomatoes or a package of corn arrives. The factory farming system does not distinguish between what once was a living animal and what was once a plant. The production of food, be it meat or cranberries, is profit driven. Production is rationalized for minimal cost and maximum selling price, be it a calf or an orange. Food is bred for shelf life in the supermarkets, not for taste or nutritional value. The variety of foods now available and the fact that we can enjoy out-of-season fruits and vegetables give rise to a spectacle of abundance which hides a Faustian bargain.

In the last century and a half, the consumption of meat has risen as a concomitant to the industrial revolution. Technological advances in transportation, refrigeration and freezing compartments have made meat available from practically anywhere in the world practically at all times. Population explosions in urban centers and lifestyle changes in "fast food" eating habits have encouraged enormous increases in meat consumption. This increase has occurred when most urban populations lead sedentary lives in climate controlled environments. These factors have altered our metabolic rates and have made the consumption of meat and fats undesirable. Fat simply cannot be burned in a modern society the way it can be burned in a primitive society, where human energy, from drawing water from a well to chopping wood and keeping warm, works most things, and human beings burn their fat in the daily needs of life. Unburned fat in a modern sedentary society becomes a health menace.

The increase in meat consumption also replaced the consumption of traditional essential foods, such as vegetables, fibers, grains and legumes, so that the Western diet has undergone the most revolutionary change since human beings appeared on the earth. For millennia, the human race lived on a carbohydrate-centered diet. Modern Western people are the first people in history to have an animal-protein based diet. The cost of this change is high-priced chronic diseases such as cancer, heart disease, stroke, diabetes, and osteoporosis.

The Jewish diet, in spite of kashrut, in spite of our declared concern with human health, underwent the same dietary changes in response to the rise of prosperity in the West as did other Westerners. Today kosher meat reflects a technical ritual determination of how the animal is killed and whether there are certain proscribed blemishes on his lungs. A "blemish" defined halachically does not convey information about the hormones, antibiotics, and pesticides that are fed to the animal, about pathogens in the meat, and whether or not the animal was irradiated or genetically altered. Kosher food animals, except for a few Jewish farming communities who raise their own animals, are raised the same way all commercially raised food animals are raised. A kosher label does not preclude the fact that this meat came from an animal which was reared on a factory farm.

The rise in meat consumption and the spread of industrialization, with its concepts of efficiency led to the rise of the factory farming system for animals. No other system of breeding animals for food has been so dangerous to the health of both animals and humans. The use of antibiotics, hormones, and sprays which are now continually required to keep the surreal world of the animal machine going is dangerous to animal and human life.

Factory farming is an automated system of breeding animals which divorces their lives from basic natural processes such as reproduction, bonding, searching for food, movement, pecking, grooming, brooding, nesting, sex, and the species-habitat relationship. By the end of the second World War, the factory farming system created the horrors of the crated veal and the battery hen chicken. Now, with the advent of genetic engineering and artificially inseminated milk cows, kept pregnant, lactating and hooked to milking machines their entire lives, farm animals have been converted into machines.[18] The formulations of kashrut do not address these animals. It is not a question any longer of this piece of meat or that piece of meat or of how sharp the shochet's knife is. The entire system which produces meat and meat products for the commercial market is corroded with inhumane concepts and questionable health practices which defy Torah and Judaism at their very heart.

Jeremy Rifkin in his book, *Beyond Beef,* [19] points out that our traditional morality, framed by the Ten Commandments, cannot address the institutionalized evil of factory farming:

> What of evil born of rationalized methods of discourse, scientific objectivity, mechanistic reductionism, utilitarianism, and market efficiency?....A new dimension of evil...has been incorporated into the modern cattle complex--a cold evil that flows from the very Enlightenment principles that animate much of the modern world view.

Neither can traditional Jewish concepts of blessings or kashrut address the animal machine. Rabbi David Rosen has declared, "...meat consumption has become halachically unjustifiable."[20] The farm animal is the first victim in the blurring line between human being and machine that has accompanied progress since the Enlightenment, and it mocks Genesis. There are no blessings for the animal machine. Life is not a blessing for chickens kept four to six in a cage the size of *The New York Times* folded in half; whose reproductive systems are altered and maneuvered to yield many times the eggs nature designed them to yield, who never feel earth or sun or smell grass, who spend their entire lives as egg-laying machines. Death, not life, is the blessing for this creature. For the animal machine, we ask what evil force created this creature and we bless the death that releases her from life.

To Rabbi Dresner's complaint that kashrut "lacks a satisfying modern formulation of its meaning and relevance,"[21] we respond that a vegetarian Judaism can give kashrut meaning and relevance, can restore kashrut to dignity, can cancel its inattention to the evil of the animal machine, and can relieve kashrut of its present meaninglessness. Many Torah-observing Jews find their vegetarian instincts upheld and justified by Torah. Rabbi David Rosen wrote in his article,"Vegetarianism: An Orthodox Perspective:" [22]

> As the mitzvot are intended to ennoble us, and as the ideal images of the Torah are vegetarian, it is natural to similarly see the laws of kashrut (as does Rabbi Kook) as actually designed to wean us away from meat towards the vegetarian ideal.

The historical development of the dietary laws for Jews has been stated many times[23] and is reviewed here briefly. Vegetarianism is conceived in *Genesis* as the ideal state for human beings. Meat is permitted for the first time after the flood, when Noah set up a slaughter site at his own bidding, with the dire divine foresight that human beings will now know war and will be separated from other animals who will flee from them. (Gen. 9, 3). Permission to eat meat is also given with the proviso that the human race is not to bite into the living animal or eat its blood (the law of *ever min hahai*, Gen. 9, 4)). Isaiah called this commandment "the ancient covenant" and regarded violations of it with intense aversion:

The earth is withered, sere;
The world languishes, it is sere;
The most exalted people of the earth languish.
For the earth was defiled
Under its inhabitants;
Because they transgressed teachings,
Violated laws,
Broke the ancient covenant.
That is why a curse consumes the earth,
And its inhabitants pay the penalty....(24: 4-12)

The law of *ever min hahai* singles out the human race from other predatory animals. It is considered applicable to the whole human race as one of the Noachic laws: we are not to take our meat as predatory animals do. Hunting, which was considered essential to all great empire-building states in the identification of hunter and warrior and in the training of the warrior, was prohibited to the Jewish people. Jews had permission to eat meat, but not to be predators. The meat they ate was to be chosen from their flock and was to be properly sacrificed before it could be eaten. There is no commandment to eat meat, but there are strict commandments regarding the kind of meat to be eaten and how the animal was to be sacrificed before it could be eaten. Walter Burkett's observation in his book, *Homo Necans,* that "For the ancient world, hunting, sacrifice, and war were symbolically interchangeable,"[24] was not true for the Jewish people, who broke that connection for themselves. By prohibiting hunting, Judaism severed an historic relationship between hunting and the consumption of meat, and between hunting and war. Judaism does not know the camaraderie of the hunt. What remained was the sacrificial system which gave to Judaism the association of eating meat with holidays and festivals. This association was later denied by the Talmud, after the fall of the Temple. Furthermore, as Burkett states, Judaism in the diaspora could spread precisely because sacrifice was concentrated in the Temple in Jerusalem. Diaspora Judaism had been "a religion without animal-sacrifice." After the fall of the Temple, the Jewish association with a meat-centered diet was not inevitable, but developed in the West with the same response pattern of other Western or Westernized people. It is essentially a response of cultural assimilation.

Observant Jews limited their meat to those animals who were vegetarian animals, in accordance with traditional kashrut, which mandated that not only were Jews not to take their meat as predators do, but they were not to eat *predatory* animals. Meat for kosher Jews is limited to the "clean" animals, who are ruminants and vegetarians. Within the parameters of the permission to eat meat, this food chain is efficient and natural. This is no longer true under the factory farming system which, in spite of its worship of efficiency, is not efficient, and the animal machine is not natural. With respect to beef cattle, grain has been largely substituted for grass, which is a very inefficient and costly way to feed animals; animals are often given ground-up meat from other animals, sometimes from sick animals who could not make it to the slaughter house. The only efficient achievement of this system is short term profit for the agribusiness investor, while civilization pays the debt in health bills and a degraded environment.

The Bible tells us that there were "food riots," during the forty years in the desert, tensions caused by the lack of meat. It relates that these conflicts were caused by "the riff raff":

> The mixed multitude, or the riff-raff, that was among them, began to lust [for meat]; and the Children of Israel also cried out, 'Would that we had flesh to eat!' (Num. 11:4)

The reference to "the riff raff" suggests derision, a derision we meet elsewhere in reference to meat. Upon entering Canaan, the Israelites are given permission to eat "the meat of lust. " As Rabbi Dresner points out, the reference is derisive,[25] and has been traditionally interpreted as such by the rabbis.

Rashi's comment on the food riots, that "It was right for the Jews to cry for bread, but not for meat, for one can live without meat," reflects the derisive sentiment towards "meat of lust." We see a similar derision towards meat in the incident in Numbers 11:4 in the designation of the grave in which the "meat-eaters" were buried, as "Kibroth-hataavah," or "graves of lust." [26] The entire description of this incident is told in the language of anger and derision. After the Hebrews stuffed their mouths with quail so that "the meat was still between their teeth, unchewed...the anger of God blazed out against the camp and struck it with plague."

There was indeed contention about the eating of meat in the formation of the Hebrew nation, and compromises were struck. In Deuteronomy 12:20, God promises to allow meat to be eaten once the Hebrew nation enters Canaan, "because your appetite craves eating meat." (Deut. 12:20) In the passage in Numbers 11:4, we gather from Moses' words, the strain which the argument put upon him:

> Moses was distressed and said to the Lord, 'Why have you dealt ill with your servant...And laid the burden of all this people upon me...Where am I to get meat to give them when they whine before me and say, 'give us meat to eat!'

Rabbi Dresner interprets the final position of the Bible and the rabbis as a reconciliation between idealism and reality:

> Human consumption of meat, which means the taking of an animal life, has constantly posed a religious problem to Judaism, even when it accepted the necessity for it. The Rabbis of the Talmud were aware of the distinction between man's ideal and his real condition, regarding food. Referring to Deut. 12:20, they said: "The Torah teaches a lesson in moral conduct, that man should not eat meat unless he has a special craving for it, and shall eat it only occasionally and sparingly."[27]

Eating meat poses a problem in many societies. Meat of one kind or another is the most universally tabooed, controlled, or ritually eaten food, suggesting discomfort with the eating of meat in many societies. For Jews, Rashi's comment is closer to the truth and truer to the sentiment the rabbis wished to inculcate, for meat remained for the Jewish people without the status which the seven sacred species have. These are figs, dates, pomegranates, wheat, barley, olives, and grapes. Later discussions in the Talmud indicate that though the rabbis believed meat to have nutritional value, they regarded it negatively and contrived to circumvent its consumption:

> Man should not eat meat unless he has a special craving for it, and then shall eat it only occasionally and sparingly. (Chulin 84a)

> A man should not teach his son to eat meat.
> (Chulin 84a)

There is a "provegetarian bias in Torah," as Rabbi Arthur Green has discerned,[28] which time has clarified. The original instincts of kashrut sought to limit the consumption of meat; the general rabbinic judgment in the Talmud reflects an uneasy compromise with the human lust for it. After the fall of the Temple and the end of the sacrificial system (which at the least lent dignity to the consumption of meat) the rabbis were even less comfortable with the idea of eating meat. Since eating meat was historically embedded in the sacrificial system, after the Temple fell there was much discussion in the Talmud about what the status of meat would now be. The association of eating meat with the festivals bequeathed to Jews the tradition that joyous occasions (*simchat yom tov*) should be celebrated with meat and wine. This association with meat was declared no longer to be in effect after the sacrifices ended. *Beit Yoseph* states: "In the days when the Temple was in existence, there was no rejoicing without meat...but now that there is no longer the Temple, there is no rejoicing without wine...." Jews are commanded to celebrate the holidays and Shabbat with wine and with joy, but there is no halachic requirement to celebrate them with meat. In*The Journal* *of Halacha and Contemporary Society,* Rabbi Alfred Cohen writes that, "...there seems to be little halachic controversy concerning vegetarianism and the Sabbath. If a person is more comfortable not eating meat, there would be no obligation for him to do so on the Sabbath." In examining other halachic statements, Rabbi Cohen concluded that there is "...support for the view that eating meat is not necessarily a *mitzvah* on *Yomtov....*" [29]

After the fall of the Temple, the focus of Jewish celebration shifted from the Temple to the synagogue and the home which, we should remember, was the focus for all Diaspora Jews--which was the majority of Jews at the time. The table in one's home, prepared properly for Shabbat and the holidays was to be considered as an altar. The shift in religious concept testifies to the flexibility of the rabbis who were able to take command of the historic hour, as we should be able to do with ours.

> Today we have no Temple in Jerusalem, no altar there, no sacrifices, no priests to minister. But in their stead we have something even greater. For every home can be a Temple, every table an altar, every meal a sacrifice and every Jew a priest. And what was formerly an animal function, a meaningless, mechanical behavior, is suddenly transformed into an elaborate ritual full of mystery and meaning. [30]

This is the way eating was intended to be for Jews, for whom food has always been holy. In *Berakhot Talmud*, the rabbis laid out a scheme for the blessing of food in order of importance in values: 1) it must be pleasurable; 2) it should be one of the seven species, subject to the obligation of first fruits; 3) it should be offered on the altar; 4) it should have food value; 5) it should have dignity. This last requirement is noteworthy, because it arose in the context of whether there should be a blessing for eating poultry.(39a-b) It was decided that poultry had the same status as a vegetable in terms of pleasure and nourishment, but that it lacked dignity. Eating should also be done in an orderly fashion, as the word "*seder* "(order) means. It is not only what we eat, but how we eat that matters. In addition to our nutritional needs, there is a spiritual dimension to food. Deborah Kesten examines this spiritual dimension in Judaism, in her chapter, "Judaism: Divine Dietary Tradition," as well as the spiritual meaning of food in a number of other societies.[31]

Why did the Talmudic rabbis feel that the consumption of poultry lacked dignity, why did they withhold a special blessing from the consumption of meat, such as bread and wine have, and yet not denounce meat altogether? The key to the situation seems to be that they took a position of neither encouraging nor discouraging vegetarianism, but of definitely discouraging meat. The explanation must lie in problems in Talmudic times: that the rabbis felt that open encouragement of vegetarianism might be regarded as a break with the tradition of animal sacrifice; they were also concerned about advocating vegetarianism because most vegetarian practice at the time was associated with non-Jewish values such as celibacy and the condemnation of creation and matter.[32] Such ideas have always been perceived to rupture the affirmative impulses in Judaism: Choose Life, Be fruitful and multiply. As John Cooper observes, the vegetarian bias in the Bible is strongly implicative: "During the wanderings of the children of Israel in the wilderness the Torah continued to hold meat eating in low esteem....Despite these concessions to human weakness, the Torah and the prophets came down firmly in favor of a vegetarian diet."[33] Jewish vegetarianism today arises out of the life-affirming impulses of guarding one's health, protecting the environment, and reverence for all life. As Rabbi Green has written:

> If Jews have to be associated with killing at all in our time, lẹt it be only for the defense of human life. Life has become too precious in this era for us to be involved in the shedding of blood, even that of animals, when we can survive without it. This is not an ascetic choice, we should note, but rather a life-affirming one. A vegetarian Judaism would be more whole in its ability to embrace the presence of God in all of Creation.[34]

This early uneasiness with meat consumption exhibited itself at a time when biblical Jews ate very little meat. Since the consumption of meat for Jews was originally embedded in the sacrificial system, it had the effect of limiting the amount of meat most biblical Jews ate. The main diet of biblical Jews, as of the Greeks and the Romans, was vegetarian. The restriction against eating meat, as Elijah Schochet points out in *Animal Life in Jewish Tradition,* is underscored by the law in Leviticus (17:3-4) which "condemns as murder the slaughter of animals outside the precinct of the altar of the sanctuary." [35] This suggests that God-fearing Jews in the Diaspora ate no meat except for the three occasions of pilgrimage to Jerusalem.[36] The exhortation of the prophets not to permit a temple in Judea other than the one in Jerusalem may have been motivated by the desire to minimize the consumption of meat, as much as by any other reason.[37]

Meat has always been associated with wealth and for this reason attracted the criticism of the prophets who understood its divisive nature. The meat of the sacrificed animals was eaten by the Temple priests, who apparently glutted themselves on meat so much that a special medical officer was needed to attend to the bowel sickness caused by their overindulgence.[38] Isaiah's disgust with such meat gluttony goes hand in hand with his criticism of the sacrificial system and his concern for the poor.

The relationship between meat and poverty is omnipresent in our world as well. The deplorable policy of one-crop farming that is prevalent in many poor countries that wish to raise a crop that can be sold quickly to rich nations, impoverishes those nations which practise it. The tracts of land (about 1/4 of the globe's earth) set aside for cows destroy and make useless much arable land that could be used to feed the world's population at a fraction of the expense that a meat diet costs. Meat, now as in the time of Isaiah, feeds the rich and impoverishes the poor. In the United States, its impact upon our health care system and its costs has been so corrosive that medical costs threaten millions of people. A study by the Physician's Committee for Responsible Medicine cited in *The New York Times* article by Jane Brody (November 21, 1995), reported that "the yearly national health care costs of eating meat are comparable to the estimated $50 billion spent each year to treat illnesses related to smoking."

The Jewish arguments for a vegetarian Judaism are those of our five mandates: human health, compassion for animal life, environmental health, charity, and concern for the community. A Jewish vegetarianism grows out of Jewish values. It is profoundly related to tikkun olam and reverence for life, not to ascetic denials of the world, of the body or of life.The animal machine casts a warning shadow over human life, for the circle of death today goes from animal to human. The animal machine lays the foundation for the dehumanization of human life. Vegetarianism is a rebellion against the usurpation of "bios" by the machine; Jewish vegetarianism is not a break with Jewish tradition, but a return to traditional concepts and values. For these reasons, the last hundred years has witnessed greater sympathy towards Jewish vegetarianism by the rabbis. As Rabbi Arthur Hertzberg stated in his address, "The Jewish Declaration on Nature": [39]

> Judaism as a religion offers the option of eating animal flesh, and most Jews do, but in our own century there has been a movement towards vegetarianism among very pious Jews. A whole galaxy of central rabbinic and spiritual teachers including several past and present Chief Rabbis of the Holy Land have been affirming vegetarianism as the ultimate meaning of Jewish moral teaching. They have been proclaiming the autonomy of all living creatures as the value which our religious tradition must now teach to all of its believers. Let this affirmation resound this day, and in days to come. Let it be heard by all our brethren, wherever they may be, as the commandment which we must strive to realize.

Among rabbis,[40] Rav Avraham Kook (1865-1935) has come to serve a special place in delineating what vegetarianism should mean for the Jewish people. His publication, "A Vision of

Vegetarianism and Peace" has had a seminal influence, so that a digression about his ideas is warranted.

Rav Kook was the first Ashkenazi Chief Rabbi of Pre-state Israel, during the British mandate.[41] He was a highly respected and beloved Jewish spiritual leader in the early 20th century, a mystical thinker, a forceful writer, and a great Torah scholar, whose writings helped inspire many people to move toward spiritual paths. He urged religious people to become involved in social questions and efforts to improve the world. What is important for our purpose is that his writings provide the strongest support for vegetarianism as a positive ideal anywhere in Torah literature. He believed strongly that God wants people to be vegetarian and that meat was permitted as a concession to people's weakness. He interpreted the many prohibitions related to the slaughtering and eating of meat as a scolding and reminder that people should have reverence for life.

> Indeed a hidden rebuke is to be found within the folds of Scripture regarding the eating of meat. For only after "thou shalt say, I will eat meat, because my soul longest to eat meat", only then, "thou mayest eat meat". Behold you can only inhibit your appetite for meat by an act of moral self control, and the time for the exercise of this power of self-control has not yet arrived.

But he believed that that time would arrive, because the permission to eat meat was only a temporary concession; because a God Who is merciful to all creatures would not institute an everlasting law permitting the killing of animals for food; eating meat was God's concession to the depraved moral status of human beings. Rav Kook believed had people been denied the right to eat meat, they might have eaten the flesh of human beings due to their inability to control their lust for flesh. The permission to slaughter animals for food, given to Noah, was a "transitional tax" or temporary dispensation until a "brighter era" would be reached when people would return to vegetarian diets. For Rav Kook, the Galut could be characterized by that time between our ideal diet and the time when that diet would return.

> Once man's appetite for meat has been aroused, then had flesh of all living creatures been prohibited, the force of moral disintegration which is waiting for an opportune moment would make no distinction between man and beast, fowl or reptile....All violations would be committed, at one fell swoop, in order to surfeit the gluttony of "civilized" humanity.

Carnivorism was the manifestation of moral degradation. The high moral level involved in the vegetarianism of the generations before Noah was a virtue of such great value that it cannot be lost forever. In the future ideal state, just as at the initial period, people and animals will not eat flesh. No one shall hurt nor destroy another living creature. People's lives will not be supported at the expense of the lives of animals. Rav Kook's emphasis on the messianic era as vegetarian, is entirely within traditional Jewish and rabbinic understanding.The tradition suggests that meat-eating prevents the messianic age from coming to birth and perpetuates the spiritual galut.

> The progress of dynamic ideals will not be eternally blocked. Through general, moral and intellectual advancement, 'when they shall teach every man his neighbor, and every man his brother saying, 'Know the Lord; for they shall all know Me, from the least of them unto the greatest of them' (Jeremiah 32:34) shall the latent aspiration of justice come out into the open, when the time is ripe.

"When the time is ripe!" The response put forward in this book is that "the time is ripe." The time is ripe to reshape kashrut according to its original vision. Rabbi Samuel Weintraub expressed the need to re-relate kashrut to our basic Jewish values: "...the original biblical system of *kashrut* served as a reminder to people of the world when they believed it was first created, pure and whole." [42] Quoting from Mary Douglas' anthropological analysis of the biblical system of kashrut, "The Abominations of Leviticus," Rabbi Weintraub writes:

> For Douglas, *kashrut* sustained a collective Israelite consciousness of the origin and preciousness of the natural world. By their food laws, the Israelites appreciated order and wholeness in the natural world and joined in the holiness of that world's Creator. *Kashrut,* then, is a kind of spiritual ecology....We must re-cultivate a spiritual appreciation of the natural world if we are to cherish and preserve kashrut....fortunately, we have, in modern ecological consciousness and in the traditions of *kashrut,* possibilities to inspire that sense of awe towards the natural world. [43]

A vegetarian Judaism returns us to the biblical mandate; it gives us a relationship and harmony with the earth and with the other creatures. A vegetarian Judaism contains a moral symmetry in its concern for human health, for animal life, for nature. It reaches down into the deepest level of moral insight that what is good for human health is good for the health of the planet and for other life on it. A vegetarian Judaism does not negate the past, nor pass judgment on the Temple or on the conduct of our patriarchs and matriarchs. Rav Kook showed a discriminating insight into the flow of history when he said, "If that which was appropriate for later were put earlier we would be lost." We do not judge the past in becoming vegetarians. Rather, like Noah who was *righteous in his generation*, we accept the imperatives of our generation, and seek a renewed covenant with the earth. As Andrea Cohen-Kiener observes, the lesson of that interesting qualifier, "*righteous in his generation*," is that "the exact 'medicine' for world repair is subtly unique for each generation." The medicine for our generation is vegetarianism. Unlike Noah, we do not begin the new age with the construction of a slaughter site, recognizing with Ecclesiastes that, "Unto each thing there is a season": Now is the time to heal and to build up. History has prepared the Jew for vegetarianism and the arguments for it today are imperative. If not now, then when?

2

From Living Soul To Animal Machine

God said: "Let the earth bring forth every kind of living creature: cattle, creeping things, and wild beasts of every kind." And it was so. God made wild beasts of every kind and cattle of every kind, and all kinds of creeping things of the earth. And God saw that this was good. Genesis 1:24-25

"We are entitled to believe...that we can create anew all the substances and creatures that have emerged since the beginning of things...." Marcellin Berthellot, chemist, 1885

The concept of the animal machine was born in June, 1637, in the pages of *Discours de la méthode*.[44] Its father was René Descartes, a brilliant French mathematician and philosopher whose ideas concerning the relationship of matter to the immaterial, of body to soul, helped establish the view that reality exists primarily in extension, or in that which can be measured. Though what is known as the "mind-body" problem had been delineated by Plato, Descartes' work decisively divorced "soul" from matter, and laid the philosophical materialistic basis for science. His impact has been immeasurable. The definition of reality became monopolistically centered in number and measure, and rendered all that which could not be measured disrespectable.[45] Subjective experiences, sentiment, imagination, morals, religion, much of what human beings live by, the "inward" life, experiences which cannot be subject to measurement and therefore proven in the scientific sense were reduced in value as indices of reality. Ironically, it was through the deduction from subjective consciousness that Descartes promoted this mechanistic view of human and animal life. His famous dictum, "I think, therefore I am," argued that it is only from consciousness that one can establish the reality of the body. However, he viewed the body mechanistically, with consciousness or the soul as a kind of engineer of the body.

The impact of Descartes, in conjunction with the work of Galileo and Bacon--whether they intended it or not--changed the way Western people hereafter thought about life and nature. Leon Kass sums up their effect upon modernity:

> Science deliberately broke with ordinary human experience and gained knowledge through the mathematization of nature. It rejected natural teleology, the belief that living things are purposive and goal-directed beings, who pursue naturally given ends, fulfillments, or purposes; it denied not only that animals have purposes relative to some larger scheme of things but also that they naturally seek ends for themselves. Science adopted an analytic and reductive mode of understanding wholes in terms of parts, living things in terms of dead matter and motion. [46]

The effect of this break with teleology, with past religious understandings of nature and life, upon the animal world was nothing less than horrific. If animals had always been at the mercy of human beings, human beings now had the backing of science and philosophy, of the highest intellectual classes, to wreak its worst upon animal life. Its worst was the doctrine that animals had no emotions, could not feel pain, were nothing more than dead objects to be cut, hammered, burned, flagellated, starved, suffocated, torn from their newborn, caged, subject to experiments of every kind. Descartes declared that animals were machines without souls or consciousness; that they were "automata." He believed that soul was related to rationality, and that rationality was related to language. If a creature had no soul, it was *ipso facto* a machine. "Bios" or life was either one thing or the other. If an animal had no soul or inwardness, it was dead matter.

There were many reasons why Descartes took this view, reasons embedded in the philosophical and religious arguments of his time. A controversy in the Catholic Church concerned the issue as to whether animals too could be resurrected after death. Ecclesiastes had already stated a point of view with respect to this issue:

> That which befalls the sons of man befalls the beasts.
> As the one dies, so dies the other.
> They have all one breath and man has no preeminence above the beasts.

In one way or another, whether concerning "resurrection," "soul," "consciousness," or "free will," Western civilization has been haunted by the question of its difference from and its similarity to the animals, as if an atavistic sibling rivalry exists between people and animals. Many religious people identify immortality with religion or religiosity: i.e., if there is no afterworld, there is no God. Religious ideas are often experienced like a domino effect: resurrection or the immortality of the soul is related to the existence of God, which is related to the creation of the world, which includes human beings, animals, vegetation, etc. When one idea is attacked there is concern that the whole edifice of Western religion is under attack. Thus, Descartes' notion that animals are automata immediately engaged theologians as well as philosophers and scientists, for it was perceived then, as it is perceived now, that there was a continuity between human and animal life that did not permit an easy answer. How far down or up the scale of creation would resurrection apply? Mammals? rodents? insects? The problem challenged the sanctity of the idea of human resurrection, but the controversy demonstrates the impossibility of definable separation between species, a problem that has also haunted the Western mind in its determined effort to define itself as something other than animal.[47] Leon Kass' wonderful meditation on food, *The Hungry Soul,* is marred by the effort to mark the human territory from animal territory by defining human beings as "the animal who does not get eaten," but eats others. We may disapprove of cannibalism, but its existence proves that human beings are no more exempt from being eaten than the lion is. Even if it could have been said that in the past cannibalism was the act of desperation or depravity, modern methods of manufacturing feed for animals sometimes includes human remains.[48] But Kass is probably right in sensing that human carnivorism is related to marking our territory: "To mark his self-conscious separation from the animals, man undertakes to eat them." [49] Carnivorism, however, is hardly a distinguished way of being a human being, nor even physiologically warranted since other animals are also carnivores. In the animal world, we find all gradations of satisfying the need for food, vegetarians, omnivores and carnivores, as we find all gradations of forms. Separatist notions, as Kass concedes,"are no longer tenable; they are permanently embarrassed by the theory of evolution."[50] Neither does the Bible support strict separatist notions, even while supporting human dominion. Genesis 2:4 ff stresses Adam's kinship with the animals. As Kass remarks on this passage: "God Himself thought the animals sufficiently similar to man to have fashioned them as his possible companions."[51] These concerns, as does Kass's book, illuminate how diet is allied to our perception of our place in nature.

Descartes argued that animals do not have souls [52] and therefore would not be resurrected. His arguments for the animal automata were based on other hypotheses as well, hypotheses which placed his work on the Papal Index. The Catholic Church perceived that while Descartes' argument supported the superior status of human beings, it degraded the status of creation. "It is blasphemous to attribute such excellent actions as occur in beasts to such a humble cause as mechanism,"[53] one theologian argued. Descartes countered this argument by admitting that animals appeared ingenious, but that it was "From the very perfection of animal actions that we suspect that they do not have free will,"[54] and are therefore automata. The argument over whether animals were *truly* living creatures was as lively in the 17th century as comparisons between computers and human beings are in our century. There has always been a fascination with the possibility of inventing a machine that could imitate human life.

Attempts to define "human" vis à vis animal or machine is related to our radical insecurity about ourselves. A century after Descartes, La Mettrie, a French physician, published his work, *L'Homme machine*. It was understood that if you could define animals as automata, you could define humans as automata or as machines, just as you could define machines as "living." The interchangeability of machines and humans is prefigured by our fascination with puppets and, again, with the problem of defining human life. In the 17th century, the issue created what Leonore Cohen Rosenfield has called "a complete 'crise de la conscience' with respect to the riddle of animal nature," [55] a crisis of conscience which has returned in all its intensity in our century, with a curious difference: we are unwilling to grant the status of "life" to animals, but we are willing to grant this status to machines, at least metaphorically for the time being.

The Jewish view, stated unequivocably in the *Encyclopedia Judaica,* in Volume 1, under "Animals, Cruelty To," is antithetical to the Cartesian view:

> Moral and legal rules concerning the treatment of animals are based on the principle that animals are part of God's creation towards which man bears responsibility.

Either animals are part of God's creation or they are not and if they are not, Genesis is false. The antithesis, foreseen in the 17th century, has come to its final crisis: You cannot support the Cartesian view of animal life and the biblical view at the same time. Throughout Jewish history, commentators and rabbis have supported the view that animals are not only part of God's creation, but demand our unyielding attention to their welfare.[56] Rabbi Samson Hirsch wrote in the 19th century:

> ...you are faced with God's teaching, which obliges you not only to refrain from inflicting unnecessary pain on any animal, but to help and, when you can, to lessen the pain whenever you see an animal suffering, even through no fault of yours.
>
> (Horeb, chapter 60, verse 416.)

In Judaism, animal suffering is taken seriously; it is part of the Jew's moral and religious world in a way in which it is not part of the Cartesian world. With respect to the animal, these are irreconcilable worlds.

Descartes' thesis had supporters and enemies in every sphere of intellectual life. Another eminent mathematician and philosopher, Pascal, defended Descartes' thesis. Other philosophers, many poets and eminent men of letters, were opposed: Montaigne, Bayles, Fontenelle, Cyrano de Bergerac and, later, Voltaire, who separated the notion of soul from rationality: "Soul is common to man and beast. Its principle essence is not thought....Does a man's soul cease to exist when he is not engaged in reasoning?" His remark foreshadowed Jeremy Bentham's objection to vivisection: "The question is not can they reason? Nor can they talk? but can they suffer?" Humphrey Primatt, a Christian theologian at the end of the 18th century who wrote a defense of animals, accepted the fact that animals were not immortal, and argued that *because* they were not immortal all the more reason we should see to it that this one life here was good for them. For him too, animal suffering was not to be ignored. He summed up this position in a dynamic aphorism: "Pain is pain, no matter who suffers it." Only if we accept Descartes' view of animal life can we ignore animal suffering.

The broad question behind animal suffering is what defines life? What defines animal life? What defines it for the Jewish people--and everyone else who embraces the Hebrew Scriptures as the foundation of their religion? What is the relationship between creation and Creator? If we decide that language and reasoning constitute soul, where do we place infants and the mentally handicapped in the order of things? Madame de Sévigné, a contemporary of Descartes, thought Descartes was joking about his theory of the animal machine. She wrote her daughter:

> ...machines which love, which show preference for someone, machines which are jealous, machines which are afraid; come, come, be serious, never did Descartes intend to make us believe that.[57]

But he did, and he understood that his "beast-machine" had implications for the definition of "human," which he did not shrink from explicating. Descartes' view of animal life is the antithesis of Maimonides' view, who wrote: "With respect to the joys and sorrows the animal feels for its young, it is no different from the human being." But the medical world, and later the agricultural communities, had much to gain from Descartes' philosophy of the animal machine: It relieved them then as it relieves them now of moral responsibility for their actions.[58] A century later, the poet, La Fontaine, described the heartlessness of the Port-Royal vivisectors:

> They administered beatings to dogs with perfect indifference, and made fun of those who pitied the creatures as if they had felt pain. They said that the animals were clocks; that the cries they emitted when struck, were only the noise of a little spring which had been touched, but that the whole body was without feeling. They nailed poor animals up on boards by their four paws to vivisect them and see the circulation of the blood which was a great subject of conversation.[59]

Compare this world view with Rabbi Hirsch's:

> In relation to [the animals] man so easily forgets that injured animal muscle twitches just like human muscle, that the maltreated nerves of an animal sicken like human nerves, that the animal being is just as sensitive to cuts, blows, and beatings as man. Thus man becomes the torturer of the animal soul....
>
> (Horeb, Chapter 60, Verse 415)

Western philosophy denied animals the capacity to suffer. Farm animals which, even when eventually eaten, were often regarded as near members of the farming family as long as they lived, were relegated to the same category as research animals. They became solely objects to be manipulated for human gain. Joy Williams declares in her article, ironically entitled, "The Inhumanity of the Animal People:" [60]

> Factory farmers are all Cartesians. Animals are no more than machines--milk machines, piglet machines, egg machines--production units converting themselves into profits. They are explicitly excluded from any protection offered by the federal Animal Welfare Act....The factory farm today is a crowded, stinking bedlam, filled with suffering animals that are quite literally insane, sprayed with pesticides and fattened on a diet of growth stimulants, antibiotics and drugs. Two hundred and fifty thousand laying hens are confined within a single building....Cows are kept pregnant to produce an abnormal amount of milk, which is further artificially increased with hormone injections....

No law in the United States covers cruelty to farm animals. Why would a "sane" government pass laws about cruelty to machines? If a paradox is observed because there are anti-cruelty laws (poor ones that are frequently not enforced) regarding other animals such as privately owned pets, this paradox is no more paradoxical than other laws and philosophies human beings live by. Western civilization was at pains to define slaves as human. Aristotle defined them as "a tool with a speaking tongue." Human is what "we" are, and "animal" is what our pets are. Machines function in our industrial world to make our lives better and to make money with. The cow as machine plays a part in the industrial world; that is the only role she plays. She does not play a part in God's world. Those who oversee the implementation of the animal machine, inspectors, cattlemen, shochtim, the United States Department of Agriculture, are also Cartesians. Those who eat the meat of these animals are excused only on the grounds that they are unconscious of what they are eating, but by playing their part in this process they also define animals as automata and as "not part of God's creation."

Genesis 1:25 tells us that God made the herd-animals after their kind...and God saw that it was good. How did this animal become a machine which the laws of a civilization that considers itself advanced and benign cannot protect?[61]

The status of animals was higher during the millennia when animal sacrifice was practised. It was in fact because the human race regarded some animals (particularly domestic animals) as akin to themselves that they were able to sacrifice them: They were seen as substitutes for human beings. We see this interchangeability in the substitution of the ram for Isaac in the Akedah. The art historian, Kenneth Clarke, believes there was an early stage when human beings did not clearly differentiate between themselves and other species; they did not know themselves as separate from the animals. There is a suggestion of this stage in Genesis 2:18-20. In this version of Creation, Adam is created first. Because God desires "a fitting helper" for Adam, God creates the animals. Adam reviews and names the animals. But no "fitting helper" is found among them. Then God creates Eve to be Adam's "fitting helper." The passage suggests an early hesitation about Adam's species.

Some animals were considered sacred in some empires surrounding Judea, such as Egypt. However, this divine status did not protect the animal, for even in kingdoms where they were sacred they were sacrificed, hunted and eaten. The animal has been sacrificed, hunted and eaten in kingdoms where they were exalted and in countries where they are degraded.[62] Some scholars believe that animals were sacrificed because they *were* exalted, others that the sacrificial system developed from hunting rituals. The sacrificial system hearkens back to a stage of human development and a state of mind that most anthropologists believe may be beyond recall. The relevance of the sacrificial system here is to point out that in Judaism, eating meat was embedded in this system, and is often confused with it. There is no commandment to eat meat. The commandment is that *if* you do eat meat, it must be the meat of a properly sacrificed animal. Moreover, as Leon Kass argues, "...there is no evidence that God *for His part* wants sacrifice."[63] Kass notes that God establishes the institution of sacrifice *after* human beings commit an act of sacrifice, such as when Noah alights from the ark. The act is *first* committed by human beings, then the institution is established. This is an important distinction which Kass argues:

> ...what if the crucial fact about the law of sacrifices is not that God desires or enjoys sacrifice but that He

> restricts and regulates the ambiguous human impulse under the strictest laws and confines it to a single and special place? [Might this explain the exhortation by prophets to confine sacrifice to the temple in Jerusalem.] Because we simply assume that the human disposition to sacrifice is good,we fail to see its questionable character.... The connection between these two activities was severed after the fall of the Temple; that severance was recognized by the Talmud, and in the establishment of the 'table as an altar.'[64]

Noah undertakes sacrifice on his own initiative. God cancels the request to Abraham to sacrifice Isaac, and does *not* request the substitution of the ram. (This point is frequently misread) Abraham substitutes the ram on his own initiative.

When the Temple fell, not only Judaism, but nascent Christianity had to forge a new relationship to meat. There are suggestions in the New Testament of the conflict over diet in Christianity, not only about whether the Jewish dietary laws should be breached, but whether meat should be eaten. Though Paul himself was not a vegetarian, several of his speeches reflect a conflict between vegetarians and meat-eaters:

> If your brother is outraged by what you eat, then your conduct is no longer guided by love....It is a fine thing to abstain from eating meat or drinking wine, or doing anything which causes your brother's downfall. (Romans 14:15)

In Corinthians 8:13, he says, "If meat makes my brother stumble, I will eat no more flesh." Jesus' brother, James, was a vegetarian as were the Ebionites, a sect of Jewish Christians. [65] In his encylopedic study, *James, the Brother of Jesus,* Robert Eisenman, relates James' vegetarianism to his nationalism, in the same way in which Judas Maccabeus' vegetarianism was a rejection of Hellenism, of "idols in the temple," and of idolatrous foods on the tables.[66]

Sacrifice at one time bound animals and humans in rituals of piety, but by the time the Temple fell the practice had become corrupt in Judea, Greece, and wherever it was practised. Criticism and storm clouds over the corruption had been gathering for centuries, as we know from the writings of the prophets.

Judaism demythologized animals as well as human beings, but retained an articulated system of dignity and respect for animals which gave them a status only slightly lower than human beings. Dr. Noah Cohen describes the early Jewish view of animal life:

> ...from the very outset, the Bible admits, the animal kingdom occupies an exalted position in God's realm. Reinforced by this concept...the Hebrew sages emphasized the doctrine that providential solicitude for the lower animals was not unlike that for man. Though man, they conceded, was neither subservient nor subordinate to them, but rather commissioned to exercise 'dominion over the fish of the sea, and over the fowl of the air, and over every living thing that creepeth upon the earth,' yet, they asserted, the wall of partition between man and beast was rather thin and the legal rights and privileges of the latter must neither be neglected nor overlooked. [67]

The biblical Jew used animals as laborers. Laws regulated this relationship, as if there was a contractual relationship beweeen humans and animals. The biblical commandment that "you may not muzzle the ox in the field," for the ox is entitled to the food he can eat--which is the reward of his labor--is often regarded as the first law concerning animal rights. Unfortunately, Paul interpreted this law allegorically, depriving it of its meaningful application to the animal.

> It is written in the law of Moses, 'You shall not muzzle an ox when it is treading out the grain.' Is it for oxen

> that God is concerned? Does He not speak entirely for our sake? (1 Corinthians 9.9-10).

James Gaffney, in his article, "The Relevance of Animal Experimentation to Roman Catholic Ethical Methodology,"[68] calls Paul a "heretic" because his interpretation departed from the traditional Jewish meaning of the original passage.

> ...the passage about the ox was as non-allegorical as everything else in the book of Deuteronomy, where it is found as part of the law of Moses....Thus, for at least one constituent tradition of the Torah, Paul's assumptions are simply mistaken. It is indeed 'for oxen that God is concerned'....

Gaffney restores the proper reading of this commandment. Paul's allegorical interpretation of the passage underlines a serious problem for Jews who do not read the Bible for themselves. Christianity is the only religion whose religious leaders read their religious scriptures in translation. They come to know the Bible, including Torah, through translations which impose Christian values on Jewish concepts. Since it is Christian values and Christian interpretations of the Bible which are normative for the Western world, many Jews give the Torah a Christian reading. The restoration of Torah values to Torah text would restore dignity to animal life.

Where did Paul get his interpretation from? Paul was a Greek Jew; he got his interpretation from Greek civilization, which regarded the animal as irrational. Greek civilization suffered from the suspicion of the inordinate lover of rationalism for the instinctual emotional freedom of the animal.[69] Greek rationalism, exalted as it is, was born of the fear of the irrational, the unpredictable, and the uncontrollable--qualities rationalism has always eschewed--qualities thought to be embodied in animal life. (In reality, animals are more predictable than human beings--but to say this is to invite Cartesian disdain.) Christianity received much of its values and concepts from Greek philosophy and from neo-Platonism. In the Middle Ages,

Thomas Aquinas, who knew Aristotle, articulated the Hellenic view of animals.[70] With the rise of Medieval rationalism, animals were again re-evaluated as "irrational" creatures. Jewish Medieval philosophers, influenced by the spirit of rationalism, also defined animals as creatures without intelligence. "Instinct," which was used to explain animal behavior, was regarded as establishing an unbridgeable hiatus between animal and human life. Animals were guided by instinct; they lacked free will; therefore, they could not be included in moral matters of judgment, punishment or redemption.

As the idea of human individuality grew, so did the idea that God cares for animals only as a species, but not for their individual lives, since only individuals can be judged, punished, and redeemed.[71] Animal suffering posed an insoluble problem for the theologian, and still does. Animal suffering offers no consolations of transcendence, transformation, or redemption. It appears barren of all ideas about divine rescue, and threatens human ideas about grace and mercy. Animals suffer in the wilderness; they suffer in a state of nature, they suffer at human hands.[72] Nevertheless, both early Jewish and Christian faith included animals in divine empathy. Jesus' observation that "God notes the fall of every sparrow," derives from the Jewish faith that "God's mercy is over all His works," and speaks the native language of Torah. Worldly and interesting as many of the Jewish medieval philosophers were, ultimately as Rabbi Joseph Soloveitchik noted in *The Halakhic Mind*: [73]

> ...the most central concepts of medieval Jewish philosophy are rooted in ancient Greek and medieval Arabic thought and are not of Jewish origin at all. It is impossible to reconstruct a unique Jewish world perspective out of alien material.

The unique Jewish world view included not only concern and compassion for animal life, but justice for them, as the law concerning the ox's right to his food for his labor states: animals are entitled to their due: They should be treated according to their nature and the concept of equivalence.

Often the dreary history of defining the animal reveals the human obsession with finding a characteristic which humans have which can be denied to the animal, whether it be language, soul, communication, the ability to make tools, individuality, rationalism, intellect, or a collapsible thumb. The view of the animal as irrational, lustful, carnal, bestial, without sexual control, was rooted in Greek mythology.[74] Many of these definitions were also applied to human beings who were regarded as "inferior." Jews throughout the Middle Ages were defined as "carnal," African Americans were described as lustful and sexually out of control, women historically were viewed as irrational ("unreasonable" beings) and often as "femmes fatales," creatures of inordinate sexuality. These categories, irrational, lustful, bestial, carnal, have been a subterranean force in Western thought whose impact has been enormous on all sorts of creatures. It is no accident that the Animal Rights Movement gained prominence in the 19th century when the Women's and the Abolitionist movements arose, for they are not only movements about social justice, but about new paradigms concerning human and animal life.

It is never easy to destroy a deeply entrenched stereotype, but women, Jews, African Americans and all other human beings are able to combat the mythic and historic distortions about themselves through human activities of writing, voting, demonstrating. The animals have no voice, they have no literature, though they have the same history other victims of bigotry have. Moreover, their oppression is more complete than any other creature. First they were denied a divine status; then they were denied rationalism, then they were denied soul; domesticated, they were denied their natural habitat; then they were denied consciousness, then they were denied free will; then they were denied their bodies; and ultimately they are denied their lives. With genetic engineering, they are denied the nature God created them with.

In *Prisoned Chickens, Poisoned Eggs*, Karen Davis quotes the predictions of an engineer: [75]

> 'Mature hens will be beheaded and hooked up en masse to industrial-scale versions of the heart-lung machines

> that brain-dead human beings need a court order to get unplugged from. Since the chickens won't move, cages won't be needed. Nutrients, hormones and metabolic stimulants will be fed in superabundance into mechanically oxygenated blood to crank up egg production to three per day, maybe five or even ten.
> Since no digestive tract will be needed, it can go when the head goes, along with the heart and lungs and the feathers, too. The naked headless, gutless chicken will crank out eggs till its ovaries burn out. When a sensor senses that no egg has dropped within the last four or six hours, the carcass will be released onto a conveyor, chopped, sliced, steamed and made into soup, burgers and dogfood.'
>
> And probably chicken soup!

This is the future of the creature God created on the fifth day and found good and blessed. We can only halt this impending dystopia by refusing to eat animals and the products of their bodies. With respect to the animal machine, it is right and moral to be an absolute Luddite.[76] For the Jew, the animal is enshrined in the covenantal statements in the Bible. Human beings deprive animals of what God gave them. To recover the biblical vision, we must respond to Descartes' dictum, "I think, therefore I am," with the vegetarian slogan on shirts and bumper stickers, "I think, therefore I am a vegetarian."

3

Pikuach Nefesh: Guard Your Health and Your Life

Choose Life, Not Meat

"You may not in any way weaken your health or shorten your life. Only if the body is healthy is it an efficient instrument for the spirit's activity....Therefore you should avoid everything which might possibly injure your health...."

(Rabbi Samson Hirsch, Horeb, chapt 62, verse 428)

In an article in the *Harvard Divinity Bulletin* [77] the esteemed anthropologist, Mary Douglas, raised the question as to why there was no cult of the dead in Judaism. Her speculations are interesting, but missed the central point that Judaism began with a slave revolt against an empire whose prominent ritual was rooted in a cult of the dead. From its inception, Judaism invested its religion in praise of life and in a God Who delights in life. This passionate thrust towards life is stated in Moses' exhortation to the slaves he formed into a nation:

> I call heaven and earth to witness against you this day:
> You have before you life and death, blessing and curse.
> Choose life so that you and your offspring may prosper.
> (Deut. 30:19)

While Mary Douglas missed this point, she shrewdly speculates that the omission of a cult of the dead gives a nation a forward-looking, optimistic direction to its national spirit.

> Excluding the dead frees the living from institutional controls. Cults of the dead are usually conservative. In this sense, a religion that is getting rid of ancestors is a modernizing religion. Doing without idolatry and superstition changes the flow of resources...[78]

For Jews, contact with dead human bodies has always been limited to a quick burial. The health of the living body is the central occupation. Because life in this world is regarded as the highest good, commandments evolved to teach Jews that they have a duty to protect their health. Though Judaism is a ritualistic religion, health is regarded as more important than ritual. No one is expected to fast on Yom Kippur if there is danger to health. One may violate the Sabbath and even eat forbidden foods when a person's health is in question. The list of prohibitions in Talmudic and rabbinic literature against placing one's life in danger or exposing it to unhealthy conditions is long.[79] Rabbi Hirsch's teachings state the general Jewish position that to preserve health is a religious duty:

> Limiting our presumption against our own body, God's word calls to us: 'Do not commit suicide!' 'Do not injure yourself!' 'Do not ruin yourself!' Do not weaken yourself!' 'Preserve yourself!' (Horeb, chapt. 62, verse 427)

Yet we weaken our bodies and injure ourselves every day with the food we eat. This is wondrous strange for a people who place so much emphasis on diet and health. From its inception, a prominent experience which shaped the Hebrews in the desert was the discipline of diet. Manna focused the desert experience, symbolically and historically. We enshrined the experience in our haggadot. But today we neglect diet and the fact that the injuries due to the consumption of meat are more dangerous than the injuries due to cigarette smoking. An article in *Self* magazine about Michael Jacobson, the director of The Center for Science in the Public Interest, wrote:

> A poor diet combined with a sedentary lifestyle contributes to approximately 400,000 deaths a year--the

> same as cigarette smoking--and yet the government's response does not go much beyond ineffectual public-service announcements and pamphlets. 'The health establishment has made tobacco enemy number one,' Jacobson maintains. 'It's a worthy enemy, but an easy enemy because there's one message: Don't smoke. Nutrition is a more complicated hazard to fight. As a result the public hasn't been persuaded that diet is crucial to its health. Maybe people will worry about it sometime down the road. Or maybe they'll eat better after a heart attack. In many cases, they understand the importance, but the pleasure overwhelms them.' [80]

In this respect, Jews are like everyone else. Even within the confines of kosher meat, the pleasures of the palate overwhelm them: chopped liver, a good brisket, a roast chicken, chicken soup, chopped eggs with onions. Like everyone else, they are lulled into ignorance by propaganda from the meat and dairy industries, while diseases from a meat-centered diet increase with every decade. There is a mountain of evidence that the standard Western diet is dangerous, but reading this material does not make the tongue salivate. Unfortunately, the choice between a moist tongue and stomach cancer is stark.

Diseases Related to a Meat-Centered Diet

The Hebrew word for "meat" (basar) was explained by the Talmudists with the following acronym:

bet: shame
sin: corruption
resh: worms
the more flesh the more worms

The diseases that are linked to a meat-centered diet are cancer, heart disease, kidney stones, gallstones, stroke, arteriosclerosis, high blood pressure, obesity, osteoporosis, Creutzfeldt-Jakob disease (the human counterpart to mad cow disease in cows), diabetes, food poisoning with emerging new pathogens, and the re-emergence of antibiotic-resistant diseases. These diseases represent a formidable and mostly avoidable strain on our health care system.

Cancer

The relationship between the increase in meat consumption and the rise of major chronic diseases in the United States, particularly cancer, has been studied for almost a century. One of the earliest studies was by Dr. Albert Leffingwell, a Harvard University doctor, who wrote *American Meat* in 1916, in which he paralleled the rise in cancer rates with the rise in the consumption of meat. He attributed this parallel rise to the disturbing fact that meat from cancerous cows was being sold to the public; their tumors were cut out, but there was no regard for--and perhaps no knowledge of--the fact that metastasis might have taken place. His statistical judgment was right, but the connection between meat and cancer and other diseases is more complex.

The fact that meat is a leading cause of some cancers is related to our having replaced our historic diet which was rich in fiber foods with animal food. Dr. James W. Anderson examined this exchange between meat and fiber-rich foods: [81]

> The American diet has changed drastically over the last ninety years. Consumption of meat has almost doubled since 1909, and consumption of dairy products has increased 25 percent. Americans eat 50 percent more fats and oils than they did in 1909, with most of the increase coming from margarine and cooking and salad oils.
> Although Americans now eat more citrus foods than they used to, consumption of fresh fruits has decreased by 36 percent and consumption of fresh vegetables has decreased by 23 percent....Consumption of grain products has also decreased by about one-half. All these changes translate into more fat and less carbohydrate and fiber in our diet.
> During the same ninety years, U.S. rates of chronic diseases have also changed drastically....U.S. death rates

> from cancer have more than tripled and death rates from heart disease more than doubled during the same period....today five of the leading ten causes of death in the United States are diet related. Heart disease, cancer, stroke, ...diabetes, and arteriosclerosis...account for 68 percent of all deaths in the United States...

Study after study about the relationship between our standard American diet and some cancers confirm Dr. Anderson's analysis. The relationship between diet and cancer appears to be strong for colon, ovarian, breast and prostate cancers. Based on information taken from articles dating from 1983, Physicians' Committee for Responsible Medicine writes (Footnotes given are from their sources.):

> Cross-cultural studies have revealed that the populations with the highest levels of fat consumption are also the ones with the highest death rates from breast and colon cancer. The lowest rates are in groups with the lowest consumption of fats. [82] Migration studies help to rule out the influence of genetics.[83]

> Fat clearly increases one's risk for cancer, and it may adversely affect breast cancer survival rates for those who have cancer....Meat and milk are also linked to both prostate and ovarian cancers.[84]

Fat may be involved in breast cancer because it increases hormone production in the body; it is dangerous for colon cancer because it stimulates the production of bile acids which is linked to colon cancer. Fiber reduces estrogen in the body because fiber binds with estrogen and moves estrogen out of the body.The Physicians' Committee for Responsible Medicine comments that, "Without adequate fiber, the estrogen can be reabsorbed from the intestine into the blood stream." The University of California at Berkeley's Wellness Letter [85] corroborates these findings:

> Diet causes about one-third of all cancer cases, almost as many as tobacco use. Having a diet that consists predominantly of fruits, vegetables and grains...is the most important factor in the prevention of cancer through diet. The evidence for this is overwhelming: study after study has confirmed that people who have the highest intakes of fruits and vegetables have the lowest rates of most cancers. It's not certain yet to what extent diet affects the risk of breast and prostate cancer, which are influenced by hormones. Diet may well be a major factor in such cancers.

While vegetarianism may seem novel in the West, most people in the world eat a largely vegetarian diet. Even in the West there is a substantial population that is vegetarian or largely vegetarian. This population furnishes us with important evidence of the relationship between diet and cancer.

> Vegetarians experience a lower death rate from all forms of cancer than do non-vegetarians. Studies comparing vegetarian Seventh-Day Adventists with similar non-vegetarian Seventh-Day Adventists have reported 50 percent less cancer in the vegetarian group. In comparison to the general population, Seventh-Day Adventist vegetarians suffer 59 percent less cancer of all kinds, and 97 percent less colon cancer. [86]

There are indications that diet may also be a factor in recovery from cancer,[87] and in dealing with the effects of chemo and radiation therapy.[88] However, in all cases it is not enough to remove the meat from one's plate; one must replace the meat with sensible foods that are high in fiber, minerals and plant protein that can maintain health. In the event of sickness, one should replace one's standard diet, even if it is a vegetarian diet, with healing foods that are targeted to one's disease. Since the scientific study of nutrition is still in its infancy, it is important to educate one's self and, in some cases, to a consult a professional nutritionist or a doctor who is knowledgeable about nutrition. Amounts of food and combinations of foods may have to be adjusted in individual cases, depending upon the illness and personal factors of age, gender, etc. It is important to learn that there *is* a relationship between diet and certain diseases, and that it is possible to tip the balance of health in one's favor.

Traditional medicine cannot always offer guidance in these matters, for most medical schools include only about a week of human nutrition study in three years of medical school. Up to the third decade of the nineteenth century, many medical schools in England included herbal gardens on their grounds, and doctors were required to know herbal medicine. Then herbal medicine, like mid-wifery, was relegated to the ranks of "quack" medicine. The knowledge the human race had acquired empirically through centuries of trial and error about the medicinal qualities of food, was dismissed in favor of experimental medicine and the modernity that it seemed to symbolize.

The study of human nutrition today is at the same point as was the study of the relationship between hygiene and health in the 19th century. Many people then did not know that you can die of dirt and bad hygiene. In the 19th century pregnant women feared puerperal fever as much as we fear cancer and heart disease today. In Europe, about one third of women who went to the hospitals to give birth died of puerperal fever. A Hungarian doctor by the name of Ignaz Semmelweis (1816-1865) discovered that the highest rates of such deaths occurred in women whose labor rooms were near the autopsy and dissection rooms. He traced the cause of their deaths from puerperal fever to the fact that doctors often went from performing autopsies to delivering babies, carrying the bacteria from corpses on their hands. The cause of puerperal fever was the doctor's inattention to this connection.

The story of Dr. Semmelweis is tragic and instructive. When he published his ideas, they were ridiculed. It is believed the poor reception to his ideas depressed him so severely it led to his death in an insane asylum. Eventually, however, as everyone knows, washing one's hands became standard procedure not only for the medical world but for the public. We learned that there could be common sense causes of diseases, such as dirt and lack of healthy ventilation. Bad diet is another common sense cause of disease.

We are fortunate that the study of nutrition has returned, that pioneers such as Nathan Pritikin, T. Colin Campbell, and Dr. Dean Ornish, have researched the relationship between diet, specifically animal food, and our high death rates from chronic diseases. Nathan Pritikin was among the first to recognize the necessity of fiber in our diet. Recently, T.Colin Campbell completed a study which may change medical practice in relation to certain chronic diseases.

The China Project

The most ambitious and thoroughgoing study in nutrition has come to be known as "The China Project." It was conducted by T. Colin Campbell, Ph.D., in the Department of Nutrition at Cornell University, Jacob Gould Schurman, Professor of Nutritional Biochemistry at Cornell University and former Senior Science Advisor to the American Institute of Cancer Research/World Research Fund, co-author of the National Academy of Sciences' landmark report on *Diet, Nutrition and Cancer*; and Dr. Chen Junshi of the Chinese Academy of Preventive Medicine in Beijing. China was chosen for this study because the populations and diets in rural areas of China are relatively stable. The study was begun in 1983 as a collaborative effort between Cornell University, the Chinese Academy of Preventive Medicine, the Chinese Academy of Medical Sciences and Oxford University in England. It represents a fifteen-year epidemiological study of the diet of 6,500 people in 65 Chinese provinces. (Nutritional studies do not lend themselves to crash or crisis studies.) These provinces and their populations were chosen for their genetic similarity and the dietary stability of their populations, though the diets *from province to province* varied. These populations furnished Dr. Campbell's group with a natural human laboratory which allowed the group to build a data bank on the relationship between diet and disease. The study represents the most comprehensive data bank on the multiple causes of disease ever compiled. When it was published, *The New York Times* hailed it as "the grand prix" of nutritional studies. What it established about many of our diseases was revolutionary:

> The findings on cholesterol and urea were remarkable, because they showed that only small intakes of animal products were associated with significant increases in degenerative diseases....In other words, there's no threshold or stopping point at which the benefits of eating plant foods stop. Quite simply, the more you substitute plant foods for animal foods, the healthier you are likely to be. [89]

The China Project not only established links between diet and cancer, heart disease, diabetes and osteoporosis, but showed that these diseases, which have come to be known as "diseases of affluence," often occur together and usually occur because of the same high-meat, low plant, low fiber diet. The study found that "deaths from breast cancer were associated with five things--high intake of dietary fat, high levels of blood cholesterol, estrogen, and blood testosterone, and early age at first menstruation."[90] The highest rates of breast cancer occur in the countries where people eat the most meat.[91] Ashkenazi Jewish women, who have been told that they may carry a gene for breast cancer can take assurance from the study's conclusions on breast cancer and diet:

> What this means is that, no matter, if both your grandmothers died of breast cancer, you have the power to help avoid a playing out of any genetic tendency to this disease. [92]

It also turned out that the diet that was good for disease was good for weight problems. The Chinese people eat about 300 calories a day more than Westerners, but there is practically no obesity in China. Dr. Campbell concluded that a higher percentage of calories are burned up in a low-fat diet. His study also illustrated that animal protein in addition to animal fat was a culprit in degenerative diseases.

Campbell concluded that the decisive difference in the rates of chronic degenerative diseases was diet.

The Lifestyle Heart Trial

In a dramatically different undertaking, Dr. Dean Ornish of The Preventive Medicine Research Institute in Sausalito, California, demonstrated that one could reverse advanced coronary degeneration through diet, stress management and moderate exercise. His study was called The Lifestyle Heart Trial. Dr. Ornish studied 48 patients who were very sick with heart disease. Twenty-eight of these patients were treated with his experimental regimen, which involved a change in diet, moderate exercise and stress control. (The remaining twenty patients served as the control group.) The first twenty-eight patients were put on a strict vegetarian diet, with a fat content of 10 percent of their daily calories, and a cholesterol intake of 5 mg. per day. The arterial clogging of 23 of the patients disappeared. One patient, Werner Hebenstreight, 75 years old at the time, could hardly walk a block without chest pains when he entered Dr. Ornish's program. When he concluded the program, he was hiking six hours a day in the Grand Tetons.

The control group followed the recommendations of the American Heart Association, which allowed 30 percent fat in daily diets and up to 300 mg of cholesterol per day. There was no improvement in these patients, and some conditions worsened.

Dr. Ornish's findings were published in the *Lancet* in England in 1990 and in the *Journal of American Medical Association* in 1995. In spite of initial skepticism on the part of the medical establishment, insurance companies were interested in Dr. Ornish's work, since diet represents a significant reduction in cost over other heart treatments such as bypass and angioplasty.

Obesity

Diets which proved good for patients with heart disease were often found to be good for people who suffered from obesity, from the constant physical and psychological strains of losing and regaining weight, losing and regaining. The goal became to change the way we think about food; to change the foods we find desirable; to teach our taste buds to salivate at what is good for the heart and the body. It can be done because diet is influenced as much by habit and social and psychological expectations as by physical necessity. Because most of us care about how we look, Dean Ornish, whose work was revolutionary with respect to heart disease, wrote a book, *Eat More, Weigh Less.* [93] In the introduction, he wrote,

> Besides helping you to lose weight and keep it off, this program has other benefits that mean even more to me, as a physician, than weight loss. But if I wrote a book entitled *How to Prevent Heart Disease, Obesity, Stroke, Breast Cancer, Prostate Cancer, Colon Cancer, Osteoporosis, Diabetes, Hypertension, and Lots of Other Illnesses,* you might not read it.

There is an interconnection among these disabilities: a high fat, meat centered diet is the common factor that unites them.

Arteriosclerotic Diseases: Stroke, Heart Disease, Hypertension

Animal fat is the only fat that contains cholesterol, and cholesterol is involved in heart disease and high blood pressure. Animal fat clogs arteries so that the blood cannot properly flow through them. Arteries should be smooth and blood should flow through them uninterruptedly.

Modern food animals have more fat in them than wild animals do, or than farm animals had in the past. Modern meat is marbled with fat. The animals our ancestors ate were leaner because they led more natural lives, they ran, they migrated, they searched for food. The modern meat animal is deliberately fattened by modern breeding habits. Science journalist, Colin Tudge, describes the process:

> ...farmers interested in efficiency cannot simply let an animal grow at its own pace. A beef animal that grew as nature intended--first skeleton, then muscle, then fat, with periods of no growth in winter--would be four years old by the time it was ready for the butcher. Modern beeves [cattle] are destined for slaughter at eighteen months if fed on grass, and as little as ten months if fed on cereals....[94]

The modern meat animal lays down muscle first before its skeleton has grown, and accumulates fat before it has muscle to carry it. The aim of the breeder is not to grow a healthy, normal animal, but to fatten the animal and bring it to the slaughtering house as quickly as possible. Animals are bred for profit, not for healthy food. A cow that used to take four years to reach slaughter weight can now reach it in ten months. This is a tremendous telescoping of the animal's normal growth pattern. What is true for cows is also true for chickens and turkeys: their growth patterns have been telescoped to suit market and profit demands.

> In genetic terms...the breeders have selected genes that alter the *timing* of events within the genomes. This effectively is the *opposite* of neoteny: the imposition of adult features into a young, growing animal. [95]

The Crated Veal: From A Sick Animal To Your Plate

The crated veal exemplifies the worst of the factory farming system. A factory farmed animal is often a sick animal kept alive until slaughtering time by continual subtherapeutic medication. The crated veal is a notorious example of the system. Deception is practised on the public in the very description of this animal as "milk-fed veal," which conjures a picture of health. This calf is not fed milk, but a whitish fluid made of proteins, vitamins and minerals, powdered skim milk, starches and fats, which is a milk-replacer gruel laced with antibiotics.

Veal is the meat of a male calf born on dairy farms which used to represent a loss to the dairy farmer. About the end of the second World War the Dutch firm, Provimi, developed the diabolical idea of converting a dead-loss animal into a gourmet status symbol. Since the male calf will never become a milk producer, he is useless to the dairy farmer and is taken from his mother at birth or, at most, after two days (though Jewish law mandates that newborn animals be kept with their mothers for eight days). He is put into a pitch-dark stall or box about his own size and tethered at his neck to restrict his movement. He is kept stationary and never develops muscle tone. The farmer deliberately makes the animal anemic because anemia gives veal its white meat look prized by gourmets. Hence, the calf's iron intake is minimal, in order to induce anemia. The calf is never given straw or bedding to lie on, because the calf will eat it out of his desperate need for roughage. "Calves, like all animals that 'chew the cud,' have a biological requirement for roughage; it stimulates the ruminating compartment of their digestive systems."[96] This ruminating system no longer works in the veal calf as it was meant to do, and veal calves suffer from frequent diarrhea. The floor of the stall is designed to channel the calf's excrement into the ground beneath him, or into troughs alongside, but the excrement usually builds up faster than it can run off. The calf often lies in his own excrement and acquires painful body sores. He also frequently will try to drink his own urine because he is denied water in order to force him to drink the whitish gruel. Nature knows what the calf needs--iron--which is used up in the calf's body by eight to ten weeks, but the farmer knows that he wants to produce a calf with white meat that will fetch a high price. The calf is given just enough iron for the remaining six to eight weeks of his life to keep him from dying.

The calf is ready for market when his anemia is very severe, usually at fourteen weeks. At this time the farmer must choose between keeping the calf a bit longer to gain more weight and value, and run the risk of the calf's untimely death from the diseases he has developed. The calf is kept alive just long enough, but often when he is taken from his crate, he collapses from the exertion of movement for the first time. Thus, milk-fed veal is the palatable tender meat produced by careful timing between disease and death.[97] Because this calf is a very sick animal, "Calves in crates require five times as much medication as calves allowed to range free." [98] About twenty percent of the calves die of this treatment, but the price that the other eighty percent fetches for the farmer makes the system worth his while.

In 1982, Rabbi Moshe Feinstein condemned the eating of the veal calf when he declared, "that it was forbidden to cause suffering to the animal by feeding it food which it does not enjoy and which causes it pain when it is eating, and also which causes it to suffer illness from which it will suffer pain." But feeding animals food which are unsuitable for them, such as feeding animal protein to ruminant animals is practically the universal basis of feeding animals today, and is thought to be the cause of mad cow disease. Rabbi Feinstein also wrote that, "There is a Biblical prohibition against causing pain to animals in such a fashion simply for the sake of some benefit, and for the sake of deceiving people to imagine that the meat is better." The benefit of feeding ruminant animals the waste products and parts of other animals is greed. Rendering animal parts for food to other animals is an enormous industry, inextricable from the modern meat business, and it has had horrendous results in the form of what has come to be known as "mad cow disease."

The meat business is pervaded with deception. The entire industry rests on deception, on the nostalgic ideas the public has about the newly-born calf who runs alongside his mother, about the generosity of the cow's udders, the goodness of her milk; about chickens scratching in the earth, roosters crowing to the rising sun, about the bliss and virtues of the peaceable kingdom. Almost none of this exists. Such scenes should be erased from the public mind as lies and propaganda. What exists in place of this bucolic picture we inherited from the past are vast structures that resemble concentration camps. Both are the twin creations of the contemporary world. Just as the prohibition against seething a kid in its mother's milk was extended to all animals, Rabbi Feinstein's judgment about the veal calf should be extended to all factory farmed animals, for they are all fed foods that are unnatural to them, live lives that are unnatural to them; and their producers are engaged in deception that the meat of these animals is neither contaminated nor the product of torture. They depend upon the false picture the public has of "Old Macdonald's farm."

Exploitation of animals for food is not new, but the exploitation has become relentless, without surcease in the animal's life. As Ruth Harrison wrote in *Animal Machines*, "It has been taken to a degree where the animal is not allowed to live before it dies." [99] Or as one protest poster declaimed: "Before this animal is slaughtered, he will wish he had never been born." People who argue that breeding of animals today is nothing more than the continuation of an historic development would not argue that nuclear war is nothing more than the continuation of an historic development, and is therefore morally no different than war with bows and arrows. War is war, and people who die in war suffer, whether killed by an arrow, by buckshot or a nuclear bomb, but the magnitude and concentration of evil today in both war and the breeding of animals for food has changed the arguments in both cases.

Rabbi Rosen declared, as have the Jewish sages throughout the centuries: "The explicit purpose of the Biblical dietary laws is holiness...."[100] Where is holiness in meat from the animal machine? What is the premise of its creation? From the point of view of the veal calf lying in his own manure in a dark crate for weeks on end, without sunshine or wind or rain or grass or smell or warmth or sound, the world is dead and his creation was evil. John Milton's description of hell in "Paradise Lost" should be carved over the buildings that house the crated veal:

> No light, but rather darkness visible
> Served only to discover sights of woe,
> Regions of sorrow, doleful shades, where peace

> and rest can never dwell, hope never comes
> That come to all; but torture without end...

One of the earliest laws of kashrut was the commandment to choose the animal "from among your herds." But our herds are not what they were. They are often bred indoors in crates or on feedlots and kept deliberately inactive, often to the point of sickness, for which they are fed quantities of medicine. They are deracinated from their original natures. Appetite and locomotion are intrinsic to the search for food and bred in the animal's nature.[101] Does the shochet's responsibility for an animal start only in the slaughterhouse, or should it begin on the feeding lots and in the barns? How does the traditional definition of "blemish" relate to the multitude of diseases the modern food animal contracts? The modern meat animal is an intensive-cholesterol, diseased, and intensively medicated animal.

Heart Disease

The work of Dean Ornish revolutionized medicine with respect to coronary degeneration when he cured patients with advanced heart disease through diet, exercise and stress counseling. He also reminded us that while bypass surgery and other intervention approaches help diseased hearts, this help is often temporary. Without a dietary change, the condition returns:

> ...drugs, angioplasty (blowing up a balloon inside a blocked coronary artery), and coronary bypass surgery--cause only *temporary* improvement because they literally or figuratively *bypass* the underlying causes of the problem. As a result, the same heart problem often recurs or new problems and side effects may develop....Up to one half of bypass grafts become clogged again after only five years, and one-third of angioplastied arteries become clogged after only four to six months....[102]

What Dr. Ornish found out about for heart disease he postulates for osteoporosis, obesity, stroke, hypertension, and other diseases.[103]

Contrary to what the public understands about scientific evidence, there is often no clear consensus in evaluating scientific data. As Dr. Jay Lavine warns, tests are always ongoing and the "evidence" is often in flux. But his summary statement, sent in a letter, is a conservative warning:

> There is no question, though, that even when one employs the most rigorous scientific thinking, the roles of diet in the causation of cancer is tremendous. If people simply increased their consumption of vegetables and fruits to five to eight servings a day, the death rate from cancer twenty years from now would be half of what it is today. Although not every cancer is related to diet, there are links between every major form of cancer and diet, including cancer of the lungs, breast, prostate, colon and rectum, pancreas, lymphatic system, ovaries, and bladder. Just as Ornish has shown that probably 95% of all heart attacks are preventable, half or more of all cancer deaths within a given age group are probably preventable as well. As far as the role of meat is concerned, many studies, looking at beef alone or combining all flesh foods have shown links with cancer.

U.S. Government Stamp of Approval

The United States government finally put its official stamp of recognition on the relationship between diet and disease with the publication of *The Surgeon General's Report on Nutrition and Health,* published in 1988. This is a 727 page report that was free to every tax-paying citizen. It was a self-consciously revolutionary document:

> This first *Surgeon General's Report on Nutrition and Health* marks a key event in the history of public health

> in the United States....This Report reviews the scientific evidence that relates dietary excesses and imbalances to chronic diseases. On the basis of the evidence, it recommends dietary changes that can improve the health prospects of many Americans. Of highest priority among these changes is to reduce intake of foods high in fats and to increase intake of foods high in complex carbohydrates and fiber.
>
> The evidence presented here indicates the convergence of similar dietary recommendations that apply to prevention of multiple chronic diseases. The recommendation to reduce dietary fat...aims to reduce the risk for coronary heart disease, diabetes, obesity, and some types of cancer....
>
> The weight of this evidence and the magnitude of the problems at hand indicate that it is now time to take action....

Few people knew of this free publication. We need a system for informing the public of such reports. Perhaps it should be the duty of congresspeople, or HMO's and insurance companies to send notices of such reports to their constituents and members.

Genetic Effects

In spite of the strides taken in the last few decades by outstanding nutritionists and researchers, there is a present danger that the public can be diverted by genetic studies from the relationship of diet and environmental factors to disease. Important as these studies are for such diseases as Huntington's and Tay Sachs, the contribution of genes to cancer is not dominantly causal. Cancer involves genetic malfunctioning, but this genetic malfunctioning is most often caused by what Robert Proctor has called, "an insult to the genes": that is, a dietary or environmental assault on genetic function which causes the genetic information to go awry. As he writes in *Cancer Wars*, we know what causes cancer. It's not a mystery. We give laboratory mice cancer all the time.

> Cancer is caused by the chemicals in the air we breath, the water we drink, and the food we eat. Cancer is caused by bad habits, bad working conditions, bad government, and bad luck--including the luck of your genetic draw.[104]

Caution is advisable when dealing with information about genetic determinants. "...inheritable cancers account for only a tiny fraction of all cancers."[105] Perhaps five to ten%. Family histories have to be examined carefully, for families share similar environmental and dietary factors, as well as genetic inheritances.

Ashkenazi Jews, for whom a gene for breast cancer and a gene for colon cancer, seem to have been isolated, need to know how to interpret information concerning genetic functioning. They should know that among geneticists themselves there is a quarrel about the degree to which genes influence disease destiny. Comments by biologists and doctors on gene theories in a *New York Times* article, indicates the extent to which there is no consensus concerning the contribution of genes to disease.[106] Richard Lewontin, Alexander Agassiz Professor of Zoology and Professor of Biology at Harvard University, author of *The Genetic Basis of Evolutionary Change* and *Biology of Ideology*, has a common sense warning about "genomania":

> The fallacy of genetic determinism is to suppose that the genes 'make' the organism. It is a basic principle of developmental biology that organisms undergo a continuous development from conception to death that is the unique consequence of the interaction of the genes in their cells, the temporal sequence of environments through which the organisms pass, and random cellular processes that determine the life, death, and transformation of cells. [107]

Diet and environmental factors can modify genetic structure. Governmental and nutritional agencies have known about the connection between diet, certain cancers and heart disease since the mid 1920's. *Jack Spratt's Legacy: The Science and Politics of Fat and Cholesterol*, by Patricia Hausman of the Center for Science in the Public Interest, documents research that indicated a relationship between fat and cancer for over seventy years.[108] By 1988, it was time for a surgeon general's report to say so.

Pathogens in Meat: Mad cow disease

Governments are conservative institutions, but diseases are not. They can be denied by governments for only so long, as was illustrated with Creutzfeldt-Jakob disease (also called CJD, the human counterpart to mad cow disease. The scientific name of mad cow disease is bovine spongiform encephalopathy, or BSE) in England. Richard Lacey, Professor of Clinical Microbiology at Leeds University in England, consultant to the World Health Organization, and recipient of many awards, documented reported cases in England from 1985/6.[109] His book, *Hard to Swallow,* provides the model for governments whose concern is to assuage public fears and to minimize commercial losses when confronted with a meat-to-human transmitted disease.

From Dr. Lacey's first report in 1985/6 until 1992, cases of infected cattle in England continued to grow yearly, but the British government believed "that cattle will be a dead-end host and that the disease will not spread once the source of it has been cut off."[110] The source of the disease was brains of infected sheep and other animals, that are processed into a powder mixed into the cow's protein supplement. Cows, who are vegetarian animals who have lived successfully on grass for millennia, contracted bovine spongiform encephalopathy or BSE. The disease causes the cow to stumble like a drunkard, to lose control of her body, to appear deranged; hence, the descriptive term, "mad cow disease." When the sick cow's brains are examined under a microscope, they show evidence of a porous structure that is like a sponge. In human beings, the disease causes neurological deterioration and dementia. There is a conflict in the biological world about whether the disease is caused by a virus or a prion. A prion is a renegade protein, which cannot be destroyed. It is impervious to irradiation.[111]

The British government remained convinced for years that human beings cannot catch BSE. On what grounds, we do not know, but the merest suspicion should have been sufficient to put in place restraints against such an unsavory disease.

By 1990 media suspicion grew that there was something rotten in the fields of England. Cows were observed to stagger and fall. They did not behave according to their traditional bovine natures. Nevertheless and amazingly, Dr. Lacey reports that in England in 1990, consumption of beef slowly rose, because "The Meat and Livestock Commission [were] successful in promoting beef to schools." The reason for the seeming increase in beef cosumption was a government cover-up: Surplus meat was being bought up by the government, giving the false impression that great volumes of beef were still being consumed. According to Dr. Lacey's report, "Various cattle organs, such as brains, spleen, and thymus, [had] been excluded from the food chain, but all the edible organs of calves under 6 months of age still enter[ed] the food chain, and animals over 6 months--even from infected herds--[were] exported. Commercial damage to the beef industry [was] minimised."[112] By 1991, the number of BSE cases was 25,000, but the government's advisors predicted that the numbers will begin to fall. On what grounds, we do not know, and no research was undertaken "to identify how many cows are infected but not yet ill." By June, Dr. Lacey wrote, 1,000 cases a week of cows sick with BSE were evident, but the "government still believes that numbers will begin to fall by the end of 1992." We still do not know where the government got its faith from, but by 1995 and 1996 there were 50-60 reported cases of Creutzfeldt-Jakob disease in humans in England. Dr. Lacey believes the number is as high as 1500-9000, and writes:

> The study of BSE has produced overwhelming evidence of the existence of an infective agent acquired through eating.....CJD is therefore probably acquired from meat (if you don't like this suggestion, try and find an alternative).[113]

Among current frightening diseases, such as the emergence of the Eboli Virus and AIDS, CJD is the most noxious and the hardest to treat, if treatment is not altogether impossible. Richard Rhodes gives this description of CJD:

> The new disease is a stealth agent: it incubates silently for years and kills every last victim it infects. Eboli is a sickness of fever and bleeding, no worse than cholera, a quick if not a merciful death. The new disease is an atrocity of destruction--a headache, a stumble, and then hallucination, palsy, seizure and coma drawn out horribly for months. Victim's brains go spongy; their minds dim; they lose the ability to walk, to talk, to see, to swallow; they die slowly, drowning in pneumonia, or they starve to death. [114]

Alex Herschaft of Farm Animal Reform Movement and others believe that mad cow disease is not just a British problem. Certainly, it would be foolhardy not to seriously raise the question.[115] The United States took the possibility seriously enough to convene an international conference on BSE at the National Institutes of Health in June, 1989. At the time the outbreak of BSE seemed restricted to cows in England, but sheep scrapie was occurring around the world, and the practice of feeding diseased sheep to animals raised for human consumption was widespread throughout the industrialized West. Since symptoms do not appear in animals for as long as two to eight years after infection (long after the animal has been slaughtered and eaten) and not for four to thirty years in humans, we will not know the toll for some time to come. Cows in the United States are slaughtered at an even earlier age, and may be symptom free at the time of their slaughter, but be carriers of the disease. The United States took some precautionary measures: they prohibited the import of pharmacological products for animals, because the capsules are covered with gelatin made from animal products. The FDA, however, permitted gelatin and other beef by-products for human use coming from countries infected with BSE to continue to be imported here. The government asked for a voluntary ban by U.S. farmers on the use of animal products in feed for their animals.The voluntary ban was largely ineffectual. Efforts which governments undertake to contain the problem meet with enormous political resistance and tremendous pressure from lobbies. Much of the efforts come under the heading of "crisis management," and "don't alarm the public."[116] The question is whether what the United States and other governments did will prove adequate. Richard Lacey believes not, that the eventual number of CJD cases will be high.[117] His analysis is a chilling warning that "the high incidence of infected animals must present a phenomenal danger to man from around the turn of this century into the next."

Rendering Unto Caesar

Mad cow disease is inextricably involved in the growth and practice of the rendering plants, which became a major producer of animal feed in the 1970s. Often what is in the feed is considered a trade secret and is identified only as "protein content." Incredibly, sick sheep and other sick animals are sent to rendering plants to be converted into animal feed for cattle. Remains of dead sheep are often mixed with other animal waste and reduced to meal. This material may be further mixed with chicken feathers, chicken litter, citrus pulp, and sawdust. Nicols Fox tells the story of how the method of rendering this material had changed around 1981 or 1982, making it even more dangerous. Heat is used to kill pathogens (though not all pathogens can be killed this way), but in the late 1970s and early 1980s this heat was considerbly reduced "to enhance taste, to increase the nutrient value of the material, and to lower energy costs." [118] Then BSE infected animals were themselves sent to the rendering plants to be recycled out as food. In the United States, the situation is ambiguous. The question of whether mad cow disease exists here has not been resolved. There is a condition in cattle called "downer animals." These are cows who collapse after being taken off the truck that has transported them to the slaughterhouse or the rendering plant. Videos of "downer cows" show the lamentable picture of an obviously sick and weak animal who cannot get up. These animals are dragged by chains or prodded with electric prods until they manage to stagger to their feet and stumble into the plant. Kosher slaughtering houses do not receive downer cows, but the downer cows may be used in the rendering plants, where their parts may be recycled into animal feed. Nicols Fox writes that Dr. Richard F. Marsh, a renowned veterinarian from the School of Veterninary Medicine at the University of Wisconsin, Madison believes that downer cows suffer from a variant of BSE.[119] In Wisconsin, his home state, around 35,000 downer animals go to the renderers each year. No one wants Dr. Marsh to be right, but his view has the support of C. Joseph Gibbs, a researcher at the National Institutes of Health.[120]

The scare in Britain had the good results of inspiring the United States in 1997 to take some steps to prevent an outbreak of mad cow disease. Richard Rhodes feels that the measures may be too little and too late.

> ...there were disturbing compromises built into the FDA's proposed ban. It would prohibit the use of tissue from cattle, sheep and goats in feed for those ruminants but would permit the continued feeding of ruminant blood, milk and gelatin. Ruminant tissue would continue to be processed into feed for chickens, pigs and pets despite the known susceptibility of pigs and cats to spongiform encephalopathy and the possible passage of the disease agent through chickens and into their manure. Nor do the ubiquitous contamination of U.S. poultry and eggs with salmonella and the continuing outbreaks of human E.coli infection from contaminated meat inspire confidence in government inspection.[121]

"Hamburger Disease" [122]

Food poisoning from a new form of the E.coli bacteria became known to the public after a serious outbreak of E.coli infection in 1993 of seven hundred people who became sick from hamburgers eaten at the Seattle fast food restaurant, Jack-in-the Box. However, there had already been many incidents of E.coli food poisoning in Canada and the United States for close to a decade. The bacterium, E.coli 0157:H7 was identified in 1982. Gail Eisnitz, in her book, *Slaughterhouse,* documents incidents dating back to 1986.[123] The horror of this disease is not in statistics alone, but in the terribly debilitating illness, and often death, that results from it. E.coli food posioning can cause hemolytic uremic syndrome (HUS), a disease "which sends toxins coursing throughout the body and destroys the blood's ability to clot." [124] Its victims are usually the elderly and children. According to Gail Eisnitiz, HUS is "now the leading cause of kidney failure in children in the United States." [125] Since it is children who frequently eat hamburgers at cook-outs and in fast-food restaurants, [126] parents of children who have become ill with E.coli infection have founded an organization, STOP (Safe Tables Our Priority) and have given testimony at congressional and USDA hearings on the plight of their children. Mary Heersink, the wife and daughter of physicians was one of the founders of STOP. Ironically, the family is health conscious and rarely eats meat. It took only one misguided and unfortunate incident to contract a lifetime of misery. Her son, Damion, contracted E.coli food poisoning from a piece of hamburger meat the size of a marble, which he ate at a Boy Scout cookout. He had been warned by his parents not to eat rare hamburger and knew immediately that he should not have eaten the piece, but "he was ashamed to spit it out." Most children and many adults would behave the same way, ashamed to spit food out in public. Within a few hours, Damion was suffering from diarrhea and acute cramps. His stool turned so bloody, Mary thought he was hemorraghing, and rushed him to a hospital. Damion suffered kidney failure, his platelet level dropped, his lungs filled with fluid, he hallucinated, his heart became enlarged 2 1/2 times its normal size. At eleven years old he had spent seven weeks in an intensive care unit, had undergone seven surgeries, and eleven plasma changes. When he left the hospital his muscle tissue was gone and he had lost twenty-five pounds.[127] A dozen parents told similar stories at a Senate symposium. The story of ten-year old Brianne Kiner was told by her mother:

> My daughter Brianne lay in a hospital bed for one hundred sixty-seven days. For forty-five of those days she was dying....the pain during the first eighty hours in the hospital was horrific. The intense abdominal cramping continued every ten to twelve miunutes. Her intestines swelled to three times their normal size.
> She fell into a deep coma that lasted forty days. All of her body organs swelled. Her breathing accelerated to a hundred breaths per minute so she was placed on a ventilator....After Brianne's second emergency surgery, surgeons left her open from her sternum to her pubic area to allow her swollen organs room to expand and to prevent them from ripping her skin....the toxins shut down Bri's liver and pancreas. Several times her skin turned black for weeks....

These were the testimonies from parents whose children survived after months in hospitals struggling for their lives. Others did not survive. One little girl, Lauren Rudolph, died of a massive heart attack at the age of six. Those who do survive are more often than not left with a lifetime of debilitating health problems: blindness, diabetes, a colostomy, and may require kidney dialysis or a kidney transplant.

E.coli food poisoning is spreading so quickly that even produce grown in land fertilized with cow manure can carry the bacterium.There are estimates that 25% of E.coli food poisoning are now contracted from vegetables, but its origins *are always* in contaminated cow feces. As Mary Heersink told Gail Eisnitz in an interview:

> 'The USDA dropped the most basic principle learned at the dawn of mankind....Humans learned early on, probably the hard way, to keep manure off meat. But here, at the end of the second millenium, at the very moment that a new, mutant strain of E.coli appears on the scene...the USDA decides that the time has come to establish levels for allowable fecal contamination on meat.

> While epidemiologists measured that one speck of feces can contain millions of microbes of E.coli 0157, and that a mere one to ten microbes can kill a child, USDA bureaucrats were counting how many visible specks and smears of cow feces they would overlook on each animal.'[128]

The inspection process is called "risk evaluation." It derives from the philosophy and process which governs decisions effecting the ratio of the cost of human disability to the economic cost. Its origins are in the decision-making process concerning war. The Reagan and Bush administrations were responsible for instituting another process in the meat industry, deregulating it and reducing the number of inspectors, which greatly increased the risk of contamination in meat. Mary Heersink confronted USDA officials at a hearing on meat inspection in June, 1993:

> Are you brave enough to admit that the one natural reservoir of E.coli 0157.H7 has been proven to be the intestinal tract of cattle? That the avenue of infection is feces splattered on our meat? That the disease which was extremely rare only a decade ago has now become the leading cause of kidney failure in U.S. children? That all this suffering is in direct correlation to the deregulatory programs of the last two administrations? [129]

Cows stand in fecal matter during transportation due to the methods of transporting them. They are given nothing to eat or drink while in transit so that their intestines will be empty at slaughtertime; they are crowded into tight quarters, hungry, tired and frightened, and lose control of their bowels. Many are covered with fecal matter as they go into the slaughterhouse.

It is now estimated that there are 20,000 cases of E.coli infection annually, most of which cause severe illness, some of which are fatal. The estimates for fatality are between 250 and 500.[130] Nicols Fox examines the spread of "The Hamburger Bacteria." [131] It should sound familiar in its resemblance to governmental action in England and the United States with respect to BSE: the initial denial on the part of the government and meat industries, the delayed acceptance of the problem by the USDA and FDA, the avoidance of the issue by the media. Problems with food are not only health problems. They are political problems. The manufacture of food is our largest industry, surpassing health care and weapons, which are second and third. They involve problems of identification and imagery. The hamburger is our national food. It is an icon.

> Standing sentinel behind the reputations of the fast-food franchises was the U.S. Department of Agriculture, which inspected and approved the meat they used. Shoring up the agency's reputation was the assurance, repeated endlessly that 'America has the safest food supply in the world.' From the 1950s to the 1980s that guarantee fit smoothly into the image America had of itself, an image of technological superiority, the highest standards, and an enviable lifestyle. It had become a part of the American mythology--often quoted and never questioned.[132]

The myth has been sold around the world, including to Israel where the tradtional, healthy indigenous falafel is being replaced by the American hamburger as the fast food of choice. As individuals, we cannot always control government policies and decisions, but we can always control what goes into our mouths. We can boycott. In Switzerland, consumer boycott of food products brought action from the government.

There are still other pathogens such as salmonella and campylobacter which receive little attention, but which cause serious diseases which can also be mortal for the very young or the elderly. Fox calls poultry "the most contaminated product Americans bring into their kitchen."[133] Cambylobacter affects between 30% and 70% of chickens, and is responsible for "2 million to 8 million cases of campylobacterosis a year and 200 to 800 deaths.....," according to an article in*The New York Times.*[134] Campylobacter has been linked "to the rare and potentially fatal nerve damage caused by Guillain-Barré syndrome," which involves life-threatening progressive paralysis. It can cause a form of arthritis. "It has also been associated on occasion with meningitis, convulsions, and bacteremia, and, rarely, miscarriage."[135] According to an article in *TheWashington Post,* the number of cases of campylobacter has exceeded that of salmonella.[136] Furthermore, "there is no simple laboratory test to identify it,"[137] and it has become resistant to antibiotics due to the use of antiobiotics in animal feed. Salmonella now infects eggs as well as poultry, and even cases involving ice cream have appeared. The source seems to be contaminated feed. Nicols Fox describes the sad bureaucratic snafu that overtook the USDA and the FDA in efforts to contain the problem. There was a problem with defining the authority for inspection and correction. the USDA had no authority in the feed industry, nor money or personnel to devote to the problem. This problem fell to the FDA, which defined salmonella as an adulterant agent, in 1967, but did not look for it. No studies were commissioned. Eventually, the USDA did make some discoveries:

> The amount of contamination in feed was related to whether the rendering plant processed dead animals or not. Vat-pressure systems were more successful at reducing *Salmonella* (and presumably other infectious agents), but ironically, it wouldn't be long before almost everyone in the industry shifted to the more economical continuous process system, which allowed pathogens to be distributed throughout the material rather than to be confined to a batch. The recycling of dead animals to animal feed would continue without pause....The potential for contamination in what animals were eating went beyond prepared feeds. Beef cattle were increasingly being fed chicken litter and other manures, both to get rid of animal waste and as a cheap source of protein. Sometimes this material was composted; sometimes it was merely left in a shed to age eight months to a year.[138]

These are only three prominent pathogens. There are others. The government is now addressing the problem, but efforts to stay ahead of food-borne pathogens, as with the emergent antibiotic-resistance diseases, may become a similar deadly race against time.

The rise of pathogens in meat since the 1980s has dramatically changed the relationship between food and disease. With this rise, it is no longer a matter of long, chronic diseases, costly and debilitating to victims and families, but mainly affecting the mature population. The new diseases are swifter, intensely painful, affect the young in large numbers, and are growing in virulence. This new development not only makes *b'dikah,* the Jewish method of inspecting a carcass for disease obsolete, it makes modern methods obsolete. Pathogens cannot be examined by sight, taste or touch. Nor can the inspection system be relegated to the slaughtering plant alone which in any event is woefully inadequate in most slaughtering houses. In 1985, a new inspection system, called "Streamlined Inspection," was instituted. Prior to this year, in a chicken slaughtering house, USDA inspectors inspected eighteen birds per minute. With Streamlined Inspection, there were 450 less inspectors, examining a billion and half birds per year, 15,000 per day, or 35 chickens per minute. A former Perdue worker testified to Congress about conditions of filth:

> 'The floors are covered with grease, fat, sand, and roaches. Bugs are up and down the sides of the walls. Some of the flying roaches were huge, up to four and five inches long....There is so much fecal contamination on the floor from the chickens that it kept getting into one worker's boots and burned his feet so badly his toenails had to be amputated.'[139]

Nicols Fox reports similar condition that occurred in beef slaughtering houses:

> Under experimental programs the number of inspectors was reduced. Unsanitary conditions were allowed to

> continue, and repeated violations failed to lead to USDA action....Line speeds often reached four hundred cattle per hour; inspectors were asked to check as many as thirty livers per minute and found the task impossible; grossly infected cattle with such conditions as urine-filled bellies, peritonitis, pneumonia, and measles (tapeworm) were slippping past inspectors into the food chain....Cowheads, which are trimmed to provide meat for hamburger, were getting through with regurgitated food oozing out, and 'fecal contamination and other filth were getting out of control.' [140]

The Streamlined Inspection project was dropped, but not before tremendous damage, which may be irreversible, had occurred, and other damaging practices still remain. Incredibly the USDA has no authority on farms. It intersects the problem of contaminants at a point in the process of meat production far removed from its origins--the farm and the feeding lot. Similarly, with kosher inspection.

Mad Human Disease

The desire to reduce costs and raise profits produces its own diseases called hubris, greed, and willful blindness. It is otherwise unfathomable to understand why farmers and breeders would change the food habits of animals that have proven successful for millennium.Common sense tells ordinary human beings that it must be unwise to feed the remains of diseased animals to other animals, to engage in a practice which has been called "animal cannibalism." Hubris and greed may be the causes of plagues for decades to come because we have bred so much change in our foods in the rage for progress and profits. The historian, William H. McNeill, believes that infectious diseases are the result of an "ecological niche" that is created when there is instability in the biotic community.[141] Infectious diseases disappear or become weak when a population has remained stable for centuries and when those who were susceptible to the infectious diseases have died off. Change creates biotic instability and new ecological niches into which newly evolved or previously dormant micro-organisms flow. Human beings have always lived with domesticated animals in a kind of extended community. This has always carried with it the dangers of animal-to-human transmitted diseases. These dangers have become magnified because of the manner in which animals are now raised. Genetic alterations, alterations of the animals' reproductive systems, of their feeding habits, are breeding new animal diseases, with consequences we can scarcely imagine. We already see new diseases emerging, such as CJD and HUS, diseases with initials and numbers as they emerge from a catalogue of diseases. In 1964, Ruth Harrison wrote with foreboding:

> It is obvious to anyone, let alone a veterinarian, that the conditions under which intensively kept animals are reared indoors could not possibly lead to healthy animals, and animal health has deteriorated to a degree such as to cause acute anxiety to the veterinary world. But...farmers regard veterinary surgeons as the miracle men of their world able to produce drugs to combat the effects of flouting every natural need of the animal. If the drugs happen to make serious physiological changes this type of farmer does not concern himself as long as the carcass remains saleable. [142]

Although there have been historic disease boundaries between animals and humans, these boundaries are also often transgressed when conditions allow them to be. In the biotic community, micro-organisms are an equal-opportunity employer, and often do not distinguish between humans and animals.

> At every level of organization--molecular, cellular, organismic, and social--one confronts equilibrium patterns. Within such equilibria, any alteration from 'outside' tends to provoke compensatory changes throughout the systems so as to minimize over-all upheaval, though there are always critical limits which, if transgressed,

> result in the breakdown of the previously existing system. [143]

For too long modern medicine has adhered to the germ theory of the specific pathogen of disease. Epidemiologists and infectious disease specialists have now come to understand that diseases may be multi-causal and influenced by propensities; but much research still is done by scientists who prefer the narrower unicausal approach of the germ theory.

> Simple cause-and-effect analysis is inadequate for such systems. Since many variables are simultaneously at work, interacting constantly and altering their magnitudes at irregular rates, it is usually misleading to concentrate attention on a single 'cause' and try to attribute a particular 'effect' to it. Study of simultaneity among multiple processes is presumably a better way to approach an understanding. But the conceptual and practical difficulties here are enormous.... [144]

It is this model of the "simultaneity of multiple processes" that should be borne in mind when we study the impact of a meat-centered diet upon disease and the environment. The sheer numbers are consequential for disease. According to Alex Herschaft of Farm Animal Reform Movement, figures from the National Agriculture Statistical Service (NASS) for 1996, state that 8.915 billion fowl were killed for consumption; 38.6 million cattle, 4.6 million calves, 107.7 million pigs, and 5.4 million sheep. The total number of all animals killed for food in the United States was projected for 1997 at 9.3 billion. Not all these animals reach the slaughterhouse. Sixty percent of bovines die of stress, injury or disease before reaching the slaughterhouse, which suggests the enormity of the husbandry problems, and has contributed to the growth of the rendering business. Nor is it easy to know what to do with all these diseased animals. (In the egg-laying business, about 250 million male chickens are suffocated to death in plastic garbage bags because they have no market value. Among the broilers, male and female live 6 1/2 weeks.) This quantity of death is translated into a continuous impact on environment and human health. Whether we eat meat or not, or eat just a little meat, we all live downwind from the factory farm which must affect the "ecological niche" in which new pathogens establish a foothold. McNeill believes that it is possible that birth control may limit population explosion, that medicine may unveil new miracles, and that a new balance between human numbers and resources may assert itself, but he does not think it likely.

> ...for the present and short-range future, it remains obvious that humanity is in course of one of the most massive and extraordinary ecological upheavals the planet has ever known. Not stability, but a sequence of sharp alterations and abrupt oscillations in existing balances between microparasitism and macroparasitism can therefore be expected in the near future as in the recent past.[145]

By being at the end of a food chain which starts with grains that have been doused with pesticides and works its way through animals that have been over-medicalized, often themselves suffering from multiple health problems, which end with us, we expose ourselves to the cumulative effects of bad farming and bad husbandry practices. We cannot eliminate the risks in modern food, but we can control the risks by changing our place in the food chain.

Eat No Evil: If We Are What We Eat, What Are Cows?

The problem of diseased meat is potentially systemic today because of the way factory farmed animals are fed. Their food is cereal based, with vitamins, minerals, protein supplements and drugs added to the cereal. The right mixture requires skill, and only a few companies manufacture the food. Thus the food supply for cattle comes from a few sources which distribute widely. Richard Lacey observes that "This type of production is potentially dangerous, were anything to go amiss, such as the introduction of an infectious agent."[146] And the protein source often comes from other animals used in the rendering plants, whose parts are recycled.

> Exactly when the practice of incorporating this type of material, now referred to as concentrates, into animal feed began is difficult to be certain about because of the surrounding secrecy. It was probably in the late 1960s or early 1970s in most countries....The unwanted waste material can be converted to a useful and profitable industry....The rendering plant operators, the feed compounders and the farmers would not have been aware of any infectious risk in this system....we now know this is not the case....[because of Mad cow disease] [147]

Dead cows are fed to other cows, because the rendering industry is powerful and relieves the farmer of the problem of having to dispose of a cow who has died. It is certainly better from the farmer's point of view to be paid for a 1200 pound cow to be removed, than to have to pay someone to take her carcass away. New born calves, a day or two old, are often put out on the road for a truck from a rendering plant to pick up, take away and turn him into something else. Cows are viewed as recycling or garbage disposal machines. Singer and Mason catalogue a list of waste products from other manufactories that have destroyed the historic nature of the vegetarian, ruminant cow.

> In many animals' feeds, the protein supplement is a meal made from feathers, feet, intestines, chicken heads, and other animal parts discarded at slaughterhouses. Our meat and milk...is made by animals fed on plastic hay, newspaper, cardboard boxes, by-products from the manufacture of corn and potato chips, municipal garbage, and animal manure....Leftovers from breweries and distilleries go into feeds. Dried blood, meat, condemned carcasses, and other parts left over at the slaughterhouse go into feed. The rendering industry, which picks up dead and diseased animals that do not make it to the slaughterhouse, supplies animals to animal

> feed manufacturers....In some factory farms, dirty litter from broiler houses is scraped up, hauled away, and added directly to cattle feed. Raw poultry and pig manure is mixed with ground corn or shredded stalks and fed to pigs and cattle. Animal scientists have developed the 'oxidation ditch' to channel liquid wastes from factory manure pits back to the animals; they have to drink it because it's the only 'water' offered to them. Even ways of processing human sewage into animal feed are being studied.[148]

The rendering business--which means recycling of animal parts--is a vast industry today, a power structure built into the meat industry. Fertilizers for a rose garden can contain bone meal from rendered animals. Animal feed for cattle today is a complex mixture of some grass, cereal, waste products and chemicals as diversified as hormones, antibiotics, sulfonamides, nitrogen heterocyclics, nitrofurans and benzamidazoles.[149] As Singer and Mason point out, the prime movers behind factory farming are the chemical industries. And as Professor Lacey points out, the risks of introducing contaminants multiply with each substance added to the feed. Whatever became of grass?

Infection from food poisoning, such as salmonella and E.coli 0157 are increasing. Inspecting for pathogens only began in 1996, due to the mounting cases of salmonella. In 1989, an article in *The New York Times*, "Officials Call Microbes Most Urgent Food Threat," called attention to the problem:

> 'Epidemiologists at the Federal Centers for Disease Control believe that roughly 2.5 million salmonella cases a year are food-borne, that most of these can be traced to poultry, meat and eggs and that both the incidence and the severity of such cases appears to be increasing.'[150]

Singer and Mason amplify the bad news:

> Thirty-seven percent of broilers are contaminated with Salmonella, according to a 1987 USDA study. Another

> USDA study showed that as many as 76 percent of chickens had Salmonella. An estimated one in every 200 eggs is contaminated with the disease. In most cases, salmonellosis takes the form of moderate to severe diarrhea, but the National Research Council's Institute of Medicine estimates that it causes as many as five hundred deaths each year; others estimate nine thousand deaths a year. [151]

Unrecognized as yet in the catalogue of contaminants is the immunological breakdown in cattle which are causing diseases that are new and difficult to diagnose. Rifkin writes:

> According to the USDA, the cow AIDS virus is widespread among dairy cows and beef cattle, and is suspected of suppressing the animals' immune systems, making them susceptible to a wide range of diseases, including mastitis and lymphosarcoma. [152]

Genetic Engineering and Irradiation: The Great Western Hopes

Irradiation of meat and genetic engineering are sometimes hailed as remedies for our problems with modern meat. Aside from the ethical question of genetically engineering animals, Colin Tudge speculates that genetic engineering of animals invites the temptation to camouflage poor husbandry practices, or will become the means to further mechanize animals to meet profit demands, such as increased efforts to enhance the growth rate of animals, or to increase the yield of milk in dairy cattle with an engineered gene that produces bovine somatotropin, or BST, a growth hormone.[153] It is important to remember that humans who eat meat eat what animals eat: if animals are fed growth hormones and the rendered remains of other animals, these will enter the human system. The hormone, DES, once widely used in cows to promote growth, and in women to prevent miscarriage, was discovered to be a cause of vaginal cancer in the daughters of these women.[154] Milk production in dairy cows already puts an enormous strain on their systems.

The dairy cow is artificially impregnated to keep her lactating all her life. Prior to the implementation of the factory farm system, the average dairy cow yielded about 2.5 tons of milk a year. Today, she produces almost 6 tons of milk a year. Before we applaud this miracle of increase, we should remember that dairy can be as unhealthy for human beings as the animal's meat is. What goes into the cow goes into her milk, goes into us. History catches up with excess: there are health costs to animals that are stressed to produce more than nature intended them to.

> Huge deformed udders are common in dairy herds today, udders so distended they scrape the ground or are kicked and scratched by the cow's own rear hooves....The cow is sucked dry twice, sometimes three times a day--it only takes ten minutes. Meanwhile her body labors; and the unrelenting milking machine, together with the special feeds and drugs, artificially prolong her natural milk cycle. During the lactation period she must produce ten times more milk for the farmers' insatiable mechanical 'calf' than her own calf would have drunk if left to suckle its full term. [155]

As if anyone needs more milk, or milk at all, the gene called BST, or bovine somatotropin, produced from transgenic microbes, has been introduced into the dairy farm to increase milk production by yet a further 25%. The results, as Colin Tudge laments, is that "extra production implies extra strain, which, in some animals at least, has led to increased udder infection, alias mastitis." [156] David Ehrenfeld's description of this unnecessary, dangerous and foolish technological intervention into the cow's life is more graphic:

> Recombinant BGH-related problems--as stated on the package insert by its manufacturer, Monsanto--include bloat, diarrhea, diseases of the knees and feet, feeding disorders, fevers, reduced blood hemoglobin levels, cystic ovaries, uterine pathology, reduced pregnancy rates, smaller calves, and mastitis--a breast infection that can result, according to the insert, in 'visibly abnormal

> milk.' Treatment of mastitis can lead to the presence of antibiotics in milk, probably accelerating the spread of antibiotic resistance among bacteria that causes human disease. Milk from rBGH-treated cows may also contain insulin growth factor, IGF-1, which has been implicated in human breast and gastrointestinal cancers. [157]

Bad as all this is, rBGH-treated cows require more protein in their diets, and their food is further supplemented with ground-up animals, which returns us to the problem of BSE. As of this writing, the FDA approved of BGH and the government has refused the petitions of consumer advocacy groups to label milk and dairy products which come from cows treated with BGH. Like it or not, if you want to drink milk, you may be drinking milk from cows treated with BGH and animal feed from other animals. Your best option, for all sorts of reasons, is not to drink milk or eat dairy products.

Osteoporosis: Milk Is Unnatural For It

We are so accustomed to thinking of "milk as a perfect food,"--a slogan invented by the Dairy Council of America--that it would be difficult for the public to wean itself from this concept. Women, in particular, fearing osteoporosis, are cautioned by their doctors to elevate their calcium intake after menopause by drinking milk and eating cheese. They are often put on a diet of calcium pills or estrogen and dairy calcium, though calcium from a meat source may be counterproductive, because meat protein can inhibit the absorption of calcium by the body. Nutritional studies are still needed in this area, but Physicians' Committee for Modern Medicine write:

> Ironically, the high protein content of milk may actually contribute to the disease that the calcium in milk is alleged to prevent. Osteoporosis is a problem not only of calcium intake, but calcium loss. It turns out that one determinant of calcium loss is protein intake. Doubling your protein intake above that required results in about

> 50% increase in calcium losses in the urine....The negative calcium balance that results, according to an FDA report on the relationship between calcium and osteoporosis, is quite sufficient to explain the 1% to 1.5% loss in skeletal mass per year noted in post menopausal women. [158]

When we consider the fact that from 60% to 90% of non-Caucasian peoples have a lactose intolerance to some degree and eat little dairy, yet have less osteoporosis than Westerners, we should realize that the cause of osteoporosis lies in calcium *balance,* not only in calcium intake, and that calcium balance depends upon other factors, not simply on the amount of calcium consumed. Moreover, there are excellent sources of calcium in plant foods such as kale and broccoli, from which other people obtain their calcium. According to an article in *The American Journal of Clinical Nutrition*, calcium absorbability from kale is actually higher than it is from milk, and broccoli "contains more calcium per calorie than does milk." [159] Beans are another good source of calcium. Finally, vegetables and beans increase fiber intake and will not contribute to the problem of breast cancer. Epidemiological studies show that osteoporosis is more prevalent among Western women than women elsewhere. Whether the cause is the consumption of dairy or meat, in combination with other dietary factors, the disease is not, as T. Colin Campbell's study demonstrates, in our genes, but in our diets.

Tudge is not hostile to genetic engineering, nor has he moral or religious problems about implanting human genes into animals, but he is wary about the use of genetic engineering in farm animals because it will enable breeders to make bigger changes more quickly, which increases the possibility that the changes will be inappropriate. The timing and growth rates of animals will be altered: "...the breeders have selected genes that alter the timing of events within the genomes [of an animal's body]" [160] We barely know what the costs will be. Pigs, whose genetic structures have been altered, have developed arthritic legs. Modern beef bulls "...are barely able to pick up their feet...." Birds suffer leg weakness brought about by over-rapid growth. University studies in England revealed that, "A total of about 25 million broilers are severely crippled. Turkeys, which in the modern form, have extremely heavy bodies...suffer a comparable deformity of the hip." [161] The introduction of a gene into a genetically stable gene pool of a species can create unexpected and hazardous results.

A further problem is the desire of those who breed animals destined for the supermarket to streamline every breed, to create one standard cow, one standard sheep, one standard chicken, to eliminate diversity in nature in the name of efficiency in marketing and to reduce the gene pool. A diversified gene pool has always been a hedge against disease. A monogenetic breed tempts fate. We need to be reminded that, "True sophistication is not a matter simply of ingenuity, but of restraint." [162]

The most dangerous aspect of genetic engineering is "the awesome irreversibility of what is being contemplated," as Erwin Chargoff observed in *Heraclitean Fire:*

> "...there arises a general problem of the greatest significance, namely, the awesome irreversibility of what is being contemplated. You can stop splitting the atom; you can stop visiting the moon; you can stop using aerosols, you may even decide not to kill entire populations by the use of a few bombs. But you cannot recall a new form of life....This world is given to us on loan. We come and we go; and after a time we leave earth and air and water to others who come after us. My generation, or perhaps the one preceding mine, has been the first to engage, under the leadership of the exact sciences, in a destructive colonial warfare against nature. The future will curse us for it." [163]

When one considers that much genetic engineering now and in the future is and will be for the purpose of providing meat and dairy products that are counterproductive for human health, the future cost may be the most expensive burger a civilization ever produced.

Food Irradiation

Like genetic breeding, food irradiation is the siren's song of temptation, and its purpose is to camouflage the problem of contaminated food. Irradiated food will get rid of some contamination, but its benefits are uneven because it takes different dosages to eliminate different bacteria. Richard Lacey gives an admirable summation of the problems with food irradiation---the last hope of the meat dealer to put uncontaminated meat on the market:

> Gamma rays damage bacteria and viruses, but not the agents that cause BSE [mad cow disease] and similar diseases....Other bacteria that are easily removed by irradiation are salmonella and campylobacter....But others, which may be dangerous, need much higher doses and may survive or even be encouraged by removing the competition. Others are completely resistant, including those that are able to survive hostile environments, such as drying, by converting themselves into tiny tough spheres. One of these is *Clostridium botulinum* which, when actively growing, can produce a powerful poison that causes the disease botulism.....Another problem with irradiation is that the exposure of a food occurs briefly, over seconds or minutes,whilst other methods of preserving food, such as drying, salting, pickling, sugaring, canning and deep-freezing all act throughout the storage life of the product. The problem is that after irradiation and subsequent storage, many things can go wrong. [164]

Irradiation is primarily a marketing tool. It extends the shelf life of produce and eliminates the need for pesticides on produce in storage, but it does not eliminate the need for pesticides on crops in the fields. Irradiation will give the public the illusion of safety which, in the case of CJD, may be tragic. Richard Rhodes graphically describes the impossibility of killing the agent of this disease:

> The new disease agent refuses to die. Assault with pressurized, superheated steam in the autoclaves that hospitals use to sterilize instruments for surgery barely shows it. It remains deadly after hours of intense bombardment with hard radiation, months of soaking in formaldehyde, years of burial, decades of freezing. It survives even the fiery furnace of a seven-hundred-degree oven....The new disease turns up no virus in victims' brains. It creeps past the barriers of species and immunity. Evidence accumulates that it's a bad seed, a mistake of protein, a misshapen cyrstal that forces the brain to poison itself. If so, it's a new kind of disease agent that can never be eradicated.[165]

No amount of shuffling of the data can hide the potential hazard of our future with CJD. It is the result of feeding animal protein to animals who had been fashioned by millennia of evolution to be ruminant and vegetarian, and suggests that the food chain is more intimately bound into the structure of life than we imagined. Mad cow disease represents a dislocation in the food chain which may not be easily repaired.

The amount of money, time, ingenuity, research and technology that is spent on products such as meat and milk that are at best unnecessary and often counterindicated for human health is amazing. The amount of money, time, ingenuity, research and technology that is spent to refashion products that are necessary to health, but that nature fashioned perfectly well for us, such as fruits and vegetables, is also amazing. Much of the latter problem is due to urban expansion and the fact that human populations no longer live near their food source. Some of this problem can be relieved by saner farming policies than we now have. Grass roots organizations, such as Community Sustained Agriculture (CSA), where communities and farmers meet together to set standards show excellent promise, but obviously such organizations may work better in small towns than in large cities. With respect to the waste of money, time, ingenuity, research and technology spent on products that aren't necessary in one's diet, just say "no." Technology can be a drug like any other drug. It feeds on its own inner propulsion, laps at rationalizations, moves its users farther and farther from reality, and costs a lot of money. That is why "The factory farm today is a crowded, stinking bedlam, filled with suffering animals that are quite literally insane, sprayed with pesticides and fattened on a diet of growth stimulants, antibiotics and drugs." [166]

The Return of Our Worst Nightmares

The whole lunatic enterprise of trying to convert an animal into a machine is kept going with dosages of antibiotics that contribute to the invitation of every bacteria waiting for a chance to strike back at their evil empire--us. We know that the machine is a creature, because the creature gets sick. Perhaps, in the future, as machines come to resemble human beings more and more, the decisive definition of "human" and "life" will be the ability to sicken and die. Disease and mortality will define our boundaries from the machine. Death will come to define life. Our effort to sublimate the "bios" of animals with antibiotics and subtherapeutic medicines is running thin. The rise of antibiotic resistant diseases, the re-introduction of diseases we thought we had conquered, the re-emergence of old diseases in new viral combinations, appear on the horizon like the horse of the apocalypse called plague. As with Mad cow disease, warnings were issued for decades. In 1964 Rachel Carson, the "mother of the environmental movement," wrote in her introduction to Ruth Harrison's book, *Animal Machines: The New Factory Farming Industry:* [167]

> As a biologist whose special interests lie in the field of ecology, or the relation between living things and their environment, I find it inconceivable that healthy animals can be produced under the artificial and damaging conditions that prevail in these modern factorylike installations, where animals are grown and turned out like so many inanimate objects. The crowding of broiler chickens, the revolting unsanitary conditions in the piggeries, the lifelong confinement of laying hens in tiny cages are samples of the conditions Ruth Harrison describes. As

> she makes abundantly clear, this artificial environment is not a healthy one. Diseases sweep through these establishments, which, indeed are kept going only by the continuous administration of antibiotics. Disease organisms then become resistant to the antibiotics....the question then arises: how can animals produced under such conditions be safe or acceptable human food....The menace to human consumers from the drugs, hormones, and pesticides used to keep this whole fantastic operation somehow going is a matter never properly explored.

The practise of feeding antibiotics to animals began in the 1950s. It is done not only to prevent disease in the animals but because, for some unknown reason, antibiotics promote growth in animals, and farmers are interested in growth. About one half of antibiotics manufactured in the United States are fed to farm animals.In August, 1985,*The Harvard Medical Health Letter* [168] contained dismal information about a study conducted by the Centers for Disease Control which was published in *The New England Journal of Medicine:*

> [It]...provided strong evidence that a particular strain of salmonella originated in a herd of cattle that had been fed the antibiotic chlortetracycline. These bacteria...caused 18 cases of diarrhea (one of them fatal) in humans. The strain in question was resistant to multiple antibiotics, but was otherwise typical of bacteria that cause nearly 36,000 cases of diarrhea annually in the United States. All 18 of the victims studied had handled or eaten ground beef the week before becoming ill. Two-thirds of them had also been taking antibiotics to treat various relatively minor illnesses.

The May, 1987 issue of *Animals Agenda* carried an article by Dr. Kenneth Stoller, "Feeding an Epidemic":

> There is a medical nightmare going on in this country that few know about. It is an infectious disaster waiting to happen. When it does occur, it will be the result of the

> indiscriminate use of antibiotics in agribusinesses that raise animals for human consumption. And physicians have been aware of this danger for years....The over-crowded conditions of factory farms where the animals are raised are made possible only by the routine addition of antibiotics to their food. In 1979, the Office of Technology Assessment (OTA) reported that 99 percent of all poultry, 90% of swine, and 70% of cattle and veal calves routinely receive antibiotics....What is being done to deactivate this time bomb? Almost nothing.

Predictably the meat industry blames physicians and the medical industry for over-using antibiotics to cure diseases in humans which, no doubt, is true. But the creation of antibiotics was intended for medical purposes; its use in animal feed evolved out of greed. The creation of antibiotics was a miracle, and miracles should be handled economically. There are not enough miracles to go around. The least place they were needed was to promote growth and profit in the meat and chicken industries. We have learned that bacteria evolve, that antibiotics stimulate their evolution towards resistance, and that they appear to be evolving with animosity towards the human race.

Within the last few decades, biologists developed a technique called "genetic fingerprinting," which allows them to discern a bacterial phenomenon known as R-plasmid. R-plasmids are bacteria which carry a gene coded for resistance. Such genes migrate from bacteria to bacteria creating transferable multiple resistance plasmids. Dr. Stuart Levy of the Department of Molecular Biology, Microbiology and Medicine at Tufts University, is a prominent leader in this field and has written forcefully about the use of antibiotics in meat. Plasmids have existed for centuries, but resistance plasmids--genes that embed themselves into other bacteria is, Dr. Levy believes "an event of the modern world." Such genes "migrate" or hop around from bacteria to bacteria like a natural form of recombinant DNA. Hence, much antibiotic treatment becomes ineffectual. This, in turn, creates a "treatment gap," which means that doctors are forced more and more frequently to resort to new and experimental drugs, as penicillin, aureomycin and tetracycline increasingly become ineffective. This creates both an expensive and hazardous situation. A typical scenario is the high risk patient with cancer or a heart problem who survives brilliant surgery and develops a secondary infection which will not respond to traditional antibiotic treatment. In *Animal Factories*, Mason and Singer point out that the severe conditions of overcrowding of animals create natural breeding grounds for bacteria, and that animals are developing diseases entirely new in the history of animal husbandry, as well as breakdowns in their immunological systems.[169] In *Modern Meat,* Dr. Levy commented on this biotic bedlam: [170]

> We have five hundred million chickens eating antibiotics every week, and that's just the chicken population. What about the pigs, cows, goats, sheep? How many billions of bacteria does that make resistant out there each day? It's beyond me why it is so hard to understand that eventually those bacteria and their R factors are going to migrate, so that finally it doesn't matter whether you're using antibiotics on animals or on people....We're caught in a global net. Bacteria don't pay attention to international borders and customs. Bacteria don't even acknowledge the boundaries we once thought were so absolute between animals, humans and plants. They're moving around! That's their evolutionary imperative. It's getting harder and harder to stay ahead of resistance.

When the history of disease will be written in the twenty-first century, the question will surely arise as to why our civilization did not stop doing what it was doing; why it did not curb its appetite for animal food; why it did not prevent catastrophe. The simple answer will be that prevention is sane, easy, logical, reasonable, but it doesn't make anyone rich, it will not ennoble researchers, it will not get them grants or Nobel prizes, or win votes for government officials. As Sylvia Tesh points out in *Hidden Arguments: Political Ideology and Disease Prevention Policy*, politics influences theories of causality about diseases.[171] Environmental and dietary issues are multicausal and complicated; environmental and dietary reforms take years to implement and years to measure their results. Politicians like fast results and neglect long-term solutions. Unfortunately, the timing of good health policies cannot be conjoined with voting campaigns.

Environmental and dietary explanations of diseases undercut laboratory methodology. Compared to germs and genes which can be studied in a laboratory, the environment is a multi-layered place. Robert Proctor points out that genetic studies take precedence over dietary and environmental studies because "heredity is orderly, while environmental causation is chaotic...." He warns readers that we are in the grip of "medically managed genophobia." Governments like to look firm and promise the public more research: "Basic research is politically safe." The more complex answer is that our civilization does not think about health in terms of prevention. Its attitude towards health problems is to deal with them as if they are battles in a war rather than the acquisition of attitudes, behaviors and habits that must be developed.

Prevention

We are not involved in "health care"; we are involved in disease management. True health care depends on prevention, it develops long standing habits and practices and the discipline of diet. Our faith in technological progress has blinded us to its costs in health, and we have surrendered responsibility for our health to complex bureaucratic institutions. The former surgeon-general, John Knowles, wrote:

> Central to the culture is faith in progress through science, technology, and industrial growth; increasingly peripheral to it is the idea, vis-à-vis health, that over 99 per cent of us are born healthy and made sick as a result of personal misbehavior and environmental conditions. The solutions to the problems of ill health in modern American society involves individual responsibility, in the first instance, and social responsibility through public legislative and private voluntary efforts, in the second

> instance. Alas, the medical profession isn't interested, because the intellectual, emotional, and financial rewards of the present system are too great and because there is no incentive and very little demand to change.[172]

What Rabbi Rosen states for the Orthodox Jew must be true for any concerned Jew and moral person.

> ...the retention of these hormones and drugs which are pumped into livestock pose a threat to human health together with the concentration of toxins at the end of the food chain contained in animal flesh. As it is halachically prohibited to harm oneself and as healthy nutritious vegetarian alternatives are easily available, meat consumption has become halachically unjustifiable.[173]

It has become morally unjustifiable for any nation.

An anecdote is told of Maimonides, considered to have been the greatest philosopher and physician in Jewish history. The anecdote [174] relates that when he was the royal physician of the Sultan of Egypt, the Sultan never became ill. One day the Sultan asked Maimonides," How do I know that you are an expert physician, since during the period that you have been here, I have never been ill, and you have not had the opportunity to test your skills?" Maimonides replied, "In truth, the great and faithful physician is the Holy One, Blessed Be He, as it is written, 'I am the L-rd, your healer.' And this Great and Faithful Physician was able to promise his people that because He is their Physician, He will be able to protect them from all the illnesses that were put on Egypt." Maimonides concluded, "Therefore, we learn that the ability of a physician to prevent illness is a greater proof of his skill, than his ability to cure someone who is already ill."[175]

Maimonides was guided by the principle that since a person cannot properly serve God when ill, "He must avoid that which harms the body and accustom himself to that which is healthful and helps the body become stronger." [176] His attitude was traditionally Jewish in that Judaism prohibits the placing of one's health or life into possible danger.

The Talmudic sages applied the principle "You shall therefore keep my statutes and ordinances, which if a man do he shall live by them" (Lev. 18:5) to all the laws of the Torah. Hence Jews are to be more particular about matters concerning danger to health and life than about ritual matters.[177] If it could help save a life, one must (not may) violate the Sabbath, eat forbidden foods, and even eat on Yom Kippur, in spite of the commandment to fast on this holiest Jewish holiday.[178] The only laws that cannot be violated to preserve a life are those prohibiting murder, idolatry, and sexual immorality.[179] Rabbi Hertz stated that the failure to protect human life exposes one to guilt for the spilling of blood, in God's eyes.[180]

There is also a discussion of prohibitions against endangering one's life in the *Shulchan Aruch* of Rabbi Joseph Caro (1488-1575) and other Codes of Jewish Law.[181] In *Choshen Mishpat* 427, Caro devotes a chapter to "the positive commandment of removing any object or obstacle which constitutes a danger to life." In his glossary on Caro's *Shulchan Aruch*, Rabbi Moses Isserles (the *Rema*) concludes:

> One should be more concerned about possible danger to life than a ritual prohibition.Therefore, the Sages prohibited one to walk in a place of danger such as near a leaning wall (for fear of collapse), or alone at night (for fear of robbers). They also prohibited drinking water from rivers at night ... because these things may lead to danger ...and he who is concerned with his health [lit.: watches his soul] avoids them. And it is prohibited to rely on a miracle or to put one's life in danger by any of the aforementioned or the like.[182]

Life is considered so sacred in Judaism that the tradition asserts that "if a person saves one life, it is as if he or she saved an entire world."[183] The preservation of human life is so important that it takes precedence over acts of reverence for a dead person, even if that person is a leader or great hero: "For a one day-old child (that is dangerously ill), the Sabbath may be profaned...; for David, King of Israel, once he is dead the Sabbath must not be profaned."[184] Also, according to Jewish law, one must sooner rescue from flames any living infant than the dead body of one's own parent.[185]

Rabbinic literature is specific in its stress on proper hygiene to protect health. The human body is considered as a sanctuary.[186] The importance of good and regular meals is stressed,[187] and the rabbis give much advice on foods conducive to health.[188] They stress the importance of personal cleanliness and washing daily in honor of God.[189] The Talmudic sage Hillel considered it a religious commandment to bathe in order to protect his health.[190]

The implications of these teachings for Jewish physicians are that they are to put emphasis on preventive medicine, in contrast to the modern/traditional teachings in medical schools which emphasize cure and drugs---locking the barn door after the horse has fled. But Torah does not place entire responsibility for maintaining good health on our physicians. All of us bear this responsibility. To take care of one's health is a *mitzvah.* "Take heed to thyself and take care of your lives." (Deut. 4:9)

4

Frequently Asked Questions About Nutrition & Vegetarianism 191

The following questions and answers reflect the most commonly asked general questions, and are offered to stimulate consideration of issues related to nutrition. Clearly, there are individual questions, many of which may refer to serious conditions. The following questions are not meant to take the place of professional diagnosis and advice. Hence, do not change medicines or medical practice without the advice of a physician knowledgeable about the effects of dietary changes.

How can people get key facts about nutrition and improved diets?

Self education is necessary. Fortunately, there are many helpful books today, such as: *The Power of Your Plate* and *Food for Life*, both by Neal Barnard, M. D.,*The McDougall Plan* and *A Challenging Second Opinion* , both by John A. McDougall, M. D, and *MegaHealth*, by Mark Sorensen, Ed. D. Medical studies are referred to in these books. For further books, see the bibliography in the appendix.

Two excellent sources for nutritional information are Physicians Committee for Responsible Medicine (PCRM), 5100 Wisconsin Avenue, NW, Suite 404, Washington, D. C. 20016; Web: www.pcrm.org , and the Vegetarian Resource Group (VRG), P. O. Box 1463, Baltimore, MD 21203; phone (410) 366-8343; Email address: vrg@vrg.org; web: www.vrg.org.

Magazines that give useful information on vegetarian nutrition include*Good Medicine* (publication of PCRM), *VegetarianVoice* and*Vegetarian Journal* (publication of VRG.)

Can a vegetarian diet include sufficient nutrients?

Nutritionists and dietitians have concluded that vegetarians can get all the essential nutrients they need without consuming meat, or other animal products. The only question concerns Vitamin B12, which can easily be obtained.

What do professional dietitians say about vegetarian diets?

The American Dietetic Association issued a pamphlet in 1992 entitled, "Eating Well--The Vegetarian Way," which concluded:

"Vegetarian foods are the prime source of nutrition for most of the world"

"Vegetarians have lower rates of heart disease and lower rates of some forms of cancer than non-vegetarians."

"Vegetarian eating can be helpful for people of all ages."

"Vegetarian diets can be simple to plan."

Up-to-date material from the American Dietetic Association can be obtained by calling 1-800-877-1600, extension 4898

For a professional dietician's view of vegetarianism, read *Becoming Vegetarian: The Complete Guide to Adopting a Healthy Vegetarian Diet,* by Vesanto Melina, R.D., Brenda Davis, R.D., and Victoria Harrison, R.D. The book contains information on every aspect of nutrition.

What were the Traditional "Basic Four Food Groups?" Are there any health problems associated with them?

The "Basic Four" was a declaration of the Meat and Dairy Industries and predictably advised (1) meats, poultry, and fish, dry beans and peas, eggs, and nuts; (2) dairy products, such as milk, cheese, and yogurt; (3) grains; (4) fruits and vegetables. This combination of foods has been the mainstay of nutrition education in the United States since 1956, when the U.S. Department of Agriculture promoted it in its Leaflet No. 424, "Food For Fitness--A Daily Food Guide." The dairy, meat, and egg lobbies strongly promoted it, and American students were taught this diet as gospel in classrooms throughout the country.

Physicians Committee for Responsible Medicine (PCRM), a non-profit health/nutrition advocacy group argues that the heavy emphasis on animal products in the Basic Four, with its high amounts of fat, cholesterol, and protein, is a prime factor in degenerative diseases, such as heart disease, stroke, various types of cancer, and osteoporosis. PCRM recommends the "New Four food Groups."

What are the "New Four Food Groups?"

On April 8,1992, Physicians Committee for Responsible Medicine unveiled its "New Four Food Groups," a program that has had an impact on the nutrition and health in the United States.

Their new Four Food Groups are:

(1) whole grains, including bread, pasta, cereal, millet, barley, bulgur, buckwheat, and groats

(2) vegetables

(3) legumes, such as beans, peas, lentils, soy milk, tofu, and tempeh

(4) fruit.

While PCRM believes that a wide variety of foods from these four groups provides all the necessary nutrients for good human health, they list meat, dairy products, nuts, seeds, and oil as "optional foods," for those who wish to use moderate amounts.[192]

Dr. Neal Barnard, director of PCRM, presented The New Four Food Groups at a press conference which was well attended by journalists. He asserted that the new proposal would have a major impact on diet-related diseases in the U. S., where heart attacks strike 4,000 people a day, and where a third of the U. S. population may get cancer. (There are estimates that the rate of cancer may double by the year 2,030.) He added that the traditional "Basic Four," which involves animal products at the center of the American diet is a recipe for disaster; he noted the shift in breast cancer rates from one in eleven American women (getting the disease at some point during their lives) when he was a medical student to one in nine in 1991.

Dr. Barnard, a vegetarian activist, was joined at the press conference by two prominent doctors: Dennis Burkitt, M. D., whose pioneering research connected dietary fiber to the prevention of disease; Oliver Alabaster, M. D., Director of the Institute for Disease Prevention at George Washington University, and author of *The Power of Prevention;* and by the famed nutritionist and author of The China Study, T. Colin Campbell, Ph.D. While feeling that it is acceptable to eat small amounts of animal products, the conference asserted that basing the major part of one's diet on the New Four Food Groups would have consequential benefits for human health.

More information about the New Four Food Groups, as well as general information and educational material on healthier eating, can be obtained from Physicians Committee for Responsible Medicine, P. O. Box 6322, Washington, D. C. 20015; phone: (202) 686-2210.

Don't we need a balanced diet that includes meat and animal products?

We do need a balanced diet, one that includes all the essential nutrients and vitamins. But all of these can be obtained from plant-based foods (fruits, vegetables, grains, and legumes), except vitaimin B12.

How can a vegetarian get sufficient vitamin B12?

This vitamin is produced by bacteria in the soil and in animals. Ironically, people who live in under-developed countries get sufficient Vitamin B12 on their daily fruits and vegetables. Our modern farming methods tend to deplete the soil of vitamin B12. Since this vitamin is not found in plant food, but *on* plant food, its presence is easily destroyed. Modern methods of agriculture have altered the amounts of B12 in soil and on crops."[193] While only a very small amount (about 4 micrograms daily) is required, there have been some reported cases of vitamin B12 deficiencies among vegans. Still, "Most cases of vitamin B12 deficiency occur not among vegetarians but in the general population."[194] Vegans should add vitamin B12-fortified cereals or soy milk, or a vegetarian vitamin B12 (cobalamin) supplement to their diets, or have two teaspoons of Red Star nutritional yeast [195] every day. Nutritional yeast has a tasty, nutty flavor and can be sprinkled on cereal, baked fruits, casseroles and salads. It is far better to obtain vitamin B12 this way than through dairy products or eggs, because absorption of vitamin B12 from such products may not be sufficient to maintain a vitamin B12 status.

How can a vegetarian get sufficient protein?

This is probably the question that is most frequently asked of vegetarians. As Dr.Neal Barnard, director of Physicians Committee for Responsible Medicine, points out, protein has been regarded with great awe in our society, almost as a fourth color of the flag: red, white, blue, and protein.

Most people get far too much protein, often two to three times the amount required. All the protein humans require can be obtained from vegan (no animal products at all) diets. At most, 10% of calories from protein are adequate. Protein is found in most plant foods. Potatoes, for example have 11% of their calories from protein, and spinach has 49%. An average working man needs about 63 grams of protein per day, which are obtained from a well balanced plant diet.

People on meat-based diets not only get excessive protein, they also get large amounts of hormones, fat, cholesterol, pesticides, and other harmful ingredients that place major burdens on their kidneys, liver, and digestive systems. Excessive meat protein puts a strain on the kidneys and prevents the absorption of calcium, which may be a factor in osteoporosis. Getting cholesterol along with your protein is a bad way to get protein.

Do vegetarians have to "complement" proteins, that is, eat a combination of different foods containing proteins, to make sure they obtain complete protein?

This was a theory advocated by Frances Moore Lappé in her influential book, *Diet for a Small Planet* , in the 1950s. She felt that when people do not eat meat, they should combine proteins in order to obtain the same protein value that they previously obtained from meat. Nutritionists no longer agree with that theory. The American Dietetic Association stated in its 1992 paper, "Eating Well--The Vegetarian Way": "Vegetarians do not need to combine specific foods within a meal as the old "complementary protein" theory advised. The body makes its own complete proteins if a variety of plant foods--fruits, vegetables, grains, legumes, nuts, and seeds--and enough calories are eaten during the day." The fact is that vegetarian food protein contain the essential amino acids. The term, "complete protein," is obsolete. Frances Moore Lappé corrected her previous assessment in later editions of her book.

What are the negative effects of too much animal protein?

Consuming excessive amounts of meat protein can seriously damage human health. It can result in a negative calcium balance which, in turn, results in calcium-deficient bones that easily break, a condition known as osteoporosis. Countries such as the United States, Sweden and Norway, with the highest consumption of meat food, have the highest numbers of incidents of osteoporosis per person.

Calcium lost in high protein diets must be handled by the kidneys. This contributes to the formation of painful kidney stones. Excess protein may cause destruction of kidney tissue and progressive deterioration of kidney function in diabetics and in others with existing kidney problems. When people with kidney problems are placed on low-protein diets, they are better able to maintain their remaining kidney function.

How can a vegetarian get sufficient calcium? Don't we need dairy products in our diets to make sure that we are getting adequate calcium?

Many plant foods are good sources of calcium. Dark leafy greens (such as kale, mustard, collard, and turnip greens), broccoli, beans, dried figs, sunflower seeds, and calcium-fortified cereals and juices are especially good sources of plant calcium. Dairy products are a questionable source of calcium because they contain large amounts of animal fat and animal protein.

How can a vegetarian get sufficient iron?

There are many good plant food sources of iron. They include green vegetables, such as spinach and green beans, dried beans, dried fruits, pumpkin seeds, sesame seeds, prune juice, black strap molasses, soybean nuts, and iron-fortified breads and cereals. Foods high in vitamin C, such as broccoli, citrus fruits and juices, tomatoes, and green pepper, help the body absorb iron from plant sources.

Is vegetarianism an effective approach to weight loss?

Yes. Each gram of protein and carbohydrates has 4 calories, but each gram of fat has 9 calories. Since plant-based diets are lower in fat than animal-centered diets, they are generally effective at reaching and/or maintaining desired weights. Of course, other factors, such as exercise, quantities of food eaten, and individual characteristics should be considered.

Does one have to carefully study nutrition when shifting to a vegetarian diet?

The more information you have about nutrition, the better, but you don't have to be an expert on nutrition to obtain adequate nutrition on a vegetarian diet. If you have a good balance of foods from PCRM's "New Four Food Groups" and obtain adequate rest and exercise, you should be able to maintain health.

Because food has become a sensitive issue, with many political and health consequences, it is a good idea to be as educated as possible about any food you eat, and not depend on labels which people often find confusing and time-consuming to read. Books listed in the bibliography and vegetarian support groups will be helpful about nutrition, recipes, and meal planning for almost every situation: pregnancy, nursing mothers, babies, teenagers, the working vegetarian, the single vegetarian, the vegetarian who doesn't like to cook, vegetarians with allergies, etc. Today there is an enormous variety of books on vegetarian lifestyle issues. If your local bookstore or library can't find one for you, write to the various support groups listed in the back of this book.

Can a vegetarian or vegan diet be unhealthy?

Balance is a key word in diet as in life. If a person eats only primarily fruits or has a diet based almost completely on rice, or consumes a great deal of candy bars, carbonated sodas, and snack foods, one can have an unhealthy diet. But if the diet is balanced and has an adequate mix of fruits, vegetables, grains, and legumes, there should be no problem.

What health problems are associated with the consumption of dairy products?

Researchers have found that the consumption of high-fat dairy products is a leading cause of atherosclerosis, heart attacks, and strokes. Hence, countries where there is high consumption of dairy products have high amounts of many degenerative diseases. Dairy products are also the leading culprits in food allergies and have been linked to childhood illnesses such as colic and diabetes.

There are also problems of intolerance related to milk products. About 20% of Caucasians, about half of African Americans, and most Oriental people are lactose intolerant.

Dairy products are high in fat, high in cholesterol, and completely devoid of fiber. While lower fat dairy products represent an improvement, they may still increase the risk of certain diseases, such as ovarian cancer. People can get enough calcium through non-dairy products such as broccoli and other green leafy vegetables.

Milk is a perfect food for calves, ideal for their rapid weight gain. It is designed to take an infant calf, weighing 90 pounds at birth, to a weight of 2,000 pounds in two years.

What is an ideal cholesterol level?

It has been found that heart problems generally do not occur when cholesterol levels are below 150 (milligram per deciliter, or mg. per dl.) Lower levels for cholesterol are not a problem. If a person has a reading higher than 150, say up to 170, this is still a good reading, but a reading below 150 gives the best assurance of protection against heart-related problems. For every decrease of one percent in the cholesterol level, there is a 2% decrease in the risk of heart attack. A reduction in cholesterol level is an effective way to reduce risk of heart problems. Cholesterol is found *only* in animal products. No plant-based food has cholesterol.

Is a change from beef to chicken and/or fish a positive step for improved health?

Many people feel a false sense of security when they change from red meat to a chicken and/or fish diet. A scientific study by Dr. Dean Ornish showed dramatic improvements in the condition of patients with severe heart problems who changed to an almost vegan diet, while those who changed to diets recommended by medical groups, such as the American Heart Association, which recommend 30% of calories from fat, and include chicken without the skin, fish, and an ample amount of dairy products, showed no improvement, and in many cases became worse. Chicken and fish have high animal protein and cholesterol contents. For example, 3.5 ounces of extra lean ground beef has 84 mg. of cholesterol, and 3.5 ounces of chicken, without the skin, has 85 mg. of cholesterol.

As people learn that red meat is unhealthy, they exchange red meat for chicken; as they learn that chicken is unhealthy, they exchange chicken for fish. In each case, the exchange causes an enormous increase in the farming or catching and production of chicken or fish, with all the concomitant problems that excess brings. The health benefits of eating fish do not match the health benefits of plant food. "A 3.5 ounce of serving of salmon...contains 74 milligrams of cholesterol, about the same as in a comparable serving of T-bone steak or chicken."[196] Many of our waterways are polluted with run-offs from industries and factory farms, which affect the health of fish. In 1992, Consumer Reports wrote that "By far the biggest source of PCBs in the human diet is fish....PCBs accumulate in body tissue."[197] According to Earthsave, Consumers Union found PCBs in 43% of the salmon, 25% of the swordfish and 50% of the lake whitefish."[198] Michael Jacobson stated the problem: "If there's something wrong with the water, chances are something will be wrong with the fish." [199]

Isn't it true that many people in nations that don't get enough meat suffer from malnutrition?

Yes, but not because they don't eat meat, but because they don't eat enough calories. It has been estimated that 20 million people die annually because of a lack of adequate nutrition. Meat-based diets contribute to world-wide hunger, since over 70% of the grain grown in the United States (and over one third of all grain worldwide) is fed to animals destined for slaughter, while the U.S. and other developed countries import food from countries where people are severely malnourished. There are two faces of malnutrition in the world today: one is in the developing countries, where people lack sufficient food; and the second is in developed countries like the U.S., where people suffer from degenerative diseases due to too much rich food, particularly animal food.

Isn't plant protein of inferior quality compared to animal-based protein?

This mistaken idea is based on the equally mistaken premise that our protein intake needs to match the pattern of the eight essential amino acids in meat. Recent studies show that humans can extract all the essential amino acids they need from plant protein to form all the necessary protein molecules they need.

While veganism may be fine for adults, don't children need food from animal products?

Except for vitaimin B12, children, like adults, can get all the protein, calcium, carbohydrates, vitamins, and other nutrients they need from plant-based foods. Meat is a source of iron and protein, but a bad source. Children raised on strict vegetarian diets have generally turned out to be healthy. A good source for further information on this subject is *Pregnancy, Children, and the Vegan Diet* by Michael Klaper, M. D..

Are there ways to work with familiar recipes to make them as healthy as possible?

Recipes in non-vegetarian or lacto-ovo-vegetarian recipe books can often be modified to lower fat content. *The Jewish Vegetarian Year Cookbook* transforms many traditional Jewish recipes into vegan recipes. (See the chapter on "Klal Israel" for a model vegan meal.) The following suggestions are made by the American Dietetic Association:

1. Interesting choices of soy-based milk, soy margarine, soy cheeses, and yogurt can be found in health food and specialty food stores.There is also rice ice cream and almond milk. There are soy cheeses which are effective for melted cheese sandwiches and pizzas. For more information about alternatives to

cheese, see *The Uncheese Cookbook: Creating Amazing Dairy-Free Substitutes and Classic Uncheese Dishes,* by Joanne Stepaniak (Book Publishing Co., Summertown, TN.)

2. Oil, margarine, butter, and shortening can usually be reduced by one-third to one-half. In most cases, olive oil can be substituted for butter and margarine. It is also possible to sauté vegetables by a method called "sweating." Use only enough oil to coat the skillet; place vegetables on top of the oil and mix to coat vegetables with oil, add about 1/2 cup of water (depending upon the amount of vegetables), bring to a boil, cover, lower to a simmer and cook for about 5-10 minutes. This is a combination of sautéing and steaming, which will give your vegetables the taste of being sautéed without giving them the fat.

3. Regular sour cream can be replaced by a fat-free version or soy yogurt. Non-dairy sour cream substitutes are now available.

4. Cheddar and other high-fat cheeses can be replaced by nonfat or low-fat alternatives, or by soy cheeses. As a compromise, a combination of low-fat and regular varieties can be used, or a reduced amount can be used. There are also non-dairy cheese substitutes available, which work well when melted cheese is used in a sandwich, pizza, or quiche.

5. Eggs can be replaced with one of the following:

2 egg whites for 1 whole egg

1 mashed banana for 1 egg (for bread, pancakes, and muffins)

2 tablespoons of cornstarch or arrowroot for 1 egg

1/4 cup of tofu (blend with liquid ingredients until smooth, then add to the dry ingredients)

6. Bulgur wheat (cracked, rolled wheat) adds texture to soups, stews, and chili. Other meat substitutes include tempeh (cultured soybeans), tofu (bean curd), and seitan (wheat gluten), which can be used in a variety of recipes, including casseroles, lasagna, and burger patties.

7. Be an informed shopper. Producers are coming out with new animal-free products all the time. Watch your supermarket stores for them. Be an aggressive shopper. If you don't see something that you know exists, ask the store manager to order it. Most food markets are eager to know what their customers want.

Watch the bookshelves on cookbooks in bookstores. The development of vegetarian and vegan cookbooks is a very competitive growing sector of cookbooks.

5

TSA'AR BA'ALEI CHAIM

You May Not Cause Pain To A Living Creature

"There are probably no creatures who require more the protective divine word against the presumption of man than the animals." (Rabbi Samson Hirsch, Horeb, Chapt. 60, Verse 415)

Human arrogance in the guise of dominion was always the temptation, and it troubled the rabbis. Rabbi Hanina made dominion a correlative of moral behavior. "If we earn it we will have dominion, if we do not earn it we will descend." A moral hedge had to be placed around human power. Islam too teaches that pre-eminence is not unconditional, but is earned by "Godly behavior."[200] By Talmudic times, Judaism had one of the best articulated systems regarding human responsibility for animal life. This system, often referred to as "stewardship," proved to be, like kashrut, no defense against the modern world. If Jews in the diaspora exclaim that they do not live under their own stars and therefore cannot exercise their own laws, Jews in Israel do live under their own stars, and the same factory farming abominations occur. Pâté de foie gras, which is the product of extreme cruelty to a goose, is an important product of Israel, surpassed in export only by France. Egg-laying hens are raised in battery cages. What exactly is meant by a "tradition"? The word is invoked with hallowed resonance when it will serve someone's profits.

The first chapter of Mary Midgley's book, *Animals, and Why They Matter* is titled, "Getting Animals Into Focus."[201]

Comparing ourselves with animals is an ongoing obsession. We are always "getting animals into focus," or trying to. We bounce our definition of ourselves off the animals. We use them as mirrors, as measuring rods, as devices to elevate ourselves, to understand ourselves, to stretch our imaginations, to instruct ourselves in morality, to make poetry from, to find companionship with, to lower stress, and to derive goods and money and profit and industry from. We have used them, along with slavery and war, to advance our civilizations. Animals have been part of human history for as long as human history. We do not have a human history without animals any more than we have a human history without the earth. We do not know ourselves apart from earth, animals, and plant life. We do not know how we would be without these. Unquestionably a symbolic dimension that informs our psyches would be lost along with the environmental loss. Some of this symbolic loss might be to the good rather than to the bad. As Mary Midgley points out, animals often suffer from a "symbolic overload."[202] In Buddhism, Christopher Chapple, author of *Karma and Creativity*, writes:

> The world of animals is one of the three lesser destinies [gati], along with the hell beings and hungry ghosts. According to the *Jewel Ornament of Liberation*, a medieval Tibetan text, animals continually suffer the misery of 'servitude,' slaughter, and devouring each other.' Birth as an animal is said to be punishment for evil deeds.[203]

Compare this view with that of the modern naturalist, Henry Beston:

> The animal shall not be measured by man. In a world older and more complete than ours they move finished and complete, gifted with extensions of the senses we have lost or never attained, living by voices we shall never hear. They are not brethren, they are not underlings; they are other nations, caught with ourselves in the net of life and time, fellow prisoners of the splendour and travail of the earth.[204]

A third view expressed by Mary Midgley, is more consonant with the biblical view of animals:

> Beasts are neither incarnations of wickedness, nor sets of basic needs, nor crude mechanical toys, nor idiot children. They are beasts, each with its own complex nature. Most of them fail in most respects to conform to their mythical stereotype.[205]

Judaism did not see animals as divine or as demonic. It did not idealize them anymore than it idealized human beings. Animals were not held sacred nor were they deified anymore than human beings were, or should be. Judaism saw animals in the same mode of realism and naturalism as it saw human beings, as rational or perhaps semi-rational creatures with emotional lives, who feel pain and pleasure, who have interests in their biological survival, in their appetites, in conserving their biological identities, and in protecting their young--except for one difference: Judaism saw animals as innocent of evil, as David's challenge to God illustrates: "But what have these sheep done?" In the evaluation of differences between humans and animals, humans had dominion and free will but they also had the inclination to evil: humans did not have innocence.

Our knowledge of animals is, contrary to the volumes of description of animal life gathered over centuries, quite small. Until the last century Western people barely knew animals at all, except as captured creatures in circuses, on farms, in zoos or acquariums, in laboratories and carnivals. Such a knowledge of animals would be comparable to knowledge of the human race as people in a prison. We knew animals through legend and folk literature, and most of what we knew about them, came through this literature and was almost always a projection of our own fantasy lives about traits we detested in ourselves, such as sexuality. Words such as "brutish," "animal-like" "bestial," to describe human aggression and sexuality are rooted in Western thought. Mary Midgley traces their origins to the exaggerated value of Greek rationalism in the West. She quotes a description of Plato's "unpleasant desires" from Book 9 of *The Republic:*

> [These] bestir themselves in dreams, when the gentler part of the soul slumbers, and the control of Reason is withdrawn. Then the Wild Beast in us, full-fed with meat and drink, becomes rampant and shakes off sleep to go in quest of what will gratify its own instincts.[206]

This description of the human soul divided between its animal nature and reason can be traced through the centuries in Western thought to its spell-binding representation in *Dr. Jekyll and Mr. Hyde*. Animals came to represent "our worst selves," and when we commit shameful acts we describe them in animal terms. Animals are not capable of human acts of violence, such as massacres, gang rapes, auto da fés, mass bombings and gassing. Nor are they the anarchic creatures of our fantasies. Most of them, like the wolf, live lives of exemplary behavior, which bear no resemblance to the myths about them. Gertrude Stein's pithy rejection of blaming the animals for human nature, "Everything human is human," puts the blame where it should be put.

The study of animals, *as animals,* (ethiology) and not as creatures of our fantasies, nightmares, or imprisonments, began in earnest only in this century, largely with the work of Konrad Lorenz. It required people equipped with cameras, willing to do field work in jungles and rainforests, willing to live among the animals as an anthropologist lives in the village being studied, to develop a view of animal life that would be honest to the animal.[207]

Following Hans Jonas' definition of animal life in *The Phenomeon of Life,* Leon Kass stresses that animals have in common with humans appetite, awareness and action.[208] In a footnote, he explains what he means by "awareness":

> I use the broad, nonspecific term "awareness" to encompass all forms of openness and receptivity and sensitivity, from the barest irritability to the richest intellection. Sensing, perceiving, imaging, cognizing, minding, intellecting--all these are species of awareness. There can

> also be internal awareness (kinesthesia) and self awareness. Awareness need not be self-conscious or even conscious to be awareness.[209]

It is a standard Jewish interpretation of Genesis, that God breathed life into animals as life was breathed into the human form. By life is meant "soul" in the Jewish understanding, or "psyche" in the classical Greek understanding. Kass is a good instructor on this point:

> ...animal organization means 'animation,' means 'inwardness,' means the presence of what the ancients called *psyche* or *anima,* soul....*psyche* referred to and comprised all the integrated vital powers of a naturally organic body, always possessed of such a body while it is alive. Not the property of the materials alone but of the materials as species-specifically formed, the species-specific psyche might be said to be the vital form or ruling-beginning of each animal, when the animal is regarded as a unified center of awareness, action, and appetite. When soul is thus understood, we should not be reluctant or embarrassed to recognize that animals--all animals--indeed have souls.[210]

At the dawn of creation, humans had one other quality in common with animals: vulnerability. Contrary to the view of a chest-thumping Adam, our "first man," as Phyllis Trible, feelingly analyzes, was created vulnerable.[211]

> Superiority, strength, aggressivness, dominance, and power do not characterize man in Genesis 2. By contrast, he is formed from dirt; his life hangs by a breath which he does not control; and he himself remains silent and passive while the Deity plans and interprets his existence.

Kass sees vulnerability as the connective tissue between animal and human life: "...subsequent parts of the biblical story...emphasize the common vulnerability and neediness of all that lives, human beings no less than others."[212] The doctrine of original vulnerability (in deliberate opposition to the doctrine of original sin) gives us a truer biblical picture of human relationship to animals, one that brings us closer to Beston's tragic view of animal life. What does "dominion" mean in the context of vulnerability? Trible asserts the "physical, perhaps psychic," similarity between animal and human, but points out that their similarity is not equality. On another level, human beings are created "in the image of God," but they are not equal to God. An image is an image, formed by the Creator. The image is not the Creator, or equal to the Creator.

Until the most recent of times, we lived in what Mary Midgley calls, "the mixed community,"[213] made up of humans and domesticated animals. "All creatures which have been successfully domesticated are ones which were originally social."[214] We encouraged the friendship of animals who had traits of trust and bonding similar to ourselves, traits we found engaging as well as useful for exploitation. References to animals in the Bible and the prophets are largely to the social and domestic animals. The earliest symbolic relationship in the Bible, which had overwhelming consequences for our religious sentiments, is that of the shepherd and his sheep. We are always moved by it: "The Lord is my shepherd." As we are to the animals, we averred, so God is to us. It is a symbolism which evokes the relationship of trust between Jews and God. We saw in the marvelous concern of the mother hen for her chickens, of the cow for her calf, a paradigm of trust which we believed God had built into the very nature of nature and animal life. Christianity embraced the paradigm of "the mixed community" when it placed the birth of Jesus in the company of animals.

But there are two paradigms in nature, and the other paradigm--that of "beast eats beast" also captured the human imagination, and also expressed itself in religious concepts and sensibilities. The experience of seeing a lion take down a deer and bring its life to an end, of seeing hyenas hound a dying elephant or kill a weak baby rhino can exhaust one's trust in a God Who created nature. We would prefer not to live in a universe where the weak are destroyed by the powerful. We are made more vulnerable by the knowledge of it. Some of us are made wicked by it and use the paradigm to defend fascistic systems that exalt power. Arguments are deduced from nature to defend power, that we are "hardwired" for aggression. The other paradigm, the one of social bonding and trust, seems weak in comparison to the drama of violence in nature.

The first thing one must do to get animals into focus is to decide which is the correct paradigm, or if one paradigm has the monopoly of truth. Both, of course, are operative, but trust and cooperation is more often the case among animals than predation and violence. The paradigm of "the mixed community" between humans and animals, and animals and animals is the prevalent paradigm. As Midgley writes, "Competition is *not* the basic law of life."[215] It is "real but limited." So why have we been seduced by the paradigm of "beast eats beast," of a food chain which supports humans eating animals? It must be because meat-eating plays a symbolic and paradigmatic role for human beings. Carnivorism is the foremost symbolic act of power over others, animals and humans. No other act so completely destroys the enemy as to eat him. To consume him is to convert his power into yours and make him vanish forever from the earth so that he will never have his power again, for you now have it. You have swallowed it. As Mary Midgley writes:

> The symbolism of meat-eating is never neutral. To himself the meat-eater seems to be eating life. To the vegetarian, he seems to be eating death....Things are made harder still by an extra, very widespread element of social symbolism. Meat-eating indicates success and prosperity, therefore hospitality....The original symbolism, depicting a straight life-and-death clash between animals and man, is still very strong.[216]

The vegetarian sees the act of eating meat as eating death, particularly in today's context concerning the conditions under which the animals are raised, and the staggering statistics of consumption of animals in the United States alone. Look again at the statistics from the National Agricultural Statistical Service which the FARM newsletter reported: "8,077 million 'broiler' chickens, 407 million 'laying' hens, 409 million turkeys, and 22 million ducks were killed for food in 1996":[217]

> Among mammals, 38.6 million cattle and 4.6 million calves were killed for food in 1996, as well as 107.7 million pigs and 5.4 million sheep, for a total of 156 million....Thus, the total number of all animals killed for food in 1997 is projected at 9.3 billion....
> One dirty secret of animal agribusiness is that 920 million animals never reach the slaughterhouse. Most die of stress, injuries, or diseases induced by their appalling conditions....
> Farm animals account for 97% of the 9.6 billion animals abused and killed annually in the U.S. Chickens and turkeys alone account for over 95% of the total.

The statistics reflect a gristly occupation and a civilization turned into a slaughterhouse.

Genesis proclaimed the benevolence of nature. That is why we love to hear it read. In the beginning of the Bible, nothing comes into life with darkness and confusion, with struggle and terror, but issues forth with order, serenity, trust and majesty. This creation assures us that the natural world we live in is habitable and sociable, cooperative and trusting, and that the God Who created this nature is a trustworthy God. In *Job*, God appeals to creation for Self-justification. The psalms are saturated with the spirit of the natural world, of creator and creation. This paradigm had moral and spiritual consequences for the monotheistic religions. Andrew Linzey, IFAW Senior Research Fellow at Mansfield College, Oxford, in England, wrote in *Christianity and The Rights of Animals*:

> Notice how the generosity of God knows no bounds. 'How many are Your works, O Lord!' exclaims the Psalmist. 'In wisdom you have made them all. The earth is full of your riches.' To affirm the generosity of God is to celebrate creation as gift and to know ourselves as

> participators in divine beneficence....to affirm the blessedness of creation is to affirm an independent source of its work. In this sense all creation has an irreducible value.... [218]

Out of its originating view of nature as a paradigm of cooperativeness, Judaism and its sister religions evolved an ethics which elevated a morality that taught that justice resides in an equation between power and powerlessness that is different from the equation inherent in "nature red in tooth and claw." Justice, in the Jewish system, is yoked to mercy. We cannot dismiss Jewish ethics from a Jewish view of God, nor this Jewish view of God from a Jewish view of nature and a Jewish view of animals. Even in his effort to justify carnvorism, Leon Kass acknowledges that a vegetarian diet "would distrub almost not at all the order of creation."[219] Within the ascription of human dominion, Genesis valued vegetarianism over meat-eating and subtracted the primary category of food from the first power relationship humans would have with animals. When Judaism turned away from the paradigm of "beast eats beast" it opted for the paradigm of cooperation between animals and humans, for Rabbi Avraham Kook's faith:

> There can be no doubt in the minds of every thinking man that the concept of dominion as expressed in the Torah...does not in any way imply the rule of a haughty despot who tyrannically governs his people and his servants for his own personal selfish ends and with a stubborn heart. Heaven forbid that such a repulsive form of servitude be forever sealed into the word of the Lord, whose tender mercies are on all His works and of whom it is said, "He shall build a world of kindness....[220]

Where is the connective symbolic logic between a God Who creates a benign nature and a God Who is tyrannical? There is a dissonance in paradigms here. No rabbi or Jewish philosopher ever interpreted that passage in Genesis to mean tyranny over the earth. Nor did Christians interpret it that way until Francis Bacon, Descartes, and the advent of science eventually eroded compassion, justice and benevolence from the paradigm of nature. The famous definition of "human being" in Psalm 8, hovering between humility and grandiosity, lurched towards the latter:

> O Lord, our Lord
> How excellent is thy name in all the earth!
> ...When I consider thy heavens, the work of thy fingers,
> The moon and the stars which thou hast ordained;
> What is man that thou art mindful of him?
> And the son of man that thou visitest him?
> For thou has made him but a little lower than God,
> and crownest him with glory and honor.
> Thou made him to have dominion
> over the works of thy hands;
> Thou has put all things under his feet

What are the last three sentences without the first six, but dangerous boasting? The Jewish system of stewardship was humane, moral and religious. That it *was* religious, part of the Jew's entire attitude towards creation, is important; for stewardship can only work in a pious, reverential system. Without the supporting posture of "humility before the Lord," human arrogance defines the human/animal relationship. Judaism did not create hierarchy; Jewish thought wrestled with the problem of hierarchy and human arrogance, sometimes rationalized it and often sought to mitigate it, as in the following quotation:

> Humanity was created on Friday, before Shabbath, and after the creation of the animals, so that in the event of human arrogance, one should reply: 'Even the mosquito was created before you.' (Sanhedrin 38)

Without remembering that animals are creatures of God, created within the same paradigm of a benevolent nature as were humans, animals become detached and ripe for their definition as "automata." It is only a matter of time until this paradigm shift from a benevolent nature to an indifferent nature and finally to a hostile nature destroys the symbolism we drew from the animal world, of cow and hen as symbols of mother love, eternal, brooding, caring, fighting for their newborn; the marvelous experience of altruism we received from the animal world, mused upon by Rabbi Akiba: "More than the calf needs to suckle, the cow needs to give milk." The factory farming system detaches animal life from the biblical understanding of nature.

The Eternal Egg Comes to An End

For millennia, human beings everywhere regarded the egg as the symbol of eternal life, the rooster as the symbol of male fertility, the hen as a symbol of maternity, hatching, brooding, fending off enemies from her chicks. We were assured of God's beneficence through the action and interaction of rooster, hen and egg, through the experience of animal life in its mating and birthing cycles, its bringing to life and its caring for the life it brought forth.

When we eat a chicken or an egg today, we do not eat a symbolic life-giving force. If we incorporate this symbolism into our psyches, we do so with deception and should adjust the symbolism of chicken and egg to that of disease and death. The egg-laying chicken is a battered, abused, crowded, deranged and diseased animal. Battery hens are housed in buildings that resemble long factories in areas that often look like concentration camps. Many egg farms today can house from 50,000 to 250,000 chickens, piled seven cages high. Four to six chickens are packed into a cage, with living space of 48 square inches.[221]

Farms are no longer the scenes of delightful, whimsical inter-relations among animals, strutting cocks and brooding hens. One might have trouble finding such a chicken farm today. Rabbi Everett Gendler and his wife discovered what chicken farms have become by accident during a vacation in Maine and wrote about the shock of what they found:

> My own awareness of the development dates from a couple of years ago when my wife and I were in Maine, driving along a country road at night, and discovered

> time and again buildings, multistoried, with light shining from them, looking very much like urban apartment dwellings. Yet there were no signs of other habitations around, no sizable towns on the map, and it was very puzzling. A couple of days later, walking along a country road, we came upon one such building by daylight and discovered that a door was open. There was netting across the opening, making sure that none of the 'contents' of the structure would spill out, and we saw crowded against the netting, piled on top of one another, countless numbers of chickens. From an elevated vantage point we were able to discern that this particular structure contained hundreds of chickens, most of them in a semi-gloom, barely visible, obviously enclosed permanently....It is now the case that millions of animals spend their entire lives in darkness or semi-darkness, without any free exposure to the natural elements, crowded together in pitiless fashion, subsisting but hardly living.[222]

Often there is only a dirt road leading to these structures. The land around is usually dead, arid, waste, brown. The long buildings give no hint of the seething torment inside anymore than the wall around a prison does. Compressed together in a cage that gives them no room for movement, the wings of the battery hens atrophy; compressed, the hens become deranged and would peck at each other if it were not that agribusiness, in its demonic wisdom, employs a "guillotine," a debeaking machine which cuts off the chicken's beak shortly after its birth. The process is very painful for the chicken. Karen Davis describes the procedure:

> In the process of having their beaks burned off, the birds chirped loudly and defecated profusely. Many died within 24 hours of shock and blood loss...many birds are debeaked twice if the procedure is done wrong the first time. Improperly cauterized birds bleed from their wounds....'In pain, these birds flap their wings, push

> against the machine, and often lose control of their bowels.'[223]

Not to be depressed about this, however, for geneticists are working to create a transgenic chicken without nerves in its beak, as Colin Tudge tells us with an acid comment:

> This, surely, is technology gone mad; an astonishingly ingenious procedure to ameliorate a mutilation that is intended merely to facilitate a quite unacceptable form of husbandry, while the whole sorry exercise is driven by greed.[224]

Caged, the hens stand on wired or slatted floors for all of their eighteen months of life. The cages are built so that their eggs can roll down to a trough, where they mechanically roll down to the packers, just as in a factory. Because the floors of the cages are open and stacked one on top of each other, the chickens sometimes unavoidably defecate and urinate on each other. However, not to worry about this either, for they are medicated to prevent diseases from breaking out.

> The battery hen spends her entire life standing and sitting on thin, sloping wire mesh rectangles designed to facilitate manure removal and the rolling of eggs onto a conveyor with minimum breakage. Her feet become sore, cracked, and deformed. Her claws, which are designed to scratch vigorously, and thereby stay short and blunt, become long, thin, twisted, and broken. They can curl around the wire floor and entrap her, causing her to starve to death inches from her food and water. When the chicken catchers violently wrench the hens from the cages at the end of the laying term, limbs and claws are frequently left behind.[225]

Because, as Karen Davis points out, "To date, there are no federal welfare laws in the United States regulating the care and treatment of laying hens," [226] everything that is done to the laying hen, from caging to transporting to slaughtering is brutal.

Chickens are transported mercilessly from their abysmal lives to their abysmal deaths:

> The hens travel in cages without food or water for hundreds of miles, frequently across state lines or into Canada, often with missing feet, legs, and wings that were left behind during catching....At slaughter, spent laying hens are a mass of broken bones, beaded ribs, oozing abscesses, bright red bruises, internal hemorrhaging, and malignant tumors. Their bodies are shredded into products that hide the true state of their flesh and their lives: chicken soups and pies, school lunches, and other institutional food service and government purchase programs, developed by the egg industry and the Department of Agriculture to dump laying hens onto consumers in diced up form.
>
> Alternately the hens are trucked an average of 200 miles to rendering plants and turned into poultry, pig, and cattle feed. Or they are gassed or ground up alive at the farm and fed back to the hens in the cages....[227]

It cannot be expected, as Rachel Carson pointed out in her introduction to *Animal Machines* that such a system will not breed disease in addition to moral horror. Thirty years after Ruth Harrison's book, Karen Davis' exposé illustrates that nothing has changed:

> Manure is everywhere in the caged layer complex. Toxic ammonia rises from the decomposing uric acid in the manure pits beneath the cages to produce a painful corneal ulcer condition in chickens known as 'ammonia burn'....In the United States, over 70 percent of hens live from day-old to death in steel cages. The baby chicks grow to egg-laying maturity in these cages stacked four decks high....the huge chicken flocks produce tons of manure and millions of dead birds. According to one researcher, a one-million-hen complex produces 125 tons of wet manure a day....The manure

> fumes and rotting carcasses force workers in the houses to wear gas masks....[228]

It is no wonder that salmonella has become an increasing source of food poisoning from chickens and eggs. While in the past, most salmonella infections were caused by dirty or cracked eggs contaminated from the outside by chicken droppings, salmonella is now found inside the unbroken egg, suggesting that the bacteria are now transmitted from the oviduct to the egg which is in formation.[229]

On an egg farm, male chicks are garbage. All newborn chicks are put on a "sex carousel," at birth where inspectors separate the male from the female chicks. The male chicks are scooped up and put into a plastic bag to suffocate and often to be ground up for cattle feed. A male chick, like a male calf, is regarded by agribusiness as a money loss or as garbage to be recycled into chicken feed. What a striking contrast between this picture of the real world of the battery hen and the Hassidic story of Rabbi Zusya:

> Once Rabbi Zusya travelled cross-country collecting money to ransom prisoners. He came to an inn at a time when the innkeeper was not at home. He went through the rooms, according to his custom, and in one saw a large cage with all kinds of birds. Zusya saw that the caged creatures wanted to fly through the spaces of the world and be free birds again. He burned with pity for them and said to himself, 'Here you are, Zusya, walking your feet off to ransom prisoners. But what greater ransoming of prisoners can there be than to free these birds from their prison? Then he opened the cage and the birds flew out into freedom. [230]

The real world of the battery hen is a recycling of death made possible by technology and the propaganda of "progress," sold to the public on the promise of cheap meat and cheap protein. Technology has become a public compulsion, but as Hans Jonas soberly reminds us, "...progress is an optional goal, not an unconditional commitment, and that its tempo in particular, compulsive as it may become, has nothing sacred about it." [231] We *can* exercise control over the technology that has invaded husbandry and agriculture. It is morally necessary that we do. We can end the cycle of technological death almost at once by becoming vegans. We can ransom these birds by not eating them. As consumers, we vote with our mouths and our pocket-books. When sales fall, the agribusiness eggsperts can be forced out of business. Every person can exercise this power.

The facts in the egg business are ironic in the Jewish moral landscape, for among the first Jewish laws of compassion for animal life is the commandment to shoo away the mother bird before taking an egg from her nest, because the mother bird will suffer if she sees the egg being taken. It would have been kinder not to take the egg at all, but this biblical consideration for the mother bird belongs to another world where an animal's emotional life was an accepted fact --and it belongs to a world when eggs were rarely if ever eaten. Eggs did not become a diet staple in Judea until the time of the Roman occupation.

Today we go to the supermarket and buy eggs by the dozen from birds who are biologically destroyed through the alteration of their reproductive cycles and through the destruction of their nesting and brooding instincts. Eggs are put on the Pesach table to symbolize spring, renewal, life, fertility. They are used at Easter for the same symbolic purposes. Their symbolism for life is more ancient than either of these holidays. It behooves us to get our symbolism straight, to adjust our relationship to nature with more honesty, and to remember that eggs today are most often the misbegotten products of biomachines.

The life of broiler chickens are only marginally better. They are not caged, but live densely packed, as many as 25,000 and even 50,000 in houses that measure around 40' by 400'. This gives each full grown bird about eight inches of space. The litter on the floor may be changed as infrequently as every year or two. By contrast, in most European countries, the litter in chicken houses is changed after every batch of chickens moves out to the slaughtering plant. In Europe, the floors of the chicken houses are made of concrete and litter can be easily removed from them; in the United States the floors are made of dirt which tends to be swept out with the litter, it is more difficult to keep clean, and is therefore cleaned less often.

Economical Death

All animals that go through the slaughter system die painfully and brutally, but a shred of law, often violated, makes some attempt to mitigate the worst effects of the death process. Fowl are excluded from the Humane Slaughter Laws. There is no pretence or shred of legal protection for them. The law only states that "'Poultry shall be slaughtered in accordance with good commercial practices in a manner that will result in thorough bleeding of the carcasses and assure that breathing has stopped prior to scalding.'"[232] The concern is that the chickens be slaughtered in such a manner that their flesh not produce "red spots" from being improperly bled, because "red spots" reduce their value in the market. Karen Davis writes that, "Every day in the United States, at least 30,000-60,000 broiler chickens enter the scald tank alive and breathing."[233]

The chickens arrive at the slaughter house after being transported in cramped cages, they are kept waiting outside the slaughterhouse sometimes as long as nine hours, sometimes in hot weather, without food or water. They are yanked by their legs and shackled by their ankles upside down on to a moving conveyor belt. Karen Davis is our guide for the rest of the process:[234]

> The killing of birds normally involves three phases: motor paralysis by means of an electric current (inaccurately called 'stunning'), throat-cutting, and bleeding. Poultry slaughtered in the United States are neither stunned (rendered unconscious) nor anesthetized (rendered pain free)....In practice, 'stunning' is monitored only for efficient bleedout....
> There are three main methods for immobilizing birds to prepare them for slaughter: (1) chemical immobiliztion, in which a mixture of gases is administered, such as car-

> bon dioxide and reduced oxygen using an inert gas such as argon or nitrogen to stabilize and improve dispersal of the main gas; (2) mechanical, as by debraining, in which the medulla of the brain is pierced directly through the eye; and (3) electrical, in which a live current is shot through the bird by which sodium chloride (salt) has been added to improve the conductivity of the charge.
> The electrified brine-water bath is the method that is used in the large commercial slaughter plants. After the birds have been manually jammed into a movable metal rack that clamps them upside down by their feet, known as 'live hang,' about thirty seconds later their heads and necks are dragged through a 12-foot brine-bath trough called a stun cabinet for approximately seven seconds....

The purpose of all this technology is to stun the chickens (and turkeys) in order to relax the neck muscles and to contract the wing muscles for "the proper positioning of the head for the automatic killers, prevent them from struggling as the blood drains from their necks, to promote rapid breathing (under ninety seconds) and to loosen feathers." The chickens are not killed outright by the electrical bath stunner because this would prevent proper bleedout.

> During electrical water-bath stunning, currents shoot through the birds' skin, skeletal breast muscle, cardiac muscle, and leg muscles causing spasms and tremors, reducing heartbeat and breathing, and increasing the blood pressure. The birds exit the stunner with arched necks, open, fixed eyes, tucked wings, extended rigid legs, shuddering, turned up tail feathers, and varying amounts of defecation.

Sometimes birds raise their heads to avoid the stun bath, sometimes they are shocked by the splashing of other birds. The amount of electric current varies from slaughterhouse to slaughterhouse, as well as the efficiency in using the electric bath. "In reality, so-called 'humane' electrical stunning of poultry is regarded as incompatible with the goals of commerce. High levels of current are said to interfere with plant efficiency and to cause hemorrhage--a 'bloody bird.'" This would mean economic loss.

The birds are then ready to have their necks cut. This is done either manually or with an automatic neck cutting machine. The fastest way to kill the bird at this time would be to sever its two carotid arteries. Kosher ritual slaughter eliminates the electrical stunning bath, and kills by severing the jugular vein. However, it is the severance of the carotid arteries which assures a rapid death. Karen Davis writes, "...the severance of only one jugular vein...can result in a bird's retaining consciousness, while in severe pain for as long as eight minutes."[235] An article in *The Baltimore Jewish Times* about kosher slaughter wonders whether anyone can keep awareness and reverence intact when... "cutting thousands of necks a day on the assembly line."[236]

Chicken Soup For The Soul?

The titles of Jack Canfield's anthologies, *Chicken Soup For the Soul*, like the concept of "chicken soup" trades on the public's ignorance and on nostalgia for a traditional food. Most chicken soup is made from spent fowl; spent fowl are chickens whose biological use as egg producers have come to an end. These fowl are packed into transport crates and trucked to slaughter plants, which are referred to as "spent fowl plants." The word "spent" is a crucial reference to the biological/commercial state of the chicken at this point. It is these "spent fowl" whose flesh goes into foods such as soups, pies, sausages, and which is used in the food service sector, in institutions like schools, prisons, nursing homes.

I Don't Eat Red Meat Anymore, Just Chicken

The sheer numbers of chicken and egg businesses are staggering due in great part to the search for a meat alternative to beef. Around 14,000 chickens are killed in America every minute of every day. As word has gotten around that red meat is unhealthy to eat, people now eat enormous amounts of chicken, putting an equal strain on their health. Animal meat is animal meat. Animal protein is animal protein, whether white, pink or red, whether in liquid form, mashed up, broiled or steamed. The dietary transference from red meat to chicken also trades in the illusion of avoiding the problems in eating animal food. Dr. Andrew Nicolsson comments on this illusion:

> The poultry industry may not want you to know it, but chicken is no health food. In fact, it's just about as bad as beef....
> Comparing chicken and beef, 3.5 oz. of broiled lean flank steak is 56 percent fat, 42 percent protein, and has 70 mg of cholesterol. Light and dark chicken with the skin is 51 percent fat, 46 percent protein, and has 88 mg. cholesterol. In other words, beef and chicken are virtually identical....
> So chicken contributes to all the illnesses linked to low-fiber diets.[237]

The emergence of pathogens such as salmonella and campylobacter in chickens seriously disqualifies chicken as a "health food." Campylobacter is particularly dangerous because the pathogen is unresponsive to antibiotics. Indeed, there is concern that antibiotics makes this pathogen more virulent.

Analysis of this problem by *Consumer Reports* for March, 1998,[238] showed that there was virtually no difference in the pathogen problem between high-priced chickens and inexpensive chickens. Empire Poultry, which is the largest distributor of kosher chicken, fared no better than non-kosher chicken with respect to salmonella and campylobacter.

Concern for animal life is an issue about "the mixed community" and the "paradigm of cooperation," about a view of nature which requires that all creatures be given their due. It is not an issue about equality between animals and humans, for there is no philosophically legitimate way to argue the case, since only people can make the claim for superiority. The giraffe cannot make that case vis à vis the rabbit, or the rabbit vis à vis the mole. We do not know if animals contemplate their status in the universe. We only know that we do, and that we do it obsessively. Animals do not enter entirely into our philosophical community, nor entirely into the Jewish understanding of ethics, for along with the affirmation of a benign nature, Jewish understanding of morality requires that human beings be free. Evil and cruelty is the work of humankind, not of God, for God is just. Because God *is* just, human beings *can* overcome their evil natures. But it is only in human freedom that human beings can work out their moral destinies. Without that philosophical underpinning, Judaism falls back into pre-Mosaic models of fate and necessity. Thus, the story of Cain and Abel, which many biblical commentators see as a working over of pre-biblical material, contains the admonition to Cain:

> Surely if you do right, there is uplift,
> but if you do not do right, sin crouches at the door,
> Its urge is toward you. Yet you can master it.
>
> (Genesis 4:6-7)

Equality and Inequality: Questions of Status

In the fourteenth century, a book called *Iggeret Baalei Hayyim,* or *The Book of Animals and Men* was published by an Islamic association, known as the Society of Pure Brethren or the Brothers of Purity. Jews, Christians and Muslims belonged to this association where they would debate the relationship between animals and human beings. Rabbi Elijah Schochet writes in *Animal Life in the Jewish Tradition* that, while superiority over animals was delegated to the human race, the "moving and impressive" lamentation at injustice in the world was voiced by the animals.[239] The rooster's lament testifies to the uneasy conscience we bear, and should bear, towards the animals:

> At midnight I rise to pray....
> But the sleeping ones lay hold of me....
> They slaughter me and eat me.
> Have we not one father?
> Has not one God created us all?

The lower status or "subservience" of animals was acceptable to those who fought for the rights of animals in the past, and to those who preached compassion for them throughout the last two centuries when the concept of "animal rights" arose in a secular framework. All the major religions, even Jainism which has the most consistent record of compassion for animal life, are basically homocentric, certainly de facto homocentric, and accept the classical pattern of hierarchy from human to animal to vegetation. Religions such as Hinduism accommodate their view of the "unity of all life," to the hierarchical pattern. In India, humans ride elephants and use them for labor, not the other way around.

An acceptance of some hierarchy in nature may have the advantage of protecting animal life by acknowledging a division between animal life and vegetation. It has become a quaint question to ask whether the carrot does not feel pain as well as the cow! Concerning this aberrant preoccupation, in *The Phenomenon of Life*,[240] Hans Jonas renders a useful distinction between animal and plant life in his chapter, "To Move and To Feel,: On The Animal Soul": For him, it is movement, not reproduction, that defines the "higher" forms of life: thus, their relationship to space and motion is different from that of plant life:

> ...appetition is the basic condition of motility, pursuit is the primary motion. Though appetite is common to all life, the motility of animal life, in translating appetition makes a visible difference between animal and vegetable life....the great secret of animal life lies precisely in the gap which it is able to maintain between immediate concern and mediate satisfaction....This is at the bottom of the whole phenomenon of animality and of its departure from the vegetative mode of life.

Leon Kass extends Jonas' argument into a discussion about form and matter. "Form and material are interdependent,"[241] and form is "form-at-work."[242] That is the animal's form is revealed in his activity; form is not static, it is dynamic, it is revealed in behavior, and the primary activity of animal life is the act of nourishing itself to stay alive. All animal life has an interest in this. Appetite cannot be separated from form. The organic powers and activities, "activities of self-persistence (that is, metabolism) itself" persists for "the maintenance of the self, by the self, and for the self...."[243]

That is why confining animals in cages and on feedlots, which deprives them of motility and the need to search for their natural food deranges them from their basic natures. Worse, to feed an herbivorous animal meat is to ensure a breakdown in the form/strucure of that animal. One does not have to be a mystic to understand why bovine and poultry life are under microbial assault. Put simply, animals are designed to search for food and to eat the food designed for them. Deprive them of this primary search and you deprive them of their natures. (This is also true of animals in zoos and circuses. As Kenneth Shapiro of Psychologists for the Ethical Treatment of Animals, pointed out, animals are "habitat-specific.") Furthermore, animals to be animals must experience want and fear, but also fulfillment and enjoyment. In animal life as in human life, enjoyment and suffering evolved together:

> The two evolve together, and their [the animals] liability to suffering is not a shortcoming which detracts from the possibility of enjoyment, but its necessary complement. The suffering intrinsic in [normal] animal life is not that of pain (which is occasional and concomitant) but that of want and fear, i.e. an aspect of appetitive nature as such....Animal being is thus essentially passionate being.[244]

Following Jonas, Kass argues for a pre-Cartesian view of animal life, not as a vegetarian but as a Jew who is close to the biblical view of animal. The nearness of natures between humans and animals, and their distinction from plant life, is implicit in the structure of Genesis: human beings and the land animals are created on the same day. Because the basic natural emotional life of an animal is rooted in want, fear and fulfillment, justifying human cruelty towards animals by the "beast eats beast" paradigm is self-serving. Human cruelty towards animals is in a different modality that is not within the framework of the animal's natural emotional range. For the animal who experiences it, and for the human being who administers it, it is a diabolical cruelty. The Cartesian view is still pervasive, as Kass writes:

> Not since Descartes broke with his philosophical ancestors to present his doctrne of the 'animal machine' and a purely mechanical explanation of vital phenomena has any philosopher or scientist of the first rank thought to argue that some notion of form or soul or purpose was required to understand metabolism or, indeed, any activity of life with the possible exception of consciousness.[245]

It is time for everyone interested in the biblical view of animal life and of nature, to take issue with the Cartesian view. At present, those who oppose Cartesianism often promote the paradigm of "the web." It is too soon to know whether the replacement of the hierarchical pattern with that of the paradigm of "the web" will return humankind to a closer relationship with nature and animal life, but it is anachronistic to blame other civilizations for not incorporating this 20th century paradigm into their view of animal life. Within the classical framework of hierarchy, animal rights literature throughout the 18th and 19th century was written from the point of view of defending "our lesser brethren," or the "subhuman species." Inequality was not seen as a threat to compassion, nor should it, or we would be in great trouble with respect to all the meek of the earth, whether they be the untalented, the unintelligent, or the non-human. As Andrew Linzey points out, there are many illustrations in the Bible of the care and love of the Creator for the animal world, "and this despite the clearly pre-eminent place given to humans in creation."[246] Judaism incorporated into a world view human and animal vulnerability, human dominion and, at the same time, human kinship with animal life. One of the most touching examples of this is the parable the prophet Nathan uses to teach David that his seduction of Bathsheba was abhorrent:

> The Lord sent Nathan to David, and Nathan said to David: 'There were two men in the city, one rich and one poor. The rich man had many flock, but the poor man had only one ewe lamb whom he raised and nourished, and this lamb grew up together with his own children; she ate from his food and drank from his cup, and was to him like his own daughter. But a traveler came to the rich man, and the rich man wished to feast him, and he took the poor man's ewe and killed her.' David's anger was greatly kindled against this man, and he said to Nathan: 'As the Lord liveth, the man that has done this is worthy to die: and he shall restore the lamb fourfold because he had no pity.' Nathan said to David, 'Thou art that man.' (Samuel ll, 12)

Nathan uses a parable he knew would elicit David's compassion. The passage is meant as judgment upon David, but it is David's compassion for both the lamb and the poor man that endears David and the parable to us. The nearness of the poor and the animal is expressed again in Deuteronomy 24: 19-25:4, in which we are instructed to leave the second shaking of the olive trees and the grape vines for the poor, and a bit further, "Neither shalt thou muzzle the ox when he treads out the corn in the field." [247] This injunction to observe the animal's right to his appetite and to its food in the fields is within a list of commandments regarding proper relationships among humans. It endorses Noah Cohen's view of the relationship between biblical man and animals, that "...the wall of partition between man and beast was rather thin and the legal rights and privileges of the latter must neither be neglected nor overlooked."[248] This view speaks to the sense of the "mixed community," to the sense of kinship between animals and humans, that animals are included in divine laws. James Gaffney's comments about this law, in his article, "The Relevance of Animal Experimentation to Roman Catholic Ethical Methodology,"[249] are on the mark and worth repeating here.

> Like certain other passages in that same book, [Deuteronomy] it is plainly intended to be read precisely

> as a piece of divine legislation in behalf of animals, despite some inconvenience to human greed.... It is indeed 'for oxen that God is concerned,' and to at least that extent he does 'not speak entirely for our sake.' The Mosaic law does envisage animal interests, does legislate animal rights, and, to that extent, does represent animals as moral objects.

So Maimonides believed too when he wrote, "It should not be believed that all the beings exist for the sake of the existence of humanity. On the contrary, all the other beings too have been intended for their own sakes, and not for the sake of something else."[250] Any quick survey of the natural world informs us that, from the point of view of the human race, we do not know the purpose of much of creation, like mosquitoes and flies, blackflies and termites and disease carrying rodents. We can spin nice tales that they are meant to remind us of our frailty, our morality, to goad us into humility, but the fact is much of nature remains mysterious, from the point of view of human purpose.Much of insect and animal life gets in the way of human life. Gaffney reminds the reader that the passage in Deuteronomy does not indicate an "extraordinary " dispensation to animals on the Bible's part, for the animals are included in covenantal statements:

> I now establish My covenant with you and your offspring, and with every living being who is with you--birds, cattle and every wild animal. (Genesis 9:9-10)

They are included in the covenant concerning the Sabbath. :

> The seventh day is a Sabbath of the Lord your God; you shall not do any work--you, your son or your daughter, your male or female slave, your ox or your ass, or any of your cattle, or the stranger in your settlements...
> (Deut. 5:14)

How is this covenant observed with respect to factory farm animals? Do dairy cows rest on the Sabbath? Is the battery hen freed from her cage on the Sabbath? Is the crated veal invited out into the sunshine to romp on the grass? No answer from the moral void of the factory farm will detain us here.

Such a situation was discussed in the Middle Ages, for it was known then as it is known now, that if you restrict an animal's freedom, the energy which goes into his free movement, can go into his growth which could bring more profit:

> ...there is a discussion by a medieval Jewish commentator in which he asks whether the provisions for resting the beast on the Sabbath means that you simply rest the beast while being permitted to keep it enclosed, or whether this requires that the beast be permitted to graze freely on the farmland, nibbling the grass, etc. And the opinion of the commentator is that because the Bible uses the term "that your beast enjoy," it is required that it be permitted free grazing. [251]

Where are the rabbis today to ask for *at least* this modest enforcement of halakha? As Rabbi Gendler comments, previous ages knew what we know, but there was a moral difference in behavior: it is not that we are smarter in how to convert animals into cash: "The most significant difference between previous ages and our own may be that while they to some extent regarded the lives of their beasts, we seemingly manage to ignore them almost completely." [252] What a transformation of Jews into Cartesians!

In accordance with Jewish teaching vis à vis the oppressed, Jews were taught that it is our moral duty to defend animals as we would defend any who are powerless. The equation is between power and powerlessness, not between superiority and inferiority. The equation between power and superiority, and powerlessness and inferiority, is fascism. In the Jewish equation between power and powerlessness, compassion is meant to mediate. Rabbi Hirsch gave that equation its sublime 19th century utterance in the Jewish understanding of "dominion":

> There are probably no creatures who require more the protective divine word against the presumption of man than the animals, which like man have sensations and instincts, but whose bodies and powers are nevertheless subservient to man. In relation to them man so easily forgets that injured animal muscle twitches just like human muscle, that the maltreated nerves of an animal sicken like human nerves, that the animal being is just as sensitive to cuts, blows, and beatings as man. Thus man becomes the torturer of the animal soul, which has been subjected to him only for the fulfillment of humane and wise purposes....(Horeb, Chapt. 60, Verse 415)
>
> Here you are faced with God's teaching, which obliges you not only to refrain from inflicting unnecessary pain on any animal, but to help and, when you can, to lessen the pain whenever you see an animal suffering, even through no fault of yours.
>
> (Horeb, chapt. 60, verse 416)

Jewish Teaching About Responsibility for Animals

The teaching of compassion toward animals in Judaism is constant and pervasive. Lecky observed in his *History of European Morals* that "the rabbinical writers have been remarkable for the great emphasis with which they inculcated the duty of kindness to animals."[253] Judaism permitted humans to use animals, but not for frivolous purposes, never for entertainment, and never with cruelty. There is no record in Jewish history of blood sports, such as wild beast combats, bullfighting, cockfighting, dogfighting, or bloodsports of any kind. There is no tradition of the hunter as hero, romantic figure or macho exemplar.[254]

A Jew was taught that a righteous Jew does not sell or give away his animal to another whose behavior towards the animal would be suspect. Based on Deuteronomy 11:15: "And I will give grass in your fields for your cattle, and you shall eat and be satisfied," a Jew was taught that he must feed his animal before he eats, for God provides food for the cattle before people, and we are to imitate God.

According to R. Eleazer ha-Kapar, a Talmudic sage, no one should buy a domestic animal, wild beast, or bird unless he is able to feed it properly.[255] The duty to feed an animal first is so great that a person is legally authorized to interrupt the performance of a rabbinic commandment in order to ascertain that this has been done.[256] Based on similar statements in Exodus 23:12 and Deuteronomy 5:12-14, Rashi stated that animals must be free to roam on the Sabbath day and graze freely and enjoy the beauties of nature. Animals are to be provided for during the Sabbatical year; the produce that grows freely during that period is to be enjoyed by the beasts of the field as well as by the poor. (Lev. 25:6-7)

Judaism teaches that we are forbidden to be cruel to animals since animals are part of God's creation and human beings have special responsibilities to them as they do to all who are less powerful. These teachings are summarized in the Hebrew phrase, *tsa'ar ba'alei chayim*, the biblical mandate not to cause "pain to any living creature."

The Mixed Community

The biblical view of animals rests on both a homocentric assumption and the assumption of kinship between animals and human beings. In Christianity the concept of the mixed community is symbolized by the crêche. Like other motifs from the past, it is an inconvenient concept in the modern world. It is also inconvenient to remember that in the Bible God makes treaties and covenants with animals, just as God does with humans, that the Bible postulates a *serious* dignity to animal life:

> "As for me," says the Lord, "behold I establish My Covenant with you and with your seed after you, and with every living creature that is with you, the fowl, the cattle, and every beast of the earth with you; all that go out of the ark, even every beast of the earth. (Gen. 9:9-10)

> "And in that day will I make a covenant for them with the beasts of the field and with the fowls of heaven and with the creeping things of the ground. And I will break the bow and the sword and the battle out of the land and I will make them to lie down safely." (Hos. 2:20)

The Hebrew term *nefesh chaya* ("living soul") is applied in Genesis 1:21, 1:24 to animals as well as to people. While the Torah clearly indicates that people have "dominion over the fish of the sea, and over the fowl of the air, and over every living thing that creeps upon the earth" (Gen. 1:28)--a fact of existence everywhere--there was nevertheless a basic relatedness envisioned between animals and humans. Animals are also God's creatures, possessing sensitivity and the capacity for feeling pain; hence they must be protected and treated with compassion and justice.[257]

God's close identification with the beasts of the field, creatures of the sea, and birds of the air is indicated in Psalms 104 and 148. Sea animals and birds receive the same blessing as humans: "Be fruitful and multiply" (Gen. 1:22). Animals are initially given a vegetarian diet, similar to that of people (Gen. 1:29-30).

The Psalms indicate God's concern for animals, in the statement so often repeated, "His tender mercies are over all His creatures" (Ps. 145:9). They picture God as "satisfying the desire of every living creature" (Ps. 145:16), "providing food for the beasts and birds" (Ps. 147:9), in general, "preserving both man and animal" (Ps. 36:7), sustaining life and creatures. According to the Jewish tradition, God provides each animal with the attributes necessary for survival in his environment. These attributes are stripped from the animal in the factory farming system, and will most probably be further stripped by genetic engineering.

Perhaps the Jewish attitude toward animals is best summarized by the statement in Proverbs 12:10, "The righteous person regards the life of his animal." This is the human counterpoint of "The Lord is good to all, and His tender mercies are over all His creatures" (Ps. 145:9). In Judaism, one who is cruel to animals cannot be regarded as a righteous individual. What then are we to make of our wanton consumption of animal meat? How does kashrut respond to the modern appetite?

In innumerable instances, concern for children and family is voiced along with concern for animals. The parable of the ewe in which Nathan admonishes David for his behavior with Bathsheba is succinct with this sense of kinship. Animals and the young, or animals and the poor, are often coupled together as those who require special care. Jacob tells Esau that a journey he is considering will be slowed because "the children are tender and the flocks and the herds giving suck are a care to me." (Genesis 33:12-14.) Later Jacob asks Joseph "Whether it is well with thy brethren and well with thy flock." (Genesis 37:14). It would be cynical to assume that such inquiries are a matter of financial concern. They are statements of kinship between family and flock, as in Nathan's parable to David: "The poor man raised the lamb as his daughter."

Abhorrence of Cruelty to Animals

It is forbidden to cause pain to any animal. Maimonides (1135-1214) [3] and R. Judah ha-Hasid (1150-1217) [4] stated that this is based on the biblical statement of the angel of God to Balaam, "Wherefore have you smitten your ass?" (Num. 22:32). This verse is used in the Talmud as a prime source for its assertion that we are to treat animals humanely. The Code of Jewish Law [258] is more explicit and specific:

> It is forbidden, according to the law of the Torah, to inflict pain upon any living creature. On the contrary, it is our duty to relieve the pain of any creature, even if it is ownerless or belongs to a non-Jew.
>
> When horses, drawing a cart, come to a rough road or a steep hill, and it is hard for them to draw the cart without help, it is our duty to help them, even when they belong

> to a non-Jew, because of the precept not to be cruel to animals, lest the owner smite them to force them to draw more than their strength permits.
>
> It is forbidden to tie the legs of a beast or of a bird in a manner as to cause them pain.

Yet for almost a century this was precisely what has been done in shackling and hoisting.

> You shall not muzzle the ox when he threshes the corn. (Deut. 25:4).

The law which states that at the time of threshing, the ox should not be prevented from satisfying his appetite was not a pious shibboleth. It reflected the status of the animal as a laborer: the prohibition gives the animal the right to these fruits while he is working,[259] just as a laborer is entitled to his wages. (Though Paul interpreted the prohibition allegorically, he understood its intention.) Rabbi Hirsch goes even further, citing the *Shulchan Aruch* : that one may prevent an animal from eating when the food might harm him.[260]

Animals should be relieved from suffering: "If you see the ass of him that hates you lying under its burden, you shall surely not pass by him; you shall surely unload it with him." (Exod. 23:5) We must be vigilant for the well-being of a lost animal: "You shall not see your brother's ox or his sheep driven away and hide yourself from them; You shall surely bring them back to your brother. (Deut. 22:1). Lest we interpret this law as implicating a financial interest, the law also states that, in addition, the animal must be cared for until the owner's return.

Such injunctions of mercy for the animal read today like the mutterings of a bygone civilization. We do not live in this pious world any longer. Reverence for nature and love for God's creatures--even merely concern for them--fled for the Jew as it has fled from all modern countries. Factory farming is international. Al-Hafiz B.A. Masri complains that "the cruel and inhumane methods of intensive farming are being practised in most of the Islamic countries these days, even in countries where indigence is no excuse" [261]

Equation of Power and Powerlessness

Inequality exists in nature. Animals have unequal strengths, unequal capabilities. A seminal Jewish law concerning animals is the commandment that, "You shall not plow with an ox and an ass together." (Deut. 22:10). This would cause the weaker animal great pain in trying to keep up with the stronger, while the stronger animal would also suffer by being deprived of her usual routine, by having to act contrary to her instinctive nature. The Talmud extends this law to apply to any case where there are two animals involved, one strong and one weak, and to other activities such as driving carts or wagons. [262] You may not allow one task to be done together by animals of two species. You may not allow them to carry the smallest thing together, even if it be only a seed. You may not sit in a wagon drawn by animals of differing species.[263] Rabbi Hirsch concluded that one should not unite animals for any activities that God's laws have not designed them for working together in the service of the world. These teachings embrace the concept of equivalent justice for animals, that we are to recognize the *nature* of each animal and to act towards it accordingly.

Lessons were drawn from the meek animal. David, the sheep herder is depicted as concerned that the younger, smaller sheep not be pushed away from nibbling on the grass by the older sheep. In the story of Balaam's ass, it is the lowly ass who hears the voice of God's messenger while the haughty Balaam, sitting atop a warrior horse, cannot. Judaism chose the ass as the animal which would bear the Messiah, and Isaiah prophesied a world in which the power of the lion would be pacified.

The Sacred Maternal Bond

It is forbidden to sacrifice a newborn ox, sheep, or goat until it has had at least seven days of warmth and nourishment from its mother . (Lev. 22:27). "And whether it be ox or ewe, you shall not kill it and its young both in one day" (Lev. 22:28).

These prohibitions refer to a custom, usual in foreign cults, of sacrificing an animal and her young together. Maimonides commented on this verse:

> It is prohibited to kill an animal with its young on the same day, in order that people should be restrained and prevented from killing the two together in such a manner that the young is slain in the sight of the mother; for the pain of animals under such circumstances is very great. There is no difference in this case between the pain of people and the pain of other living beings, since the love and the tenderness of the mother for her young ones is not produced by reasoning but by feeling, and this faculty exists not only in people but in most living things.[264]

We are forbidden to take the mother bird and its young together. Some Jewish scholars, including Nachmanides, Bahya b. Asher (died in 1340), and the Kol Bo (late 13th century) connected the above law and others prohibiting slaughter of an animal together with its young to the preservation of species, rather than to abhorrence of cruelty toward animals. [265] Some Torah commentators saw the above laws and the prohibition against boiling a kid in the milk of its mother (Exodus 23:19, 34:26; Deuteronomy 14:21), as a rejection of an ancient pagan practice, but most Jewish commentators saw in such laws the maternal bond as a sacred trust.

It would be an exhaustive task to point out the incongruities between meat-eating today and Jewish laws concerning animal life. It is not possible to conjoin them, but it is possible to opt out of the system. Vegetarianism is not only good for one's health; it is a moral requirement to reclaim responsibility for animal life; it is a revolt against the evils of a technology that has gone mad and that is spreading across countries whose food production methods have not yet been totally industrialized; it is a revolt against the industrialization of living creatures.

Compassion

"Sympathy, empathy, imitation, identification--these are the terms...for the transmission of all culture." [266]

The Jewish Sages regarded compassion as tantamount to the act of creation: "He who sustains God's creatures is as though he had created them." (Tanhuma Noah 16a) A Jew was taught that there were lessons to be learned from brutality to animal life, that a sympathetic chain unites us in the struggle for survival. The long history of interpretation of the laws of kashrut which taught that dietary discipline was intended to civilize us spoke to this relationship between humans and animals.

History bears out the intuition that there is a subliminal connection between how we treat animals and how humans will treat humans. Modern racist theories about human beings derived in part from experiments in animal breeding in the 18th and 19th centuries. Himmler, Haas, Borman, Darré and other Nazis had backgrounds in agriculture and animal feeding. "The Final Solution" and "euthanasia" programs were part of their master plan to breed a better Aryan Germany. Nazi doctors and others learned how to experiment on human beings from their experience with experimenting on animals.[267] Syphilis experiments on animals and humans were concomitant. Hunter/warrior cultures know the synergy between killing animals and killing people.

An anomaly concerning the definition of human nature is creeping into modern life like an invisible gas because of an interchange between ourselves, machines and animal life. On the one hand, we accept the fact that computers are becoming more like us, while we ignore the fact that animals are becoming more like machines. An exchange of definition between sentient life and machine is taking place. The classical definition of the human being as "a little higher than the animals, a little lower than the angels," may soon be rerplaced with "a little higher than the robot, a little lower than the computer." As a human being's organs and, eventually, brain cells, will be replaceable and interchangeable with animal and machine parts, at what point will the definition of "human" disappear?[268] Our civilization may cling to the classical definition of "human" for some time, as the Renaissance used pagan myths of Eros and Cupid without believing in them, but the definition of "human" will become as quaint as Eros and Cupid are, cherubs for a greeting card. Technology will superimpose other realities which will be experienced in our psyches, even as technology builds a bridge via biblical imagery to temporarily accommodate itself to us.

Among biologists and other scientists there is the expectation of the brave new world being created via genetic engineering. This is not just a matter of one or another gene being discovered, or of sheep being cloned, but of being at the beginning of a new creation. The use of biblical imagery, particularly that of Genesis inevitably suggests itself in matters of creation. Chapters such as "Noah's Vessel," and "The Promised Land," in Stuart Kauffman's book, *At Home In the Universe,* are efforts to embed the world of technology and artifice into the world that we thought of as "natural" for millennia. A portentous third paradigm of "nature" is emerging. The boat that carried goats and sheep into the atoll of Bikini Island to test the effects of radioactivity after atomic bomb explosions was called "Noah's Ark the Second." The animals did not walk off this "ark." Their bodies were flattened out, one side pasted against the other as if their interior space had been sucked out of them. These animals were carried off this "ark" for further testing.

The Purpose of Animal Life

Why were animals created? Why are they here at all? Why wasn't the world created with just human beings in it? Would we like it that way? The question is no longer theoretical, since so much of animal life is becoming extinct or diseased.

Does animal life reflect the abundance of nature, the creative powers of God? The Talmud says, "All creation praises the Creator of the Universe." Rabbi Hirsch believed that animals were created for the same reason human beings were: to be called to the bar of joy. Perhaps at one time they were, but that time for the veal calf and the battery hen is past. The "biomachine" must force us to rethink our moral world, and the rewards and losses between nature and "artifice." It should force us to remember the second commandment, which is not to worship idols. The implication of this commandment is that we should know the difference between "artifice" and the living spirit of the living God which cannot be embodied in an artifice made by human hands. Protest of the abomination of the animal machine speaks with the same message, whether the voice is religious or secular. John Robbins wrote:

> To me, the fact that new born human infants and new born animal babies of all kinds glow with this ineffable sweetness testifies to our common source. They are born as we are--fresh from the lap of God, wanting to express their qualities in the service of the divine spark with them. They are born, as we are, thirsting for life. They are born, as we are, wanting to be all they are, and become all they can become. [269]

In a different rhetorical mode, the Talmud says the same thing:

> All creation praises the Creator of the Universe.
> The cows of the field gather together and sing,
> The cattle saved in Ninevah, sing
> 'Sing, oh sing, acacia, tower in all your splendor.

In Rabbi Everett Gendler's article, "The Universal Chorus," [270] he reminds us of the many passages in the Bible and elsewhere which depict all creation praising the Lord of Creation:

> This tradition is not confined to the Psalms, nor does it end with the Bible. The Song of the three Jews, found in the Apocrypha as an addition to the Book of Daniel, and probably a Hebrew composition, also summons all the works of the Lord to sing God's praise with exaltation.

'Bless the Lord, all you works of the Lord,
sing God's praise and exalt God forever...
Bless the Lord...whales
and all that swim in the waters...
all birds of the air...all beasts and cattle...
all people on earth...'

Even more striking is the portrayal of all living creatures singing their individual songs in praise of the Creator. In Perek Shira, Chapter of Song, a mystical hymn (dating from the 5th-7th century)...worded songs are ascribed specifically to land animals, winged creatures, insects, and residents of the waters. Cows, camels, horses, mules; roosters, chickens, doves, eagles; butterflies, locusts, spiders, flies; sea monsters, fish, frogs: all of these and many more offer biblical words of praise in song to their Creator, filling the universe with hymns and songs.

Does the battery hen celebrate the Creator of the Universe? What hymn of praise to creation can she sing?

Compassion for animals is not only hortatory, an exercise in good feelings. It is meant to make us more moral, more human; it is meant to remind us that we stand at a perilous crossroad between nature and artifice. For the Jews compassion for animal life played a determining role in their history. Leaders were chosen on the basis of their compassion for animals, surely a startling leadership quality. Exodus Rabbah 2:2 relates that Moses was chosen because he ran after a lamb who had strayed from his flock. When finding her, he realized the animal was thirsty, and gave her drink, then carried her back on his shoulders. It was for this reason that God said to him, "You who have shown compassion for an animal shall be the leader of my people."

The story of how Rebecca is chosen to be Isaac's wife is so charming that we easily forget its main point: that she was chosen because she showed compassion for an animal. Abraham's servant traveled back to Abraham's birthplace to bring Isaac a wife from there. As in a fairy tale, he is given a test by which to choose the right maiden: "As I stand by the spring of water, let the young woman who comes out to draw and to whom I say, 'Please let me drink a little water from your jar,' and who answers, 'You may drink, and I will also draw for your camels,' she shall be the wife of my lord Isaac.

Luckily, Rebecca knew the right answer. How much history and destiny depended upon it! How much history and destiny depend upon the fact that we no longer know the answer?

6

Bal Tashchit

"All animal life and all growing and life-giving things have rights in the cosmos that man must consider, even as he strives to ensure his own survival. The war against the spoliation of nature and the pollution of the environment is therefore the command of the hour and the call of the ages."

Rabbi Robert Gordis

The meaning of "bal tashchit" is variously given as: you must not waste anything; use all things prudently; do not waste natural resources, but these all point to the same moral. The origin of this teaching is in Deuteronomy 20:19-20:

"When in your war against a city you have to besiege it for a long time, you must not destroy its trees, wielding the ax against them. You may eat of them, but you may not cut them down. Are trees of the field human to withdraw before you into the besieged city? Only trees which do not produce fruits may be used for your siegeworks against the city that has been waging war on you, until it has been reduced."

We notice the curious quality of innocence attributed to the trees, as is attributed to the animals. The text says: nature is not your enemy; do not include it in your wars. The text admits that one must use nature's resources, but one must use exactly what is required: once your enemy has been reduced, do not continue to cut down trees. Do not cut down trees wantonly; do not use things more than is necessary to the task at hand.

The Talmudic rabbis expanded on the passage in Deuteronomy for centuries, cautioning against excess of all kinds, including excess in diet, dress, and even in burial practices.

"Whoever breaks vessels, or tears garments, or destroys a building, or clogs a well, or does away with food in a destructive manner violates the negative mitzvah of *bal tashchit* (*Kiddushin 32*a) [Talmudic rulings on *bal tashchit* also prohibit the killing of animals for convenience (*Hullin* 7b), wasting fuel (*Shabbat* 67b), and a minority opinion classifies the eating of extravagant foods when one can eat simpler foods as a violation of this precept (*Shabbat* 140b)][271] The rabbis evinced a dramatic sense that the world hangs by a moral thread: "Do not corrupt and desolate My world, for if you corrupt and desolate it, there is no one to set it right after you." (*Kohelet Rabbah* 7:28). Written centuries ago, the words have a chilling timeliness. The great, almost legendary Rabbi Yohanan ben Zakai, living through the downfall of Jerusalem and the conquest of Judea by Rome, said, in a time of fervent Messianic expectations, "If you are holding a sapling in your hand and someone should say to you that the Messiah has come, first plant the sapling, then go out to greet the Messiah."[272]

Rabbi Samson Hirsch regarded the passage in Deuteronomy on preserving the fruit trees in time of war as the whole of the moral relationship between the human and the non-human world, between God the Creator and Source of all life, and human life, a creation of God:

> Yea, 'Do not destroy anything,' is the first and most general call of God...if you should regard the beings beneath you as objects without rights, not perceiving God Who created them, and therefore desire that they feel the might of your presumptuous mood, instead of using them only as the means of wise human activity--then God's call proclaims to you, 'Do not destroy anything! Be a *mentsh*! Only if you use the things around you for wise human purposes, sanctified by the word of My teaching, only then are you a *mentsh* and have the right over them which I have given you as a human....I lent

> them to you for wise use; never forget that I lent them to you. As soon as you use them unwisely you commit treachery against my world, you commit murder and robbery against My property, you sin against Me!...In truth there is no one nearer to idolatry than one who can disregard the fact that things are the creatures and property of God, and who presumes also to have the right, having the might, to destroy them according to a presumptuous act of God. (Horeb, #56).

Wendell Berry sees the story of the Hebrews incoming into the Promised land as the beginnings of an ecological discipline:

> The story of the giving of the Promised Land to the Israelites is more serviceable than the story of the giving of the Garden of Eden, because the Promised Land is a divine gift to a fallen people. For that reason the giving is more problematical, and the receiving is more conditional and more difficult. In the Bible's long working out of the understanding of this gift, we may find the beginning--and, by implication, the end--of the definition of an ecological discipline. [273]

Jewish environmental ethics, like concern for animals, is rooted in the religious system and in Jewish teaching that there is a divine plan to creation, and that human beings do not own nature or the earth. The lines from Psalm 24 are a watchword of the Jewish attitude:

> "The earth is the Lord's, and the fullness thereof;
> the world, and they that dwell therein."

Jewish commentary is filled with loving embroidery on this statement, evincing the unity of God with creation, and the constraints on human dominion. "The awareness of God's dominion, a proprietorship anchored in creation, is the ultimate constraint erected by Judaism to stay the hand of self-destruction." [274]

We are to hold creation holy, as God is the Lord of a plan which includes commandments such as that we may not create hybrids, we may not sow with two different seeds. These commandments strongly suggest that you may not disrupt natural law, and they should bear implications for genetic engineering in agricultural products and animals, at the least.

The Sabbath itself is seen as an ecological discipline, for the foundation of it is that we do not disrupt anything on the Sabbath. On the Sabbath, creation rests. We do not work, because work changes nature and creation. The purpose of the Sabbath is for us to re-establish harmony with nature, to know God's order for the world and not to intervene in it. During the Sabbatical year, we let the land rest. In "Judaism and Environmental Ethics," Jonathan Helfand writes:

> Judaism's genuine concern to maintain what is called *sidrei bereshit*--the orders of creation, the plan and intent of the Creator, is expressed in several ways...first, injunctions against the despoliation of nature and natural resources and, second, legal imperatives regarding the development and conservation of the God-given environment.

Repeating Leon Kass' observation here that vegetarianism is the diet which least disturbs the Jewish sense of the order of creation, it is the diet most fitting for Shabbat.

Jewish environmental ethics proceed from the concept that we live in a God-given environment. The concept of planning for open space seems so modern, it is startling to come across a provision in Numbers 35:2. for "the establishment of a migrash, an open space two thousand cubits wide around the levitical cities, to be maintained free of all construction and cultivation." Helfand's comments on this provision :

> The need for such a provision is ultimately based upon the principle of the yishuv ha-arets...[which] requires man to consider the consequences of his creative activities in the world, not merely to clear stones and build

cities or to avoid acts of wanton destruction, but to maintain a proper balance in the environment, providing the necessary amenities while insuring the mutual security of society and nature.

Aryeh Carmel sees in this idea of the migrash, or open spaces around the city, "the importance of cleanliness, beauty and 'naturalness' of environment for a balanced development to the personality. These are the amenities of a civilized society: what it takes to produce a healthy and emotionally stable citizenry. For this achievement the natural environment must be given its place, it is to be honored as a source of enjoyment and as the origin of our being."

Genesis is the blueprint of creation for the Jew, the Muslim and the Christian, as well of everyone who reads in the story of Genesis the embodiment of order and justice in the natural world. Commenting on Genesis in his article, "God, Man and Creation," David Shapiro writes:

> But even though man was converted into a conqueror he was never to forget his original relationship to the earth, which was to work it and watch over it. The second chapter of Genesis emphasizes that man's origin was derived from the earth. 'The Lord God formed man from the dust of the earth.' (2:6) The earth is not only the seat of man's activities and that of other creatures; it is not only the medium of their substance, it is the very source of man's existence as well as that of the other land-animals, just as the water is the origin of life. The earth is the mother of man, from which he emerged and to which he will ultimately return....God did not create the world to be a wasteland. He made it to be inhabited....It is man who makes possible the extension of blessings to the earth, just as he is answerable for the curses that the earth suffers when he departs from God and the righteous way of life. Because of man's sinfulness, the earth can no longer perform its functions properly.

The sources of pollution in the contemporary world are industrial and agricultural. In this study we are concerned mainly with agricultural pollution--the source for more than half the world's pollution. Most of that pollution is caused by a meat-based diet, but some of the pollution defined as "agricultural" is also derived from industrial processes, such as the manufacture of pesticides and fertilizers. Eric G. Freudenstein, in "Ecology and The Jewish Tradition," writes:

> Ancient Jewish tradition stressed the maintenance of the biosphere over three and a half thousand years ago, but during the centuries of the Diaspora, divorced from their land, that message of our venerable tradition became weak. Jews were often cooped up in urban ghettos, their energies absorbed by the struggle for survival in a hostile world which they were powerless to influence. Nor was the destruction of the world's natural assets as yet a threat to human existence. In modern times, the active participation of Jews in the Diaspora, in all phases of the public welfare, the reclamation of land in the state of Israel and a general awareness of ecology, have created a new climate for a deeper understanding and acceptance of the concern for the environment evinced by Jewish tradition. Conditions are now propitious for the ancient message of *bal tashchit* to be once again proclaimed loud and clear to all men of goodwill.

That ancient message can only be reclaimed by a radical change in diet. An editorial in *The New York Times* for Monday, September 22, 1997 traced the death of fish, the rise of pathogens and the pollution of Maryland's riverways to agricultural run-off from hog farms and chicken factories. The enormous chicken industry in Maryland produces tons of waste. The waste is used to fertilize corn fields."When the rains come, the nitrogen and other nutrients in the manure flow inexorably into the surrounding watershed and nourish the microbes." The editorial asks for "a better, stronger, Clean Water Act that identifies key watersheds, sets clear targets--percentage reductions in nitrogen loading...." etc. Such proposals to identify the problem, or to nullify or remove the garbage, are useless. As Lewis Regenstein, author of *America, the Poisoned*, said in a speech: "It's no use talking of taking waste away. There's no away to take it to." *Away* is some else's river, or air, or land. The secular and religious contexts merge under the necessity for action:

> We need to realize that just as there is no action that is not recorded by *Shomer Yisrael*, the Guardian of Israel, so too there is no action without consequence to God's creation, the biosphere, no 'elsewhere' to dump our garbage that will not eventually come floating back to haunt us. [275]

It is useless to ask for better management through the recycling of fertilizers. The point is to stop the mess at its source, which is meat. In 1988, the Environmental Protection Agency blamed agricultural run off for the most extensive source of pollution. Environmental and ecological movements which do not place diet at center stage of their concerns are like ostriches with their heads in the sand. The statistics are depressing.

How Much Does That Hamburger Really Cost ?

There are approximately 2-3 times more livestock than people, not counting the billions of chickens.

More than half the water used in the U.S. for *all* purposes is used for livestock production.

In semi-arid states such as in the midwest, it takes 2,500 gallons of water to produce one pound of meat; it takes 25 gallons of water to produce 1 pound of wheat.

85% of the topsoil that has been lost in the United States is due to livestock raising.

260,000,000 acres of forest in the United States have been cleared for grazing land for livestock.

Every five seconds an acre of trees disappears. Fast food equals fast destruction. According to the World Wildlife Fund, quoted in David Coats' book, *Old Macdonald's Factory Farm,* tropical forests are being cut down "at the rate of fifty-nine acres a minute--or 31 million acres every year." An area the size of New York State vanishes every year.[276] It is estimated that at the present rate of destruction, there will be virtually no rainforests left anywhere in the world in forty years. The deforestation is so severe that scientists estimate that it would take a thousand years for the rainforests to recover. This is an area potentially filled with medical wonders to be harvested from its plant life; yet the medical world, dependent upon the pharmaceutical industries, never protests the destruction of nature's pharmacy. "Rain forests support half the different species of flora and fauna that exist on earth." [277] They constitute a vast arena of breathing vegetation which affects climate for thousands of miles. They contribute to the "stability of the oxygen/carbon dioxide balance in our atmosphere."[278] This destruction is for the main purpose of producing beef. Coats calls beef "the chief culprit in *all* Latin-American rain-forest destruction."[279] The destruction of the rainforests is possibly the worst expenditure of net loss energy.

> The soil itself is too poor to support cattle for more than three or four years. Once the soil is exhausted, the area is abandoned, more forest is cut down, and the cattle move on.
> In Brazilian Amazonia, nearly all ranches cleared before 1978 have now been abandoned. On such ranches, where land is cheap, meat production barely reached forty-five pounds per acre....[280]

Ironically, one of the recommendations proposed in an article in *Fortune* to fight global warming was to "Expand forests, whose trees absorb CO_2 and offset human emissions."[281] The author's lack of irony in this recommendation and his failure to suggest that we simply stop destroying the forests we have is astounding. Finally, the moral cost of destroying the rainforest is miserably compounded by the fact that much of the work in Brazil is done by slave labor.[282]

The Problem of Excrement

Billions of tons of animal excrement from animals treated with hormones and chemicals, must be disposed of. This has created a dangerous situation for *all* food production, even organic farming. Thousands of tons of manure, carrying the infectious E.coli pathogen are ploughed into the ground and invade fruits and vegetables as well as meat. According to *Vegetarian Voice*, 25% of E.coli infection is now from fruits and vegetables.[283] Infectious microbes spread from meat to everything else, which is why we cannot think of vegetarianism solely as a lifestyle choice, but must recognize meat to be as much of a public health issue as smoking is. The Marlboro Man is also a cowboy.

The production of excrement from livestock is 230,000 pounds per second, compared to 12,000 pounds per second from the human population. This excrement is a moving storehouse of execrable wastes--pesticides, hormones, and pathogens--which are dumped into our rivers, our lakes and ploughed back onto our land, and onto our food.

Cows contribute to 15%-25% of the greenhouse effect because of the methane gases they emit.

Entropy Is A Bad Energy Investment

Thirty-three percent of our raw materials (base products of farming, forestry, mining, and fossil fuels) are devoted to the production of livestock, while it would take only 2% of the same raw materials to produce a vegetarian diet.

> The factory-farming industry is a net consumer of energy. The production of millions of tons of feed grains requires highly mechanized, fuel-extravagant crop-

> growing methods....the result is a poor energy input to food output ratio.
> This cost is clearly understood when we see that for every calorie of fossil fuel input we get back from meat products at best only one-quarter (.25) of a calorie of food energy; a broiler hen returns only one-fourteenth (.07) of a calorie, while feedlot beef returns merely .03 food calories--*a ratio of just one food calorie received for every thirty-three fuel calories expended*....agribusiness methods in the US and other Western countries require that we put more fuel energy into the system than we take out in food energy. Where this negative flow presently exists, it cannot last indefinitely; and there are certainly not enough fossil fuel resources available in the world, for all countries to operate at the same high level of agricultural energy input.[284]

What this means for poor people, we shall see in the next chapter. What this could mean for a national policy governing matters of resources and energy, John Robbins sums up:

> The social, ecological and economic consequences as we...turn away from animal food products, are equally remarkable....The water crisis ceases. As we stop raising and grinding up cattle for hamburgers, we discover that ranching and farm factories have been the major drain on our water resources. The amount now available for irrigation and hydroeletric power doubles....As expenditures for food and medical care drop, personal savings rise--and with them the supply of lendable funds. This lowers the interest rate, as does also the drop in oil imports which eases the pressure on the national debt.[285]

Energy and power are engrained in the mythos of modernity. But energy and power are lost in our food supply: It takes 78 calories of fossil fuel to get 1 calorie of protein from beef, and 2 calories of fossil fuel to get 1 calorie of protein from soybeans. The United States leads the world in the production of soybeans. It exports much of it and feeds most of the rest to animals. Soybeans have been cited for their potential in reducing the hormones which lead to prostate and breast cancers. One might think that our agricultural system is either diabolical or stupid, but it is merely greedy and governed by the economic laws of fast profit. Modern myths govern the way we look at farming: fast profits, big machines, energy expenditures.

Agriculture, which today represents the worst of the synthesis of industrialization, capitalism, and technology, creates monumental costs in environmental decay and in an overburdened health care system.

Losing Ground

Worldwide, cattle take up one fourth of the earth's land. They not only take up much land by their presence, but "Much of the world's prime agricultural land--in the US over 90 percent of the total agricultural land--is used to grow food for animals."[286] C. David Coats describes the impact of the erosion of soil and energy that takes place in the factory farming system:

> In nature animals eat what they can get. The weak die, the fit survive, and predators keep the number in check. Seldom do wild animals destroy the food supply of their habitat--unless under pressure from the encroaching influence of man.
>
> But forced to multiply, reared in huge numbers by humans, protected from predators and encouraged to get fat, domestic animals eat more than a fair share. And they eat everything--from dry grasses and scrub on semi-desert rangeland to the high-quality grains and legumes grown especially for them....It is often argued that the land used for grazing is not suitable for other agricultural purposes....[but] Grazing is only acceptable if the stocking density of animals is kept realistically proportionate to the ecological soundness of the land--so that the effect of grazing on the sustainability of the local en-

vironment is scarcely more than that of passing wildlife.[287]

Over-grazing affects everything else in our environment: the climate, water supply, soil erosion. Eventually it causes desertification. Cattle grazing is a major cause of growing deserts in many areas of the world, because of the loss of topsoil. "Not surprisingly, the regions most affected by desertification are all cattle-producing areas and include the Western half of the United States, Central and South America, Australia, and sub Saharan Africa."[288] Eating meat products and raising animals for food does not constitute a rational, sustainable agriculture.

Meat Is An Environmental Four-Letter Word

In an article in *The Atlantic Monthly,* Robert Kaplan painted a doomsday scenario where ecological disasters will be at the heart of coming strife in the 21st century.[289] Water scarcity, soil erosion and desertification will place environmental limits on human growth, even as we enter a century of technological expansion. In Kaplan's analysis, environmental limitation will be to the planet what population was to Malthus: it will be the ultimate cause of the breakdown of social institutions, the disappearance of the nation-state, and the rise of a new kind of warfare carried on by stateless guerrilla bands, where crime and warfare become indistinguishable from each other. The source for Kaplan's analysis is the work of Thomas Fraser Homer-Dixon, head of the Peace and Conflict Studies Program at the University of Toronto, who himself published an article in 1991, "On the Threshold: Environmental Changes as Causes of Acute Conflict":

> 'In Homer-Dixon's view, future wars and civil violence will often arise from scarcities of resources such as water, cropland, forests, and fish....we need to bring nature back in....we have to stop separating politics from

the physical world--the climate, public health, and the environment.'

We also need to stop separating diet from environmental analysis. Robert Kaplan laments the lack of interest of politicians in the environment. Wait until you place "meat" on their agenda. Making the connection between diet, crops, farmland, irrigation, the totality of the biotic community and politics evades politicians, just as making the connection between meat and disease evaded them for decades. Meat *is* an environmental issue. "Soil erosion" is not something that just happens; nor does "disease" just happen. Certain natural phenomena such as earthquakes and monsoons can be said to be beyond human influence, but soil erosion, deforestation, air pollution, malnutrition and many diseases are not in the same category.

Meat is a major contributing factor to almost every environmental problem, including the greenhouse effect. No single factor is so wasteful in nature as our meat-centered diet. Jeremy Rifkin traces the history of cattle from deified animal to its sordid effect on human history.

> Domesticated cattle are responsible for much of the soil erosion in the temperate regions of the world. Cattle grazing is a primary source of the spreading desertification process that is now enveloping whole continents. Cattle ranching is responsible for the destruction of much of the earth's remaining tropical rain forests. Cattle raising is indirectly responsible for the rapid depletion of fresh water on the planet, with some reservoirs and aquifers now at their lowest levels since the end of the last Ice Age. Cattle are a chief source of organic pollution; cow dung is poisoning the freshwater lakes, rivers and streams of the world. Growing herds of cattle are exerting unprecedented pressure on the carrying capacity of natural ecosystems, edging entire species of wildlife to the brink of extinction....This once-sacred animal of bygone years has taken on a pestilent guise, swarming over the great land masses of Europe, the Americas,

> Africa and Australia like hoofed locusts, devouring the endowment of millions of years of evolutionary history. 290

Life At The Top Of the Food Chain Is Dangerous

Meat is not only a major contributing factor *to* environmental problems, a meat-based diet increases the damage *from* chemicals in the environment. Carcinogenic chemicals, such as dioxin, PCBs, DDT, chlorodane and toxaphene are fat soluble. Susan Steingraber, in her study, *Living Downstream: An Ecologist Looks At Cancer and The Environment,* writes that fish, meat, eggs and dairy, "function as a major source of pesticides in our diet."[291] Through a process called "biomagnification," toxins become more concentrated the higher up the food chain they go. In 1994, the General Accounting Office found five different pesticides in fish: chlordane, dieldrin, heptachlor, DDT, and mirex. Beluga whales dying of cancer were found in the St. Lawrence Estuary, with PCBs, DDT, chlordane, and toxaphene dissolved in their fat. As Susan Steingraber writes, our vaunted position at "the top of the food chain" may be our undoing:

> ...as organisms continue to feed on each other, any contaminant that accumulates in living tissues--such as an organochlorine pesticide--is funneled into the smaller and smaller mass of organisms at the top of the pyramid....a diet rich in animal products exposes us to more pesticide residues than a plant-based diet, even though the plants are directly sprayed. For the most part, the flesh of animals we eat contains more pesticides than the grasses and grains we feed them. Indeed, the largest contributors to total adult intake of chlorinated insecticides are dairy products, meat, fish, and poultry. In 1991, the National Research Council reported that more than half the cattle tested in a sample of Colorado ranches had detectable levels of pesticides in their blood serums.[292]

Particularly at risk are babies being breast-fed because "the residues of fat-soluble pesticides contained in the food eaten by nursing mothers are distilled even further in breast milk."[293] A woman who hopes to breast-feed would do well to change to a vegan diet well before she gives birth. Additional harm may be done to women by chemicals which mimic estrogen or stimulate estrogen production. These are called xenoestrogens. They not only mimic natural estrogen, but can enhance the effect of estrogen.[294] For men, chemicals such as DDT can interfere with the production of androgen, the hormone related to masculinity.[295] Eating at the top of the food chain, a traditional metaphor for "real men," may be counter-productive to masculinity.

Among the harmful chemicals in our environment, few surpass dioxin,[296] which is formed by burning chlorine-based chemical compounds with hydrocarbons. Ninety-five percent of dioxin comes from incinerators burning chlorinated wastes, and from the manufacture of products such as paper and plastics which use chlorine bleaching. Dioxin can interfere with the regulatory hormones and with the functioning of the immune system. Dioxin too is fat-soluble and accumulates up the food chain. It is found mainly in meat and dairy products, in chicken, pork, fish and eggs. In fish, dioxin reaches levels of 100,000 times that of the surrounding environment. Dioxin can cross the placenta into the foetus, and it is present in breast milk, making breast-feeding for non-vegan mothers hazardous to the infant.

The Summary of Negative Technology

In the light of the unprecedented effect which intensive livestock rearing has on agriculture, there is a global imperative to abolish it. Modern livestock agriculture and animal-centered diets not only contribute to the cruel treatment of billions of animals annually, they have devastating consequences for all people, for the environment, and for a world of declining available resources. Seventy percent of the grain grown in the United States and two thirds of exported grain is consumed by animals destined for slaughter, while hundreds of millions of people in the world are chronically hungry, malnourished, or dying of famine. Yet the United States is one of the world's largest importers of meat, much of which comes from countries victimized by extensive hunger. According to the Worldwatch Institute, each pound of feedlot steak "costs" about 35 pounds of eroded American topsoil. The large amount of petrochemical fertilizers used to produce feed crops for grain-fed animals creates significant amounts of oxides. The increased refrigeration necessary to prevent animal products from spoiling adds chlorofluorocarbons to the atmosphere. Finally, the environment and the human digestive track combine their lethal forces: Eating meat, fish, poultry and eggs in a carcinogenic environment increases the risks to human health.

Current livestock agriculture contributes to four major global warming gases: carbon dioxide, methane, nitrous oxides, and chlorofluorocarbons. The burning of the tropical forests primarily to raise livestock releases millions of tons of carbon dioxide into the atmosphere. The highly mechanized agricultural sector uses a significant amount of fossil fuel energy, which also contributes to carbon monoxide emissions. The production of one imported quarter-pound hamburger requires the clearing of 55 square feet of rainforest. Richard Schwartz states the problem:

> Climate scientists have linked the increases of...heat-trapping gases in the atmosphere to human activities, especially the burning of fossil fuels (coal, oil, and natural gas), cattle ranching, deforestation [a result of cattle ranching], and rice farming....Current modern livestock agriculture and the consumption of meat contribute greatly to the four major gases associated with the greenhouse effect. The burning of tropical forests releases tons of carbon dioxide into the atmosphere, and eliminates the ability of these trees to absorb carbon dioxide. Also, the highly mechanized agricultural sector uses a significant amount of fossil fuel to produce pesticides, chemical fetilizer, and other agricultural resources, and this also contriutes to carbon dioxide emissions. Cattle

emit methane as part of their digestive process, as do termites who feast on the charred remains of trees. The large amounts of petrochemical fertilizers used to produce feed crops for grain-fed animals create significant amounts of nitrous oxides. Also, the increased refrigeration necessary to prevent animals products from spoiling adds chlorofluorocarbons to the atmosphere.[297]

Prophecy

Without recourse to modern terminology, Isaiah knew that a plant-based agriculture was sounder than an animal-based agriculture. He valued agriculture over husbandry, and urged the nation to keep its sheep away from fertile areas. He understood that agriculture and the ability of the nation to feed itself was implicated in the nation's security. His condemnation of meat and the "luxurious couches of the glutton" was a condemnation of the wealthy who steal from the poor and eat up their inheritance. The larger issue for him, as for all the prophets, was social justice. Social justice grew in the soil of sound ecological principles which use the land in the most productive and equitable manner possible. Isaiah knew, as Wendell Berry has stated, "that eating is an agricultural act": using the land justly was related to diet.[298] "Trust in Ywh" meant trust in the Creator of nature. A harmony of human life with nature was possible through prudent agriculture. Nature sustains human life when humans uses nature wisely.

7

Tzeddakah

Vegetarianism As Charity

"Providing charity for poor and hungry people weighs as heavily as all the other commandments of the Torah combined."
(*Baba Batra* 9a)

"In a world in which a child dies of starvation every two seconds, an agricultural system designed to feed our meat habit is blasphemy." John Robbins, *Diet For A New America*

Feeding The Poor: The Answer is Food

In the decades from 1814-1834, France was gripped by "the gelatin controversy." Doctors and chemists thought they had discovered an inestimable value in gelatin, that it was replete with cheap protein. They decided it would be an excellent food to feed the poor, and they fed it to the poor wherever they could get hold of them, in charity wards, in hospitals, in prisons, in asylums. But the poor would not cooperate. They retched and vomited up the gelatin and refused to eat it. The scientists fed it to dogs, and the dogs refused to eat it. The French government appointed a "Gelatin Commission" to find out why the poor would not eat the gelatin---it was cheap and it was pure protein. Some of the most famous chemists of the time in both France and Germany were involved in the controversy. There was a competition among the chemists as to who would discover the proper formula for gelatin which would make the poor like it. The poor never learned to like it, and the project was finally abandoned. However, it helped launch the chemical industries of France and Germany which have been so influential in transforming husbandry and farming.

Just governments would like to eliminate poverty and feed their poor. It seems like a worthy goal, at least during campaign season. But governments only know how to feed the poor according to how lobbyists and advisors instruct them. Garbage in, garbage out. Paul Starr, in his monumental study, *The Social Transformation of American Medicine*,[299] tells the story of a few socially conscious workers who went to Mount Bayou, Mississippi, as volunteers in the "War on Poverty," where malnutrition was one of the most serious health problems:

> ...when the health center began stocking and prescribing food for the malnourished, some officials objected that its pharmacy was only supposed to carry drugs for the treatment of disease. To which the staff responded, 'The last time we looked in the book, the specific therapy for malnutrition was food.'

Governments believe that the remedy for malnutrition is politics. The food industry is the largest industry in the United States.When an industry is that large, it is inevitably political; hence, food *is* a political subject. Feeding the poor, famine, malnutrition, and diet are transformed into political subjects. Most famines are caused by politics, not by nature. England exported grain and beef from Ireland during the potato famine. The story of beef exports from Ireland is told by Jeremy Rifkin:

> The Irish food crisis only served to help the British. English bankers seized control of abandoned pockets of Irish land, turning agricultural fields to cow pastures and greatly increasing the flow of beef to English cities. Between 1846 and 1874 the number of cattle exported from Ireland to England more than doubled, from 202,000 to 558,000 head. By 1880, Ireland had been virtually transformed into a giant cattle pasture to ac-

> commodate the English palate. The statistics were staggering. Over '50.2 percent of the entire surface of the country and two-thirds of its wealth were devoted to the raising of cattle.' A decade later, over 65 percent of Ireland's meat production was being shipped to England. Irish meat accounted for 30 percent of the domestic consumption of meat in England. [300]

If it were a matter only of charity, it would be simple, and it *should* be simple. What should be simpler than feeding poor people? Almost everyone recognizes that no one should go hungry in this world, that no baby should close its eyes in death for lack of adequate food. But as Gandhi observed, "There is enough food for need, there is not enough food for greed." For greed there is not enough of anything, not enough land, not enough meat, not enough cows, not enough chickens, not enough eggs, not enough milk, not enough oil to produce these products. Food, and predominantly meat and meat products, is a multibillion dollar industry. Feeding the poor gets in the way of feeding the rich.

Patricia Hausman of the Center for Science in the Public Interest, has documented animal research, which goes back for over seventy years, that indicated a relationship between fat and cancer and arteriosclerotic diseases.[301] Just as the tobacco industry knew and hid for years that nicotine was dangerous, governmental and nutritional agencies have known about the connection between diet, certain cancers and heart disease since the mid 1920s. In 1913, two researchers from the University of Wisconsin, Dr. Elmer McCollum and Marguerite Davis, discovered the first vitamin, vitamin A, in milk fat and egg yolk fed to laboratory rats. Newborn rats, who need a high protein diet, thrived on milk fat and egg yolk. At the same time of this discovery, Russian scientists also discovered that rabbits fed milk fat and egg yolk developed arteriosclerosis. Since this discovery was not useful information to the dairy and egg business, the work of the Russian scientists was shelved while the discovery of McCollum and Davis was heralded as emblematic of what a modern diet should include, and the first concept of the four essential foods was born. Whenever nutritionists and scientists attempted to make the work of the Russian scientists known to congressional committees their findings were negated by the work of the powerful beef, dairy, farming and pharmaceutical lobbies.

In 1979, at the National Academy of Sciences' Food and Nutrition Board, chaired by George McGovern, scientists were brought in on behalf of the egg industry. Robert Olson from St. Louis University School of Medicine charged that as far as lowering blood cholesterol level goes, "A positive effect has not been proven." When Senator Schweiker informed him that, "In some animals it has been proven," Professor Olson responded with unabashed cynicism, "You can pick an animal to show anything you want."

The myth of the superiority of animal protein was born in 1914 when two scientists, Osborne and Mendel found that laboratory rats thrived better on animal protein rather than on vegetable protein. Newborn rats do. But their protein needs are not ours. The National Dairy Council, The National Egg Board, and the National Livestock and Meat Board, in a brilliant marketing move rivalled only by McDonald's appeal to children and the image of the hamburger as our national food, undertook to counsel America's schoolchildren in nutrition. Colorful diagrams of the "basic four" food groups were hung in classrooms across America. The National Dairy Council became the "foremost supplier of 'nutritional education' materials to classrooms in the United States." [302] Placing meat at the center of a diet not only made that diet a health hazard, it made it an expensive health hazard. The price of meat and cheese is not and never has been as inexpensive as lentils, soybeans, or vegetables. Furthermore, if it were not for government subsidies for water and grazing lands (subsidies paid for out of tax dollars), meat and dairy products would be even more expensive. Almost a century of urban populations, of newly arrived immigrants, were coached into eating high-priced diets. During the second world war, black market prices in meat soared in the United States, while in countries such as Denmark where butter, meat and eggs were rationed, the number of heart fatalities fell. The myth of the superiority of animal protein was based on greed and propaganda. Like all myths, it was costly. John Robbins asked Dr. David Reuben,who needs animal protein. Dr. Reuben answered:

> 'The people who sell meat, fish, cheese, eggs, chicken, and all the other high prestige and expensive sources of protein. Raising the amount of protein you eat by 30% raises their income by 30%. It also increases the amount of protein in the sewers and septic tanks of your neighborhood 30% as you merrily urinate away everything that you can't use that very day. It also deprives the starving children of the world the protein that would save their lives....it makes you pay 30% of your already bloated food bill for protein that you will never use. If you are an average American family, it will cost you about $40 a month to unnecessarily pump up your protein intake. That puts another $36 billion a year into the pockets of the protein producers.' [303]

Lentils have often been called "the poor man's protein," which is probably why many people give up eating them as soon as they can afford to eat meat. But lentils are a very good, economic source of protein. A one pound steak, which can cost anywhere from $3.00 to $6.00 or $8.00 a pound, depending upon cut and what neighborhood the steak is bought in, will feed 4-6 people. A one pound package of lentils costs around 79 cents. Made into a lentil loaf, it can feed 8-10 people. Leftovers can be served cold the next day in sandwiches or they can be combined with sautéed onions and mushrooms, tomato sauce, and made into a sauce for spaghetti or rice. You can get two full meals for four or more out of a package of lentils for 79 cents. There are many other ways of cooking lentils, but this suggestion should serve as a reminder the next time the public is told that "meat is a cheap source of protein!" Meat is not a cheap source of anything. It is there to make a profit for the meat industry.

In the last century, as a result of the rise of cattle culture in "the New World," North and South America, an exchange of food energy between animals and humans took place, with grave consequences for the human diet. As human beings consumed more meat, they consumed less fiber, less beans, grains and fruits. At the same time, grain was substituted for grass in the historical diet of the cow. In the United States, the majority of corn, oats and soybeans was now fed to animals.

The drain on the pocketbooks of average Americans is substantial, but the drain is even more marked when we add in the costs of diseases caused by a meat-protein diet, the cost of lost working days, the cost of the loss of a breadwinner to a family due to a disease caused by a poor diet The cost to citizens in Third World countries is even more dramatic. Harriet Schliefer observes that "...if everyone in the developed world became a vegetarian [as people mostly are in the undeveloped world], it would be possible to give four tons of edible grain to every starving person."[304] If governments want to feed the poor, they should wage war on meat, and teach the poor how to cook beans, rice, lentils, vegetables, soybeans and fruit. Instruction manuals should be given with food stamps. We should stop subsidizing meat and dairy, as we should not subsidize tobacco. Many of these subsidies are hidden. Tax-supported public institutions, such as prisons, orphan asylums, and hospitals, should reform their diets. The cost of food in these institutions might be cut by one-third. If we really want to do something for the poor, we should tear down the slaughterhouses and convert the areas into housing for the homeless, with vegetable gardens around them.

The House That Meat Built

America can afford its bad habits. We have not yet reached the breaking point in our health care costs, though that time seems to be arriving. Talk of rationing health care to the elderly is obscene for a country that has squandered its wealth. But Third World countries cannot afford their bad habits, or the bad food habits of the Western world. The loss of food due to land degradation which, in turn, is due to the raising of cattle for export in Third World Countries is sometimes devastating.

According to Jeremy Rifkin, The United Nations Environmental Program paints a bleak picture.

> Throughout the Third World, land degradation has been the main factor in the migration of subsistence farmers into the slums and shanty towns of major cities, producing desperate populations vulnerable to disease and natural disasters and prone to participate in crime and civil strife....such exodus exacerbates the already dire urban problems...and at the same time, it has delayed efforts to rehabilitate and develop rural areas--through the lack of manpower and the increased negligence of land.'[305]

Susan Steingraber writes of how animals have disappeared from the agricultural landscape as they have been herded into enclosed areas. Farmers have also disappeared.[306] More than half the farms in the United States are run by absentee owners. Those who do work on the land have elevated cancer rates.[307] The attack on the environment, on human health, and on the food supply is a three-pronged problem.

And the future looks bleaker. Lester Brown, president of the prestigious Worldwatch Institute, believes that the prospects for feeding the world's population are worsening for the following reasons:

1. Rapid Population Growth

The world's population was increasing by over 80 million people per year in the past few decades. At this rate the world's population increased by an amount equal to the population of the United States every three years. Most of the children were born in less developed countries. Even though this rapid population growth appears to be slowing down, the earth's population will have major impact on land, water, pollution, and other factors related to the food supply.

2. Increasing Affluence

In addition to rapid population growth, increased affluence is a major factor behind potential food scarcities. There has been a sharp increase in affluence in many countries, especially in Asia--which has increased the demand for animal products and for grain to feed livestock. China is a significant example: it was a net exporter of 8 million tons of grain in 1994, but became a net importer of 16 million tons of grain in 1995, due to the increased affluence of many of China's 1.2 billion people. While China was basically self sufficient with respect to grain in 1990, it is estimated that it will need to import 215 million tons of grain by 2030.

3. Water Scarcity

Depletion of aquifers due to increased demand for water and diversion of irrigation waters to expanding cities are decreasing available water for irrigation in many countries. Water tables are falling in many key-producing areas, including the southern Great Plains of the United States, much of northern China, and several states in India.

4. Decreasing Arable Land

The world's grainland per person has been decreasing at an increasing rate due to the combined effects of rapid population growth and the paving of land to meet the growing needs of industry and transportation.

5. Climate Changes

There is increasing concern about global warming, especially the effect of increasingly severe heat waves, on agriculture. The eleven warmest years since temperature records were kept in 1866 all occurred since 1979, and the warmest year was 1995. There is an increasing scientific consensus that human activities are having a major effect on global warming. The droughts and severe storms that may increasingly accompany global warming would be a threat to future food security.

6. Decreasing Fish Catches

While the seafood catch per person doubled from 1950 to 1989, it has decreased 7 percent from 1989 to 1995, and is projected to continue decreasing as rapid population growth continues. The U.N.'s Food and Agriculture Organization (FAO) indicated that all 15 major ocean fishing areas are being fished at or beyond their capacities, and 13 of them are in a state of decline.

The net result of these interacting factors, according to the Worldwatch Institute, is that while the recent past was dominated by food surpluses, with competition among exporters for access to markets, the future will be dominated by food scarcity, with increasing competition among importers. Extensive hunger and malnutrition in many parts of the world make rebellion and violence more likely. Professor Georg Borgstrom, internationally known expert on food science, fears that "the rich world is on a direct collision course with the poor of the world....We cannot survive behind our Maginot line of missiles and bombs." The outlook for global stability is poor, unless the problem of global hunger is solved. That problem should be solved not only for reasons of global stability, but for every civilized reason. Clearly, vegetarianism is not only the healthiest, but the most logical, reasonable, rational diet for a planet that is not only growing smaller, but one whose population is growing larger and whose resources are growing scarcer. However, we shouldn't wait for the future, because much of the world already suffers from hunger. In 1976, William Shurtleff and Akiko Aoyagi wrote a description of a desperate situation which has not become better:

> During the past decades, the population/food crisis has suddenly emerged as the most serious problem facing mankind. We are now experiencing the greatest famine in history and the situation is clearly getting worse.

> Experts estimate that starvation and malnutrition-caused diseases are now taking the lives of between 15 and 20 million people each year (45,000 to 60,000 daily), and more than half of the victims are children under five. According to the United Nations Food and Agricultural Organization (FAO), an additional 400 to 500 million children (twice the population of the United States) living in the 60 poorest countries suffer from such severe chronic malnutrition that their growth and mental capacity are permanently retarded. And more than one-quarter of the earth's present 5.6 billion inhabitants confront inescapable hunger during some part of each year. At this turning point in history, we have for the first time, rounded the bend on three dangerous exponential curves-population, resource-and-energy consumption, and pollution--and are heading almost vertically upward at a dizzying pace. These cold statistics add up to immense suffering, which is quickly becoming the dominant reality of daily life for poor people throughout the world.[308]

These world hunger statistics and predictions are staggering: It is believed that the number of people who die each year from hunger and its effects, including diseases brought on by lowered resistance due to malnutrition, will increase. Children are particularly victimized by hunger and malnutrition. Three out of four people who die from hunger are children. Over 8 percent of the world's children die before their first birthday. Many children go blind due to vitamin A deficiency in their diet. Malnourishment also brings listlessness and reduced activity and capacity for learning, which perpetuates the legacy of poverty. Population control is not sufficient to stem the tide of disaster overtaking poor countries. Zero population growth must be matched by zero animal consumption growth.

Vegetarianism: A Key to Reducing World Hunger

Prospects for a reduction in hunger are not good, unless there is a radical change in diet. In his book, *Tough Choices--Facing the Challenge of Food Scarcity,* [309] Lester R. Brown,

President of the Worldwatch Institute, indicates that the combination of increased world population and affluence, environmental strains, and climate changes have combined to reduce the world's grain stocks to the lowest level ever and to raise wheat and corn prices to grave heights. The Worldwatch Institute believes that providing enough food for the world's rapidly increasing population will be a critical issue facing the world for many decades. But we have it within our means to feed the poor. During the time that an unbalanced exchange in foods took place in the West, from a consumption of grains and fiber and fruits to meat, an equally deleterious exchange in foods took place in cattle, from grass to grains to corn, plastic and offal, a number of inspired people educated themselves about the food wisdom of the East and began the experiment of exchanging their Western diets for Eastern diets. Unfortunately, many people in the East, as they became prosperous, exchanged their ancient diet for the standard meat-based Western diet, with concomittant disease consequences. The soybean was a contribution of immense value to the Western diet as a result of this change. Not only are soybeans as economical as lentil beans, with a protein value as good and perhaps better, but discovery of their health benefits are still unfolding and their versatility as food seems limitless.

Ode To Soy

William Shurtless and Akiko Aoyagi put the case for the soybean well:

> ...soybeans can produce more usable protein per acre of land than any other known crop--33 percent more on the average (60 percent more under ideal conditions) than second-place rice and 20 *times* as much as if the land were used to raise beef cattle or grow their fodder. This fact becomes increasingly important as farmland grows more and more scarce....
> Containing 34 to 36 percent high-quality protein--more than any other plant or animal food--plus all of the eight essential amino acids, they are rightfully known

> throughout the Orient as 'the meat of the fields.' From the body's point of view, the amount of usable protein contained in 1/2 cup of dry soybeans (1 cup cooked) is no different from that contained in 5 ounces of steak. And low-cost, low-calorie soybean foods contain no cholesterol and almost none of the saturated fats so abundant in most animal-derived products.[310]

And yet--and yet to our shame--while we preach and wail and weep over famine and poverty, we feed soybeans to animals and the animals to people. The United States is the world's largest producer of soybeans. Next to corn, the soybean is the most important US crop "in total dollar value and third in total acreage. Exporting about half of the domestic crop, America is the largest international supplier, providing 70 percent of the total trade."[311] Shurtleff and Aoyagi ask: "...what happens to all these soybeans and the 18 million tons of protein they contain?" Their answer is predictable and depressing. "Virtually all of the non-exported crop is sent to huge factories where the soy oil--which contains no protein--is extracted with hexane solvent. Then, approximately, 95 percent of the protein-rich meal left over is fed directly to livestock." [312]

This returns us full circle to the evil in the house that meat builds, from the food the cow eats to the poverty eating at poor people.

> The system responsible for this immense waste is the feedlot, which was designed after World War II in an era of huge farm surpluses as a way of transforming excess grains and soy into more 'profitable' meat.....In addition to soybeans, we feed livestock a full 78 percent of our cereal grains, including about 90 percent of our corn, oats, and barley, and 24% of our wheat....The process of running grains and soybeans through animals and then eating the animals is so inefficient, uneconomical, and energy-expensive as to be virtually inexcusable. Clearly, the earth cannot support this level of waste. [313]

The tragedy is multiplied tenfold when we realize how healthy soy foods are. In addition to being a good source of protein, they contain linolenic acid, which is one of the omega 3 fatty acids, an acid that is essential in human diet. Their ability to reduce the risks for some cancers is cited frequently in scientific and nutritional studies. Soy foods may actually *lower* cholesterol levels. Louise Hagler, author of *Tofu Cookery,* cites 38 studies of the effect of soy protein on cholesterol levels, and concludes that "Soy protein lowers LDL-cholesterol (the bad cholesterol) but does not affect HDL-cholesterol (the good cholesterol).[314]

In addition to their remarkable health effects, soybeans can be made into a versatile number of foods, from soy milk to tofu, tempeh, flour or grits, miso, soy oil, soy sauce, and textured vegetable protein, a quick-cooking meat substitute, low in fat and calories, and high in fiber, calcium and potassium. There are now many soy food cookbooks with numerous appetizing dishes, including delicious desserts.

The sin of famine and hunger in this world cannot be excused. God has given us what we need for basic life and health. Maimonides knew that "Most maladies that afflict humankind result from bad food." Now we know what the good food is. "Cereal grains and soy are the most democratic of foods, for nature produces them in such abundance that there is enough to go around at prices everyone can afford." [315]

Jewish Teachings Related To Hunger

"God says to Israel, 'My children, whenever you give sustenance to the poor, I impute it to you as though you gave sustenance to Me...." Does then God eat and drink? No, but whenever you give food to the poor, God accounts it to you as if you gave food to Him." (*Midrash Tannaim*)

In both Judaism and Christianity, feeding the poor is not only an act of charity, or good politics, it is an *imitatio deo*, an imitation of God.

On Yom Kippur, the holiest day of the Jewish year, while fasting and praying for a good year, Jews are told through the words of the Prophet Isaiah that fasting and prayers are not sufficient; they must work to end oppression and provide food for needy people:

> Is not this the fast that I have chosen? To loose the chains of wickedness, to undo the bonds of oppression, and to let the oppressed go free.... Is it not to share thy bread with the hungry? (Isa. 58:6-7)

On Passover we are reminded not to forget the poor. Besides providing *ma'ot chittim* (charity for purchasing matzah) for the needy before Passover, at the seders we reach out to them:

> This is the bread of affliction which our
> ancestors ate in the land of Egypt.
> Let all who are hungry come and eat.
> Let all who are in need come and celebrate the
> Passover. (Passover Haggadah)

We are even admonished to feed our enemies, if they are in need:

> If your enemy is hungry, give him bread to eat.
> If your enemy is thirsty, give him water to drink.
> (Prov. 25:21)

This is consistent with the Jewish teaching that the greatest hero is a person who converts an enemy into a friend (*Avot de Rabbi Nathan,* chapter 23).

It is a basic Jewish belief that God provides enough for all. In our daily prayers, it is said, "He openeth up his hand and provideth sustenance to all living things" (Ps. 145:16). Jews are obligated to give thanks to God for providing enough food for us and for all of humanity. In the *bircat hamazon* (grace after meals), we thank God "who feeds the whole world with goodness, grace, loving kindness, and tender mercy."

The blessing is correct. God has provided enough for all. The bounties of nature, if properly distributed and properly consumed, would sustain all people. Millions of people are hungry today, not because of insufficient agricultural capacity, but because of unjust social systems and wasteful methods of food production, most notably the feeding of tremendous amounts of grain to animals to fatten them for slaughter. The Jewish approach to hunger was eloquently summarized by Rabbi Marc H. Tannenbaum, Former National Interreligious Affairs Director of the American Jewish Committee:

> If one takes seriously the moral, spiritual, and humanitarian values of Biblical, Prophetic, and Rabbinic Judaism, the inescapable issue of conscience that must be faced is: How can anyone justify not becoming involved in trying to help save the lives of starving millions of human beings throughout the world--whose plight constitutes the most agonizing moral and humanitarian problem in the latter half of the 20th century.

Vegetarianism Can Make A Crucial Difference In Feeding the Poor

It takes up to 12 pounds of grain to produce one pound of edible beef in a feedlot. Half of U.S. farm acreage is used to produce feed crops for livestock. A meat-centered diet requires about seventeen times the land area per person than would be required for a purely vegetarian diet. Animal agriculture also requires tremendous inputs of chemical fertilizer and pesticides, irrigation water, and fuel, commodities which are becoming scarce worldwide.

Not only are much land and many resources used in the United States to raise beef, but the United States is also one of the world's largest importers of beef. We import approximately 1 million head of cattle every year from Mexico, half as much beef as all Mexicans have left for themselves. In spite of widespread poverty and malnutrition in Honduras, that country also exports large amounts of beef to the United States.

Grains are increasingly being fed to livestock in the Third World, although the majority of people there can't afford to buy meat. Much of the best land in poorer countries is used to graze livestock, often for export. In Central America, two-thirds of the agriculturally productive land is used for livestock production, for the wealthy or for export.

Additional shocking statistics:

(1) Two hundred and sixty million Americans are eating enough food (largely because of the high consumption of grain-fed livestock) to feed well over 1 billion people in the poor countries.

(2) The world's cattle consume an amount of food equivalent to the calorie requirements of 8.7 billion people. Livestock in the U. S. consume ten times the grain that Americans eat directly.

(3) The former Tufts University President and famous nutritionist, Jean Mayer, estimated that if people reduced their meat consumption by just 10 percent, enough grain would be released to feed 60 million people.

(4) The wealthy nations feed more grain to their livestock than the people of India and China (more than one-third of the human race) consume directly.

(5) Contrary to the common belief that our grain exports help feed a hungry world, two-thirds of our agricultural exports go to feed livestock, rather than hungry people.

These facts indicate that the food being fed to animals in the affluent nations could, if properly distributed, end both hunger and malnutrition throughout the world. A change from animal-centered diets would free land and other resources, which could be used to grow nutritious crops for more people. It would then be necessary to promote policies that would enable people in the underdeveloped countries to use their resources and skills to become food self-reliant. As Sister Elizabeth Seton said, "We should live simply, that others may simply live."

Jewish mandates to feed the hungry, help the poor, share resources, practise charity, show compassion, pursue justice, support vegetarianism as the diet most consistent with the Jewish mandate to "share thy bread with the hungry." The prophets are not regarded as unique for no reason! Yehuda Feliks writes of Zechariah's vision of peace and its connection to agricultural values:

> Zechariah...used the expression 'seed of peace' in a concrete sense, namely that the seed brings peace or that the seed which yields a plentiful crop testifies to the peace and tranquility abroad in the country....We have here scriptural verses which envision truth, righteousness and peace to be connected with the seed and the work of sowing....[316]

The relationship between food and social justice is as pertinent to us today as it was to Isaiah's prophetic vision. The frequent metaphor in prophetic writing, "the seed of peace," was not a poetical metaphor, nor were the prophets painting bucolic pictures of pastoral nostalgia. For Isaiah the reward of practising frugality in diet and lifestyle is political stability. It involves a religious vision which we hear again in Rav Kook's writing, "A Vision of Vegetarianism and Peace." "Trust in Ywh" for Isaiah means trust in the Lord of Creation Who creates the good things of the earth. Isaiah's blessing for the Jewish people, "May you eat the good things of the earth," is the blessing governments should bestow on their people.

8

Klal Israel

Community and Diet

Behold how good and pleasant it is
when brethren dwell together.

Kashrut is often credited with helping to keep the Jewish people together during the centuries after the fall of Jerusalem, maintaining Jews as an identifiable, unified community. However, there is no suggestion in the literature on kashrut that its *original purpose* was for community identification. Distinctiveness seems to have been a consequence, rather than a purpose. Jews were accused by Roman writers such as Tacitus of being anti-social because they would not eat at the same table with non-Jews. During the period of Hellenic and Roman ascendancy, as at the time of its birth, diet divided Jews from other nations for good reason. During these times when the nation struggled with the temptations of idolatry and paganism, Jews were forbidden to eat at a table where "carrion" or the food of animals sacrificed to idols, such as pig, would be served. The consumption of blood was often part of a pagan meal. For these reasons, it was frequently impossible for Jews to eat at the table of Gentiles. Thus kashrut, in the Jewish struggle against idolatry and assimilation, became a cohesive force binding the Jewish people together, but it also marked them off as anti-social in the eyes of writers like Tacitus.

Other social forces kept the Jewish communities together. For the centuries during the Middle Ages, at least in Europe, Jews had no choice but to be together. They were kept in ghettos for five hundred years, behind walls whose doors were locked and opened every evening and morning; their comings and goings outside the ghettos were subject to curfews. Many forces kept the Jews together, many of them not of their own choice, where they would work and what they would work at. The diet they followed kept them healthier than the horrific conditions of the ghettos would have allowed for, because the ghettos were often founded in damp, downstream, mosquito-ridden areas into which they were overwhelmingly crowded. Frequent fasts, at least half day fasts, and the food of poor people, potatoes and roots, much as people may have chafed at these, probably helped them to physically survive. The Jewish housewife became a paragon of innovation, making tzimmes and cholents from left over food. Chicken became popular as the only food poor Jews could afford for their Shabbos meal.

Many Jews gave up kashrut after the major migrations of Jews from Europe, between 1880 and 1940, and after prosperity opened doors and food shops that had been unknown to them. But the reasons for the decline of kashrut are multifarious: The spread of rationalism and the difficulty of defending in rational terms what Jewish tradition had long accepted as a non-rational practice, was a compelling force in modernity. Practice had to be rationalized. For American Jews, modern rationalism combined with the temptation to fit in with the American way of eating. A two-tiered system grew up for Jews in America: Many kept a kosher home, but ate differently outside the home. After two generations of Jews had settled in America, it was customary to hear Jewish housewives say that they kept kashrut for their grandmothers, or their mothers, or their husband's mother. Soon there were many varieties of kashrut being practised. Some Jews kept kosher at home, but not on the outside, some bought kosher meat but served it with dairy products, some served only fish and dairy. There were gradations of kashrut, until it became a custom to call some practices, "kosher style." The dietary laws which had bound Jewish communities and Jewish families were no longer reliable. An Orthodox visitor could not be sure of what he or she would be served in a Jewish home or at a bar/bat mitzvah. It was obvious that when the older generation passed away, there would be less and less reason for the younger generation to keep kosher. They and the tradition had undergone sea changes from Europe to America, from the ghetto to modernity. Among Jewish practices, diet, kashrut, underwent changes which the Jewish calendar or the holiday cycles or Shabbos did not. The holidays and the Sabbath continued to be meaningful in a way that kashrut no longer was.

If kashrut helped keep Jews together at one time, by the mid-twentieth century it was dividing them. Many Jews would not eat in the homes of friends, in-laws, or relatives because their homes were not kosher. For many Jews the raison d'être of kashrut had been lost. Other Jews, younger Jews, Jews of the present generation, found the key to kashrut in vegetarianism.

Twenty years ago, vegetarianism was regarded as a "divisive diet, " as kashrut had been regarded two generations ago. But once the bridge was crossed, many Jews discovered that the way back to kashrut was through vegetarianism, that vegetarianism does what kashrut once did: it unifies the Jewish community, it allows kosher and non-kosher Jews, observant and less observant Jews, Jews of every background to attend the same conferences, go to the same weddings, the same bar/bat mitzvahs, eat in one another's homes again. Mothers and daughters-in-law have common food they can eat together. It permits young Jews in college or in professional life to have a diet which does not single them out. This is not a matter of a camouflaged kashrut, but of a kashrut which is responsive to today's world. More importantly, it is responsive to intrinsic, traditional Jewish values.

For the first half of this century, diet was a problem of the "generation gap." The Jewish community today faces internal problems of sectarianism and separation, different from the problems of the "generation gap," different from the problems of the immigrant generation who tried to communicate with children who were born into another world; but these divisions are more serious. Many issues separate Jew from Jew today, and diet sometimes contributes to the divisions. It can also heal the divisions.

Increasing numbers of Jews have discovered that vegetarianism can help solve Jewish sectarianism. New and alternative Jewish groups, like Jewish Renewal, or P'nai Or, which often attract Jews from many backgrounds, serve vegetarian food at their retreats and communal dinners. Jewish organizations have discovered that vegetarianism is a solution to the problem of how to feed Jews who come from a variety of different diet backgrounds, and from different parts of the world, such as India, where meat is not served. Organizations and Jewish institutions, camps, hotels, vacation places that service many kinds of Jews have pragmatic food problems to solve. They are discovering that vegetarianism is the solution to the food problem. A common complaint is that vegetarianism takes time to learn, that the transition is difficult. All transitions pose problems, whether it is getting married, graduating from college, having a baby, surviving grief or illness--or learning to drive a car or learning a new language. Becoming a vegetarian poses less of a transition problem than most other transitions. For Jews it should pose a minimal problem because kashrut has prepared the Jew for vegetarianism. Thinking about the morality of food, the holiness of food, has prepared the Jewish mind for vegetarianism. As Louis Berman pointed out, Jewish vegetarianism is less a break with tradition than the fulfillment of tradition:

> Jewish vegetarianism is an expression of radical traditionalism. It holds that what is worth preserving in Jewish life are its values--compassion for all that lives, concern for health and life, and regard for the welfare of those who live in want.[317]

Vegetarianism is good for Jewish community life. Jews who can break bread together and eat together have a better chance to re-create the spirit of klal Israel than Jews who cannot sit at the same table together, or attend the same functions together. Jewish tradition elevated the table as an altar. Let us make it an altar to our unity as well as to our holiness.

A vegetarian diet is good for interrelations between all peoples. According to anthropological studies, almost all cultures have food taboos, but meat is the most tabooed food everywhere. The taboos on the specific animals for meat consumption vary from country to country. In the United States, the idea of eating dogs and horses is repulsive, but acceptable elsewhere. It is acceptable in some European countries, particulary in France. Approximately three million horses slaughtered in the United States each year are exported to Europe for consumption. In India, cows are tabooed, but it is acceptable to eat cows in the West. According to Bharti Kirschner, (author of *The Bold Vegetarian* and *Healthy Cuisine of India*,) who has travelled widely and studied many food cultures, an international diet is emerging which will include fish but which will otherwise be vegetarian. Vegetarianism is seen as a necessary diet for the coming century, not only because resources are growing scarce, but because the planet is shrinking, and populations are intermingling at unprecedented rates. Vegetarianism facilitates co-existence.

The latest tourist information estimates that half a billion people are on the move around the world and it is expected that by the year 2010, that number will reach a billion. When Frances Moore Lappé wrote her book, *Diet For A Small Planet*, she had in mind the requirements of feeding a burgeoning human population. We should add to this requirement the need to feed a burgeoning human population *on the move* from country to country and from continent to continent. We need a diet that travels well, and that diet is a vegetarian diet. It travels well on the land and in the air--most airlines now recommend a low fat diet to prevent jet lag. Some health magazines recommend that the plane traveller order kosher or vegetarian food to ensure freshness of food and light eating.

Diet has always been a factor in Jewish distinctiveness. Jewish vegetarianism will also be distinctive. It will be different from other forms of vegetarianism practised in the past, because of Jewish values. Many earlier practices of vegetarianism, such as the rabbis met with centuries ago, were associated with a denial of life, with pessimism and dark forces. This vegetarianism, such as the practice of the Cathars,[318] was accompanied by celibacy, asceticism, a general denial of matter, and the created world. It was often associated with the denial of life forces, such as sexuality and bearing children. For these reasons the rabbis were right not to embrace vegetarianism in the past. It carried with it too great a burden of negation of everything Judaism embraces. But in this century, with so much real and potential death abounding, vegetarianism is a call to life, and the Jewish life force can shape it.

Jewish vegetarianism springs from all the life-affirming values of Judaism. Its purpose is the same as the purpose of traditonal kashrut: to refine our appetites and to teach us reverence for life. A Jewish vegetarianism will be Jewish because it will be invested with Jewish values, with the values of life and health, with our traditional understanding and practice of kashrut. Vegetarianism does not guarantee kosher, but kosher can guarantee vegetarianism. A label of "kosher" will *guarantee* the vegetarian purity of a food. An Orthodox Jew, or any Jew concerned with the *true* vegetarian content of his or her food, should not take anyone's vegetarianism for granted. The committed Jewish vegetarian who wishes to know that his or her food has not been contaminated by a meat product would seek the kosher label. As contaminants such as E.coli spread to non-meat products, the kosher label on vegetarian products would be sought as a matter of health for all Jews and concerned non-Jews. Kashrut and vegetarianism reinforce each other. The committed Jewish vegetarian will enforce the discipline of kashrut in a vegetarian diet.

Vegetarianism responds to pragmatic problems of diet in the relations among people. It spiritualizes kashrut, as Judaism spiritualizes vegetarianism by seeking the highest dietary standards, its blessings on food, its concept of the table as an altar. Vegetarianism plays a special role for Jews because it responds to both practical problems and to spiritual hunger at the same time--the combination of concerns which has made Judaism unique. Rabbi Arthur Hertzberg's address, "The Jewish Declaration on Nature" concluded with a summary and a prophecy:

> Judaism as a religion offers the option of eating animal flesh, and most Jews do, but in our own century there has been a movement towards vegetarianism among very pious Jews. A whole galaxy of central rabbinic and spiritual teachers including several past and present Chief Rabbis of the Holy Land have been affirming vegetarianism as the ultimate meaning of Jewish moral teaching. They have been proclaiming the autonomy of all living creatures as the value which our religious tradition must now teach to all of its believers. Let this affirmation resound this day, and in days to come. Let it be heard by all our brethren, wherever they may be, as the commandment which we must strive to realize. This cannot be achieved in one generation, and it will not happen through pressure from within or without: Jews will move increasingly to vegetarianism out of their own deepening knowledge of what their tradition commands as they understand it in this age....
> We have a responsibility to life, to defend it everywhere, not only against our own sins, but also against those of others. We are all passengers, together, in this same fragile and glorious world. Let us safeguard our rowboat--and let us row together. [319]

The task is to build a new food culture. Food traditions change. What is often called "traditional food" is not more than a century old in its tradition. A short article in *The Jerusalem Report* described the eating habits of first-temple-period Israelites, who "breakfasted on bread dipped in olive oil, toasted wheat and figs; and in the evening ate legume broth, seasoned with Dead Sea Salt."[320] The preface by Chaim Raphael to a Jewish cookbook published in 1846 notes that many Jewish foods, like bagels and lox, gefilte fish and chopped liver, which practically personify traditional Jewish food today are missing, while there are dishes "which seem to be rooted in a very un-Jewish background."[321]

Food is not an isolated phenomenon, certainly not for Jewish people, and not for most people. It changes in response to social and historical forces. Food conveys symbols, it talks a language of history, of the senses, of etiquette, of class systems, of social relationships, of pleasure, of memories of holidays and of special occasions. While all the reasons given in this book to become a vegetarian are cogent, there is one reason we have not yet dealt with, which is a very Jewish reason. That reason is that vegetarian food is a great joy and therefore belongs on the Jewish holiday and Shabbos table. It belongs in our daily lives, but especially on our occasions of *simcha tov.* Vegetarian food is as much a joy as flowers, the sight of autumn plenty, of a good garden, of a farm which is alive with produce, of a country road through an apple orchard. Vegetarian food speaks the language of colors: red, yellow, green, orange. The Jewish calendar is a calendar of the senses and the seasons as well as of historical moments. Jews have always known the deep sensuality of food as evident in the wonderful custom of baking Jewish letters and dipping them in honey to be given to the Jewish child to eat as a way of learning the Hebrew alphabet. What wonderful wisdom in that custom of combining learning with eating. Jews do not divide the body from the soul. Neither should we do so in our food. Everything we eat should nourish body and soul.

The Jewish Grandmother's Or Parents' Survival Guide To Vegetarianism

A midrash states that the creation of flowers proves that the soul exists--for why else was pleasure created--and why else were the good things of the earth created? We launch out into learning a new tradition, which we will learn with our hearts and our souls and our stomachs. So enjoy.

It is easier to become a vegetarian today than at anytime in history. There are more food manufacturers responsive to the growing vegetarian movement, stocking supermarkets with "veggie burgers," soy products, rices and beans, and organic vegetables. There are more vegetarian books of every kind: books for the beginning vegetarian, for the single vegetarian, for the pregnant mother, for the lactating mother, for the bachelor, for the cook who loves to cook, for the vegetarian who hates to cook, for the fast food junkie. There are vegetarian cookbooks for every lifestyle, and there are vegetarian support groups.

The food world is abuzz with new terms like "tofu," and with new products which may be mystifying to some of us. Our children come home from college and ask for "tofu turkey."

The difficult problem arises acutely at holidays, for it is then that we most urgently want our food to be traditional: that is as we knew it at the table of our parents. But most traditions are actually much shorter than people imagine them to be. Jews did not eat brisket, chopped liver or gefilte fish in biblical times or the Middle Ages. Such foods are no more than a few generations old. Jews have adapted to many diets and have changed many diets to their own liking and purposes. There is a lingering notion that the holidays require meat, though there is no halachic requirement which says this. Many Jews think that it is necessary to eat chopped liver, gefilte fish, chicken soup, and roast chicken in order to properly celebrate Jewish festivals.

According to the Talmud (*Pesachim 109a*), since the destruction of the Temple in Jerusalem, the celebration of Jewish holidays does not require the consumption of meat. Many rabbis, including Rabbi Alfred Cohen, editor of the *Journal of Halacha and Contemporary Society* and Rabbi J. David Bleich, Professor of Judaic Studies at Yeshiva University, have written articles that reinforce this assessment. Also several Israeli Chief Rabbis, including the late Rabbi Shlomo Goren, former Ashkenazic Chief Rabbi of Israel, and Rabbi Sha'ar Yashuv Cohen, Chief Rabbi Of Haifa, were or are strict vegetarians. The *Beit Yoseph*, states:

> Our rabbis taught that a person is obligated to bring joy to his wife and children and members of his household during the Festivals. He rejoices with wine....Rabbi Judah ben Betairah says, " In the days when the Temple was in existence, there was no rejoicing without meat...but now that there is no longer the Temple, there is no rejoicing without wine....

Vegetarianism is the diet that best puts into practice the values reflected in the Jewish holidays.[322] It is consistent with the universal message of the Jewish New Year, which involves the prayer that "all the world's people shall come to serve God," since it best shares food and other resources with the world's people. It is consistent with Rosh Hashanah as a time when Jews are to "awake from slumber" and mend our ways, and with Passover, which is associated with cleansing and rebirth, since moving away from meat means changing habits that are detrimental to health, hungry people, animals, and ecosystems.

Vegetarianism should be associated with Chanukah, since the Maccabees lived on vegetarian diets while they were fleeing the Syrian Greeks and hiding in the mountains. The traditional food for Shavuos is dairy and the Tu b'shevat seder is historically vegetarian.Vegetarianism is the ideal diet for Shabbos. In his book, *The Sabbath*, Abraham Heschel wrote,

> ...the Sabbath is a day of harmony and peace, peace between man and man, peace within man, and peace with all things. On the seventh day man has no right to tamper with God's world, to change the state of physical things. It is a day of rest for man and animal alike.

Vegetarianism enhances the Sabbath and the Jewish festivals. But we yearn to share a common diet with friends and relatives, at least to speak a common food language. Some of our grandchildren seem to speak a food language we don't understand. They ask for ingredients, like tamari or rice milk or sesame oil, mung beans, sunflower seeds, dandelions, foods we never heard of or thought they were food for birds. We think they're eating grass and wonder if they will procreate. They ask if we baked our challah with eggs, if there's butter in our cookies. If we say "yes," they won't eat it. They like tofu, which is a mystery to us, and drink miso soup, which is more of a mystery. They've become macrobiotics or lacto-vegetarians, or ovo-vegetarians, or ovo-lacto vegetarians, or vegans. They ask if your eggs are "free range," they speak of intermarriage between a vegetarian and a vegan. Are these concerns Jewish?

To prevent another "generation gap" between grandparents and grandchildren (or between spouses or friends) caused by diet, we have prepared a short guide to behavior between vegetarians and non-vegetarians, and to the world of vegetarianspeak, with some suggestions for how to feed the apples of your eye when they come for dinner.

What To Do When Your Grandchild or Child Is A Vegetarian: [323] A Survival Guide for Jewish Parents and Grandparents

Just as relationships involving racial or religious differences require tolerance, so do relationships between a vegetarian and a non-vegetarian, particularly between a vegetarian and parent or grandparent who has nostalgic memories of former holiday meals, and the child or grandchild who believes that present problems require a more responsive diet and that holidays should be celebrated with this diet. Here are some factors to consider:

1. This change is probably very important to your child or grandchild. Take it seriously. Don't tease by saying, "I remember when...." or "Don't you miss my meat knishes?"

2. How strongly does your child or grandchild hold his/her view? Does she/he regard it as a moral crusade or only as a personal preference? Is he/she revolted at the sight of meat? Some people really are. Take that seriously too.

3. If she is pregnant, don't tell her she is weakening herself or will cause harm to her baby. If she is nursing a baby, don't tell her she needs meat for her milk. First of all, neither of these ideas are true. Secondly, new mothers already have much to worry about without being told that they are threatening their child's life by their diet. Chances are she has read Dr. Michael Klaper's books on *Veganism and Pregnancy* or *How To Raise Your Child Vegan.* It would be a good idea for you to read them too. Buy them as a family gift. Educating one's self about the facts can do wonders for a relationship.

4. Recognize that our culture is going through an important food change that will affect the future of our food. Your child or grandchild belongs to this future.

Suggestions for Negotiating the Problem

1. Recognize that the issues that you agree on and the affection you have for each other are greater than those you disagree about.

2. Recognize that your child or grandchild did not adopt their diet to hurt you or to make life more complicated for you. Try to respect their decision, whether it is based on what she/he regards as a moral principle, convenience, conformity, or habit. Don't tell her that she is just buckling into peer pressure or that this is

another food fad that will pass. (There are strong indications that this is not so. Vegetarianism is growing.)

3. Take advantage of the vegetarian substitutes for hot dogs, hamburgers, and other meat-based meals. Ethnic dishes, such as pastas, offer many ways to cook a vegetarian meal without fuss or need to change your own habits.

4. Try to be creative in experimenting with new dishes that do not compromise your position. Cook a tsimmis without meat.

5. Never attack your child's or grandchild's point of view, especially in public.

6. Compensate for any friction related to dietary differences by stressing important areas of agreement.

7. Try to find restaurants where you can eat together, without either of you feeling strange. Chinese food is helpful here.

8. Show you're interested. Ask for help, suggestions, some easy vegetarian cookbooks to read. Ask for recommendations. Have a recipe party and ask different members of your family to suggest their favorite ingredients for a dish or a salad---and then name it after your family, or have a "Mystery Dish of The Month" party, or invite your child's or grandchild's friends to a potluck dinner and see what they bring. If they're very young, ask their parents to help. Channukah or Purim are great times to do this. Make the learning fun.

9. Form your own support group: Jewish Grandparents and Parents of Vegetarian Children---And How They Cope. Ask others for suggestions.

10. If your grandchild is a teenager, buy a vegetarian cookbook that "swings." One recommendation is *The Sensuous Vegetarian Barbecue* by Chelf and Biscotti (Avery Publishing). A few recipes from the book, like "Ophelia's Onions," "Autumn Bouquet," "Intermezzo," "Seventh Heaven Kebobs,"

"Bathsheba's Eggplant" should put you in your child's or grandchild's orb.

Suggestions for the Vegetarian Child/Grandchild

1. Play an active role in shopping and preparing meals. Try to show that vegetarian meals can look appealing and be tasty.

2. Invest in a few good cook books for Grandma and your parents, and try to come up with perhaps 7 or 8 easy recipes that you can all enjoy without too much bother. Make sure the vegetarian cookbooks are easy for a beginner. Two suggestions are *How To Feed A Vegetarian: Help for Non-Vegetarian Cooks,* by Suzanne D'Avalon (Amid the Noise Pub. Co., P.O. Box 16914, Colorado Springs, CO 80935-6914.) and *Vegetarianism For the Working Person*, by Charles Stahler and Debra Wasserman (Vegetarian Resource Group). Be helpful. Don't lecture your parents or grandparents, don't tell them that "meat is killing them," or that "it's animal murder." Of course, it is difficult if she--or anyone else--asks why you are a vegetarian, to give your honest answer without sounding "holier than thou." You must find the line between standing up for your integrity without standing on their toes. Perhaps pointing out how diets always change as we discover new values in food would make the issue less personal. No doubt your grandparents' and parents' diets changed when they moved from one country to another or from one part of the country to another. Ask them how their diets changed from when they were young.

3. If you lack time for meal preparations, you might find valuable ideas and recipes in *Meatless Meals for Working People - Quick and Easy Vegetarian Recipes* by Debra Wasserman and Charles Stahler and *Conveniently Vegan* by Debra Wasserman (Vegetarian Resource Group). For The Jewish holidays, try *The Jewish Vegetarian Year Cookbook,* by Roberta Kalechofsky and Rosa Rasiel, which has menus for each holiday.

4. Be a positive role model. Let your good health, cheerful attitude, and tolerance serve as an example of a vegetarian life.

5. Don`t talk about your diet and the many benefits of vegetarianism unless your parents and grandparents are interested. Don't be surprised if they're not.

Suggestions For The Carnivorous Grandparent/Parent

1. Try to see the positive side of your child's or grandchild's diet. Recognize that she/he may be having a hard time defending their diet, especially if she is young or a new vegetarian. Your support can be very helpful.

2. Don't tell your child or grandchild "how much easier life could be if you could just throw a steak on the stove".

3. Appreciate any improved health and increased vitality your child or grandchild shows due to a vegetarian diet. Ask them to take responsibility for some meals.

4. Recognize that if you eat vegetarian food you are not compromising any principle or belief, but your child or grandchild would be doing so if they ate meat. Consider, for example, that all meals served by the Israeli military are kosher so that nobody's beliefs will be violated, even though many Israeli soldiers do not normally keep the kosher laws, Additionally, there are now vegetarian kitchens for Israeli soldiers who want to eat vegetarian food.

Vegetarianspeak

The Vegetarian Union of North America (VUNA) defines a <u>vegetarian</u> as "a person who lives upon a diet of grains, legumes, fruits, vegetables, and other products of the plant kingdom with or without the use of dairy products and eggs, to the entire exclusion of the flesh of animals (meat, fish, and fowl). A lacto-ovo vegetarian is included in this definition. Twenty or thirty years ago, many vegetarians were lacto-ovo vegetarians, eating dairy products and eggs as part of their diet. But as vegetarians learned about the cruelty and health hazards involved in dairy products, many vegetarians became vegans.

A vegan is a vegetarian who eats no meat or animal products of any kind. The word "vegan" comes from the Greek word for life.

A macrobiotic is a vegetarian who eats no meat or meat products, but who will eat fish. This diet was developed in Japan and proved helpful for victims suffering radiation sickness from the Hiroshima and Nagaski atomic bombs. The macrobiotic diet strongly recommends eating produce that is in season. The word, "macro/biotic" means "great life." Dairy is absolutely forbidden. Aside from other problems, dairy raises the level of mucous in the body (the way meat raises the cholesterol level) and is felt to be responsible for asthma and breathing problems. Macrobiotics recommend cooking with gas and in stainless steel or cast iron cookware. They make much use of sea vegetables and many traditional Japanese foods, such as umeboshi plums or paste, which are credited with healing virtues. Some claim that the macrobiotic diet has led to cancer cures.[324] An example of this is discussed in Elaine Nussbaum's book, *Recovery From Cancer*. Another book, *Double Vision*, by Alexandra Todd, describes the use of a macrobiotic diet to diminish reactions to chemotherapy and radiation treatments.

Miso is a condiment greatly esteemed by macrobiotics. Miso is a fermented product made from soybeans, grain (rice or barley), salt, water, and an aspergillus oryzae culture. Miso comes in many varieties and tastes, so you have to experiment and learn one miso from another, just as you learn one vinegar from another. It tends to resemble peanut butter (though it doesn't taste like it) or a paste. Miso can be used to replace salt as a flavoring, particularly in soups. Because it has a high protein value, it can be preferrable to salt.

It is advisable not to undertake a macrobiotic diet without a nutritional counsellor, or with reading about this diet. Vesanto Melina, Brenda Davis and Victoria Harrison, who are registered dieticians, are skeptical about some aspects of the macrobiotic diet. They give this summary:

> For adults, macrobiotic eating patterns can be expected to have very favorable consequences for health. On the other hand, macrobiotic diets have been shown to offer insufficient protein, energy, fat, vitamins and minerals to support the rapid growth and development of infants and young children....When feeding an infant or child, the principles of macrobiotics must be carefully balanced with current knowledge of infant and child nutrition....[325]

Grains, Beans and Rices

There are 40,000 different kinds of rices in the world and dozens of different kinds of beans. Something to wonder at, the richness of the earth! Become acquainted with some of the grander varieties, such as basmati rice (white or brown), whose fragrance surpasses any chicken soup. There's wild rice, and long grain rice, short grain and medium grain in brown and white; Minnesota wild rice, arboria, Thai black; there are now mixtures of rices, wild rice with white rice and rices with herbs, with wheat berries or rye berries. You can make risottos and rice puddings, and all kinds of sauces for rices.

Among other grains, there's kasha, which everyone knows about---so traditional and so modern because it's so good and so healthy; there's bulgur wheat and couscous and quinoa, which is a perfect protein. How about a vegetarian bean and barley cholent for Shabbos?

Some of the more interesting beans are mung, aduki, appaloosa, anasazi, cannellini, white, and kidney. Experiment with them because some people find certain beans more digestible for them than others. Learn how to soak and cook them. It is really easy and gas problems from first eating beans often pass away in time as the digestive systems adjusts to the diet. Often gas simply indicates that a shift in your intestinal bacteria is taking place, which means that your body is responding to the vegetarian diet. Sometimes it takes only two-three weeks to adjust, though some people need longer. In Japan, the sea vegetable, "kombu" is used to help in digestion, by adding a little to the cooking beans. Fennel is also sometimes useful.

Sea Vegetables

Sea vegetables such as agar agar, alaria, arame, kombu, wakame, and others with strange names, can usually be found in health food stores. Many large chains now stock these traditional Japanese foods, or ask your local supermarket to get them. It's best to find out how to use them, in what proportions, etc., since some have a strong "ocean" flavor. But experiment, because sea vegetables are very healthy. In designing a diet for your lifestyle and nutritional needs, it's not only what you eliminate like meat or eggs, but also what you *include* in your diet. Many people make the mistake of thinking that vegetarian diets are automatically healthy. They're not! A diet of peanut butter, potato chips and spaghetti is vegetarian and unhealthy. *All* diets should be balanced diets. Some nutritional education is advisable, but you don't need a degree in chemistry or nutrition. Common sense and one good book on the subject is all you need. The bibliography at the back of this book has many recommendations.

It takes only a few weeks of working with an ingredient for it to become familiar to the taste and touch. Reach out for what the East has to offer in the way of ingredients. Along with yoga, karate, the martial arts, meditation and acupuncture, the "revolution of the 60's" introduced the West to many Eastern foods which are changing the way we eat, the way we look at food and its relation to health.

> Nutritional concepts with Eastern origins...offer valuable ideas on balancing food choices in a way that is quite different from our Western food group model. People can experience the benefits of both worlds when Western scientific concepts are used as the basis for building a nutritionally adequate diet and Eastern ideas of health

and nutrition are added to this foundation. With this kind of approach, excellent nutrition can be achieved in people of all ages.[326]

Demystifying Tofu

In the beginning there was tofu. Our grandchildren rave about it. They advertise it on their t-shirts and brag about it on their license plates. We're convinced it's healthy, but it looks and tastes like plaster of Paris. By itself tofu has little taste, so don't make the mistake of buying a package of tofu and eating it as is. (It isn't harmful to eat it that way, it just isn't tasty.) Do not eat it unadorned. Mix it, marinate it, stew it, sauté it. Tofu is a great mixer and can accompany many dishes. It is an inexpensive form of protein, which can be used in a variety of recipes, such as tofu loaves, tofu burgers, sloppy joes, stir fries, sweet and sour dishes with green peppers and pineapples. It can be fried, baked, and marinated. One of the virtues of tofu is that it marinates quickly, within 30-60 minutes. Almost any marinade will do, even simple tamari or soy sauce.

Tofu is extraordinarily adaptable and versatile. It can be used in main courses, or to make dips, spreads, desserts, creams, and cakes. Soy foods broaden the kosher taste experience. Kosher soy products now include pareve ice creams like Tofutti, soy cheeses, and soy meat analogs for foods.

You can buy 1 pound or 10 ounce blocks of tofu in many supermarkets. (Always check the expiration date as you would for any food). Tofu is packaged in liquid to keep it moist and fresh. To use, slit the package open and drain well. Place in a colander for about 10 minutes, then pat dry with kitchen towelling. Or place a heavy dish over the block of tofu in the colander and press down to squeeze out the moisture.

Tofu blocks are available in "firm," "extra firm," "regular," "soft" or "silken" textures. Recipes generally specify which type you will need. Firm and extra firm are the most useful; they contain the least water and hold their shape best in cooking. Once the package of tofu is opened, it is best to use it up or freeze it. It can be stored in water for about three days in the refrigerator in a closed container. The water should be changed daily. Drained and wrapped well in plastic wrap, it will keep in the freezer for many weeks. To defrost at room temperature takes about six hours, so if you use frozen tofu, plan accordingly. After defrosting, squeeze out remaining moisture with kitchen toweling. Frozen tofu marinates well and adds "heft" to dishes like chili.

Tofu's cousin, tempeh, is a cultured food, like yogurt. It is made of a mixture of cooked soybeans and grains, or of soybeans alone, bound together by a harmless mold. (Spots on the surface are a result of this mold.) Tempeh is sold frozen or refrigerated. Like tofu, it can be marinated, cubed, sliced, fried, oven fried, used in sandwiches with onions, sauerkraut or ketchup. It makes for a fast, easy sandwich, high in protein and if not fried, low in fat. Always keep refrigerated or frozen.

Tofu Recipes To Knock Your Socks Off

The following recipes and advice are from *The Jewish Vegetarian Year Cookbook.*[327]

Walnut Mushroom Pâté

1 teaspoon canola oil, or spray, or vegetable broth
1 medium onion, finely chopped
1/2 pound mushrooms, sliced
2 cups walnuts, toasted
1/2 pound firm tofu, patted dry and crumbled
2 tablespoons nutritional yeast flakes
2 tablespoons tamari

Heat large skillet; add oil, spray or broth. Add onion, brown quickly over medium high heat so that onion stays crisp.

Add mushrooms, cover, cook for 3 minutes. Uncover and cook, stirring occasionally, until mushrooms release their juices, and are lightly browned.

Put mixture into food processor and blend until smooth. Add remaining ingredients; process until smooth. Transfer to serving dish; cover, refrigerate at least 1 hour, preferably more. Spread on crackers or stuff in cherry tomatoes, celery boats, etc. Makes 3 cups.

Chocolate Tofu Pie

A dessert recipe that is so good, it's hard to believe it's healthy:

Graham Cracker Crust:
1 1/2 cups graham cracker crumbs
1/4 cup (1/2 stick) margarine, cut in small pieces

Filling:
1 cup semi-sweet chocolate chips
2 tablespoons water
1 pound soft or silken tofu
1/4 cup soy milk
1/3 cup honey
1 teaspoon vanilla extract

Preheat oven to 350^0 F.
Grind graham crackers thoroughly in food processor. Add margarine and continue processing until it is well combined with the crumbs. Press mixture in the bottom and sides of a 9" pie pan.
In a heavy-bottomed saucepan or in the top of a double boiler, melt chocolate chips with 2 tablespoons water.
Wash and dry the work bowl of the food processor. Put tofu and melted chocolate in it and process until perfectly smooth. Stir in remaining ingredients.

Pour filling into the crust and bake 30-35 minutes, until filling is firm and crust is golden. May be served at room temperature or chilled. Serves 6-8. Best made a day ahead.

Those are two examples of what can be done with tofu. Try them and find out what everyone is raving about.

Cooking Without Eggs

The following suggestions are from *Instead of Chicken, Instead of Poultry,* by Karen Davis.

It is easy to forego eggs when you remember that they contain about 70% fat, and an average egg contains 250 milligrams of cholesterol, and may be contaminated by salmonella bacteria, and that they are the products of biomachines whose lives have been spent in tortured conditions. Generally, if a recipe calls for only one egg, it can be omitted altogether.

To hold foods together in casseroles, burgers and loaves, do the following:

For white sauces made with soy milk or nondairy cream, use mashed potato. Amounts will have to be adjusted to specific recipes.

To leaven, bind, and liquefy batter in baking. Each of the following is for one egg.

1 tablespoon arrowroot powder plus 1 tablespoon soy flour + 2 tablespoons water (if needed).

2 tablespoons flour + 1/2 tablespoon vegetable shortening + 1/2 teaspoon baking powder + 2 tablespoons water.

2-4 tablespoons tofu, blended with liquid called for in recipe.

2 tablespoons cornstarch or potato starch.

2 tablespoons arrowroot flour.

1 heaping tablespoon soy powder + 2 tablespoons water.

1/2 to 1 banana, mashed.

1 tablespoon flax seeds + 1/4 cup water. Blend flax seeds and water in blender for 1-2 minutes, till mixture is thick and has the consistency of unbeaten egg white.

Free Range Eggs

If you absolutely must use eggs, you can purchase "range free" eggs in most health food stores and in some supermarkets. The price of range free eggs varies from neighborhood to neighborhood, but you should be able to purchase a carton of a dozen eggs for about $1.75. These are eggs which come from chickens who are not kept in cages, but in barns. Unfortunately, in many instances, the chickens are severely crowded in the barns as well. Many chickens are often still kept in barely acceptable conditions. "Range free" chicken farmers will state whether their eggs are free of pesticides and hormones. Read labels on the cartons. If your local supermarket or health food store doesn't carry free range eggs, ask them to do so. Become the Ralph Nader of Food. As a consumer, it is your right to insist upon safe food as much as it is your right to insist upon safe cars and seat belts.

A Vegetarian Shabbos Menu

You are now ready for your first vegetarian meal as a hostess. The following suggestions largely include ingredients we are all familiar with. It is not necessary to begin the vegetarian life with a larder of strange foods. In fact, most of what we eat almost every day will do very well for vegetarian meals. But if this meal is in the nature of a conscious new level of life, it might be fitting to say the Shehecheyanu blessing to commemorate the occasion. Fittingly and symbolically for the new vegetarian, this blessing is the same as the blessing for a fruit or vegetable from a new crop.

We bless You, HaShem, Creator of the Universe, for keeping us alive, taking care of us and bringing us to this season.

All specific blessings for food in Judaism are for vegetarian food, such as the blessings for wine and bread.

Blessing For Wine

We bless You, Hashem, Creator of the Universe,
Who created the fruit of the earth

Blessing For Bread

We bless You, HaShem, Creator of the Universe, Who makes bread come out of the earth.

Blessing for foods made from flour, such as pasta, and for rice:

We bless You, HaShem, Creator of the Universe,
Who creates many kinds of nourishing foods.

Blessing for Vegetables

We bless You, HaShem, Creator of the Universe,
Who creates vegetables out of the ground.

Blessing for the Fruit of the Tree

We bless You, HaShem, Creator of the Universe,
Who creates the fruit of the tree.

Blessings for Fruits and Vegetables From the New Crop:

We bless You, HaShem, Creator of the Universe, for keeping us alive, taking care of us and bringing us to this season.

A Shabbos Menu

Eggless challah, wine, walnut tofu pâté or mock chopped liver, Golden Glow Shabbat soup, bean and barley cholent, chocolate tofu pie.

Challah

2 packages dry yeast
2 cups warm water (105-115 ^{0})
1/2 cup sugar, divided
3 tablespoons flaxseeds
3/4 cup water
6-9 cups unbleached white flour
2 tablespoons honey
2 teaspoons salt
3 ounces vegetable oil
1/2 teaspoon turmeric
raisins (optional, but include for Rosh Hashanah challah)

In a small bowl, dissolve yeast in 2 cups warm water. (Use a thermometer, if possible. Otherwise, add 1 cup boiling water to 1 cup cold water.) Add 1/4 cup sugar, and allow the yeast to work for about 10 minutes while you prepare the dry ingredients.
Place flaxseeds and water in a blender and blend for about 2 minutes or until the mixture is the consistency of unbeaten egg white. Or grind the seeds in a spice mill or coffee grinder; place ground seeds and water in bowl of food processor and beat to desired consistency.

Place 6 cups flour, salt, remaining sugar and raisins (if using) in a large bowl.
Add flaxseed mixture, oil, honey and yeast. Mix until dough forms, adding more flour if needed. Turn the dough out onto a floured surface, flour your hands and knead the dough for about 10 minutes. Add flour as necessary until the dough no longer sticks to the board or your hands.

Oil a deep bowl. Put the dough in it, turning to grease it on all sides. Cover the bowl with a damp cloth or with plastic wrap, and allow to rise for about 1-1/2 hours, or until doubled in bulk.

Punch down and allow to rise a second time. Punch down again and knead briefly. Use a heavy, sharp knife to cut the dough in half. Cover one half while you shape the first loaf.

Oil a baking sheet. Divide one dough ball into three equal parts. Roll each one into a "snake," using a back and forth motion and keeping the dough under the palms of your hands. Each "snake" should be about 16" long. Allow them to rest a few minutes, then pinch the three strands together at one end, braid them, and pinch them together at the other end.
Remove the first loaf to an oiled baking sheet. Shape the second loaf, place it on the baking sheet, and allow the loaves to rise again.

Preheat oven to 350^0 F. For a crisp crust, brush loaves with cold water before placing in oven. Bake 25-35 minutes. The usual criterion for doneness is that the loaf sounds hollow when rapped on the bottom with your knuckles, or you may insert a thermometer in a crease on the bottom of the bread. It should register 200^0 F.

Cool loaves on a cooling rack. Makes 2 large loaves. Freezes well.

Preparation tip: You can make the dough the evening before and refrigerate it after the first or second rising. Extra dough can also be used for dinner rolls.
To form round challot for Rosh Hashanah, and the first Shabbat of each month: Divide the dough into two balls. Roll each one into a thick rope and coil the rope upon itself. If you prefer, divide the dough into thirds and make 3 loaves.

Mock Chopped Liver

1/2 package brown lentils (1/2 pound)
1 large diced onion
1 cup chopped walnuts
Salt to taste

Put lentils in a 2 or 3 quart pot, and cover with water. Use water sparingly so that lentils absorb all the water. More water can be added as needed. Bring water to a boil, partially cover and simmer for about 45 minutes. Check occasionally to make sure water has not boiled off, and add water as needed.

Sauté onions until lightly golden and tender.
Put lentils, walnuts and onions in food processor, purée until slightly coarse. Salt to taste. Chill about 2 hours. Serve with crackers or rye bread, or on lettuce leaves.

Golden Glow Shabbat Soup

1 pound package yellow split peas (2 cups dry)
1 cup grated parsnips
1 cup grated carrots
Salt to taste
3 bay leaves

Cook yellow split peas according to directions on package.
Halfway through cooking time, add parsnips, carrots, salt and bay leaves. Simmer with partially covered lid. Remove bay leaves before serving.
For a golden color and smoother taste, purée. Serves 8.

Bean and Barley Cholent

1/2 pound Great Northern beans
1/4 cup vegetable oil
2 large onions, chopped
1 large carrot, sliced thin
3 cloves garlic, chopped
1 tablespoon sweet paprika
1 tablespoon honey
1/2 cup pearl barley
5 cups boiling water
Salt and freshly ground pepper to taste

In a large pot or bowl, soak beans, covered, overnight. Water level should be 2" above beans. Preheat oven to 350^0 F.

Heat oil in a large, heavy oven casserole. Add onions, sauté until golden.
Stir in sliced carrot, cook 5 more minutes.
Stir in garlic and cook 1 more minute.
Remove vegetables with a slotted spoon, drain well and set aside.
Stir in paprika and honey. Return vegetables to pot. Stir in barley.
Drain beans and add them to pot.

Add boiling water, cover and bake for 30 minutes. Reduce heat to 250^0, and bake 30 minutes longer. Remove cover and season with salt and pepper. Serves 4-6.

Add your favorite salad, if you wish, remember the dessert.

B'tay-avon.

Appendix

Key Jewish Vegetarian Groups

1.The International Jewish Vegetarian and Ecological Society (often referred to as the "International Jewish Vegetarian Society" (IJVS), or just the "Jewish Vegetarian Society" (JVS)).

Adam Jackson, chairperson. Bet Teva, 855 Finchley Road, London, N. W. 11 8LX (telephone and fax: 01-181-455-0692;). The society has published a quarterly magazine, *The Jewish Vegetarian*, since September 1966.

2. Jewish Vegetarians of North America (JVNA)

Israel Mossman, coordinator. 6938 Reliance Road, Federalsburg, MD 21632; phone: (410) 754-5550; email address: imossman@skipjack.bluecrab.org. The group sends out a newsletter, edited by Eva and Ziona Mossman, about once every three months.

3. Jews For Animal Rights (JAR)

Roberta Kalechofsky, founder and director. 255 Humphrey Street, Marblehead, MA 01945, U.S.A.
phone: (781) 631-7601) fax: 781-639-0772
(Email address micah@micahbooks.com)
website http://www.micahbooks.com

4. Micah Publications

Roberta Kalechofsky, founder and director. 255 Humphrey Street, Marblehead, MA 01945, U.S.A. (781) 631-7601 fax: 781-639-0772 website http://www.micahbooks.com

(Email address micah@micahbooks.com) Publishing arm of Jews for Animal Rights, and have published many books on Jewish perspectives on these issues.

5. The Jerusalem Centre of the International Jewish Vegetarian Society.
Adam bar-Tura, director; 8 Balfour Street, Jerusalem, Israel. (02) 561 1114; Email address: ijvsjlem@netmedia.net.il

6. CHAI (Concern for Helping Animals in Israel)
Nina Natelson, director; P. O. Box 3341, Alexandria, VA 22302 phone (703)658-9650.
Email: 74754.654@compuserve.com

7. Anonymous (Animal Rights Group in Israel)
David Massey, director. 48a Ben Yehuda Street, Tel Aviv, Israel. (03) 525 4632 dmassey@netvision.net.il

8. Chaymeshek (Farm Animal Group in Israel)
Avi Pinkas, director; 8 Geulim Street, Rishon L' Tzion 75280, Israel; FAX: (03) 962-4086

9. New Jewish Vegan Lifestyle Group
Menachem Bahir, founder and director. 5515 North 7th Street, Suite 5-442, Phoenix, AZ 85014, USA, or via email to tjvmab@goodnet.com.

10. ProAnimal Magazine
Suzanne Trauffer, editor. P. O. Box 2039, Rehovoth 76120, Israel;
U. S. contact: Dr. K. Zupko, 51 Pine Lane, Barnstable, MA 02630
Local Jewish vegetarian contacts and groups can be located by contacting the above groups.

11. Israel Society Against Vivisection (ISAV)
Amnon Jonas, director;
(02) 652-8302
Email: amnon@rdc.active.net.il

Other Important Organizations

The issue of safe food will be paramount for the foreseeable future. Its issues are so enmeshed in bureaucracies, that a single person alone cannot effect change. Join an organization, get their newsletter, get informed and find out how to organize in your community.

The following addresses are for national organizations, but if you contact them they may be able to give you the name and address of an organization in your area. These organizations are not necessarily vegetarian, but are involved with the cause of safe food. The list is not an endorsement of any particular organization.

Americans For Safe Food
1505 Sixteenth St., NW
Washington, DC 20036
202-332-9110

Mothers and Others For Pesticide Limits
P.O. Box 96641
Washington, DC 20090

National Coalition Against Misuse of Pesticides
530 Seventh Street SE
Washington, DC 20003

Pesticide Action Network--North America Regional Center
P.O. Box 610
San Francisco, CA 94101

National Coalition To Stop Food Irradiation
P.O. Box 59-0488
San Francisco, CA 94159
415-626-2743

National Nutritional Foods Association
125 East Baker Avenue, #230
Costa Mesa, CA 92626
714-966-6632

Feingold Assocation for Information on Food Additives
P.O. Box 6550
Alexandria, VA 22306
703-768-3287

Organic Crop Improvement Association (OCIA)
125 West Seventh St.
Wind Gap, PA 18091

Organic Foods Production Association of North America
P.O. Box 31
Belchertown, MA 01007

Organic Growers and Buyers Association
P.O. Box 9747
Minneapolis, MN 55440

Community Sustained Agriculture of North America (CSANA)
e-mail: csana@bcn.net telephone: 413-528-4374.
An important movement with over 600 communities working with farms to set standards of organic produce. Membership includes fresh farm food and meetings with farmers and community. There are CSA groups in big cities like New York as well as in small towns.

Action-Centered Ideas

Four steps to action:

Join a group
Become informed
Write letters
Speak out

Vegetarianism is increasingly becoming a societal imperative because of the economic and ecological costs of producing and consuming animal products. For those who want to help move the world toward vegetarianism and the concept of "Just Food" the following suggestions are provided:

(1) Become well informed. Learn the facts about vegetarianism, and health from this and other books (see bibliography). See Dr. Jay Lavine's website for a Jewish view of nutrition and health.
http://members.aol.com/Sauromalus/index.html.

(2) Check out the website, http://www.USDA.Gov/NASS to get the latest statistics of how much livestock is being slaughtered and eaten, how many feedlots there are, etc. Call your congressperson or senator and ask them to send you pamphets on free information on the issue: for example, what laws about food, irradiation, labeling, are pending Most congresspeople have local telephone numbers listed in telephone directories.

(3) Don't underestimate the power of letters to local papers. Write! Ask papers to include vegetarian recipes for holiday menus. Contribute your favorite recipes. Set up programs and discussion groups at local religious, business and social organizations. Interest the Social Action Committees of your temples to table a discussion on the idea of "Just Food." Get newsletters from appropriate organizations to give them.

(4) Stickers and rubber stamps with the world vegetarian symbol can be obtained from the International Jewish Vegetarian Society. Use them on all your mail.

(5) Always ask for a vegetarian meal at Jewish functions and celebrations. Ask school and camp directors at your children's schools and camps to serve vegetarian meals.

(6) Arrange a synagogue or organizational session where vegetarian dishes are sampled and recipes exchanged.When applicable, indicate how values of the Sabbath and festivals are consistent with vegetarian concepts. For example: point out that the *kiddush* recited before lunch on the Sabbath indicates that animals are also to rest on the Sabbath day; on Sukkot, note that the sukkah is decorated with pictures and replicas of fruits and vegetables (never with animal products); on Yom Kippur, consider the mandate expressed in the prophetic reading of Isaiah to "share thy bread with the hungry," which can be carried out best by not having a diet that wastes the land, grain, water, fuel, and fertilizer.

(7) Get vegetarian books into public and synagogue libraries by donating duplicates. Request that libraries purchase such books. If you can afford it, buy some for them. Try to get your local library to have a special exhibit on vegetarian food.

(8) Work with others to set up a vegetarian food co-op or help support such places if they already exist.

(9) Join support groups for your good and theirs. Support charities that work to reduce world hunger in accordance with Maimonides's concept of the highest form of charity, to make people self-reliant in producing their own food.

(10) Vegetarianism is only part of the struggle for "Just Food," justice, compassion, and peace. Try to affect public policy with regard to *all* the issues raised in this book. **Join a group, become informed, write letters, speak out.**

BIBLIOGRAPHY

Jewish Literature On Vegetarian Issues and Kashrut

Aleichem, Shalom."Pity for Living Creatures," *Some Laughter, Some Tears* . New York, 1979. A young boy becomes aware of the concept of tsa'ar ba'alei.

Berman, Louis.*Vegetarianism and the Jewish Tradition* . K'tav, 1982. Good review of historical connections between Judaism and vegetarianism.

Bleich, Rabbi J. David. "Vegetarianism and Judaism," *Tradition*, Vol. 23, No. 1 Summer, 1987.

Cohen, Rabbi Alfred. "Vegetarianism From a Jewish Perspective," *Journal of Halacha and Contemporary Society,* Vol. I, No. II Fall, 1981.

David, Nathan S. ed.*The Voice of the Vegetarian* (Yiddish). Walden Press, 1952. Essays on ethical vegetarian ideals.

Dresner, Rabbi Samuel H.*The Jewish Dietary Laws, Their Meaning for Our Time*. Burning Bush Press, 1959. Religious and ethical meanings of kashrut.

Frankel, Aaron H. *Thou Shalt Not Kill or The Torah of Vegetarianism* . New York: 1896.

Green, Joe.*The Jewish Vegetarian Tradition*. South Africa: 1969. Discusses vegetarian aspects in the Jewish tradition.

--------------------"Chalutzim of the Messiah--The Religious Vegetarian Concept as Expounded by Rabbi Kook." (Text of a lecture given in Johannesburg, South Africa) Outlines some of Rabbi Kook's vegetarian teachings.

Groner, Arlene P. "The Greening of Kashrut--Is Vegetarianism the Ultimate Dietary Law?" *The National Jewish Monthly* . April 1976. Good summary of reasons for Jewish vegetarianism

Hakohen, Yosef Ben Shlomo, *The Universal Jew: Letters to My Progressive Father* . Jerusalem, New York, 1995. Discussion of people's obligations to the earth and its creatures.

Hirsch, Rabbi Samson Raphael. Horeb, translated by Dayan I. Grunfeld. Soncino Press, 1962. Classical work on the mitzvot of the Torah, and principles of love and justice, and the mitzvot related to the earth and its creatures.

Kalechofsky, Roberta, *Haggadah for the Liberated Lamb.* Micah Publications, 1985. Valuable material for conducting a vegetarian Passover seder. Written as a poetivc saga. Connects nature to history.

-------------------------------*Haggadah for the Vegetarian Family.* Micah Publications, 1990. Excellent for intergenerational seders.

----------------------------*Journey of the Liberated Lamb: Reflections on a Vegetarian Seder.* Micah Publications, 1996. Describes how Judaism grew through substitutions of religious symbols. Recommendations for substitutions for shankbone and egg on the Passover table, and projects for children.

---------------------- editor, *Judaism and Animals Rights: Classical and Contemporary Responses*. Micah Publications, 1992. Articles on animal rights and vegetarianism from Jewish perspective. Section on shechitah.

------------------ editor, *Rabbis and Vegetarianism: An Evolving Tradition.* Micah Publications, 1995. Articles on vegetarianism by 17 rabbis from different Jewish backgrounds.

------------------ *Vegetarianism and the Jewish Holidays.* Micah Publications, 1993. A Green Mitzvah Booklet. Questions and answers about vegetarian connections to Jewish festivals. Some recipes included.

--------------------- *A Boy, A Chicken, and The Lion of Judea: How Ari Became a Vegetarian.* Micah Publications, 1995. Seven-year old Ari overcomes family and peer-pressure to "take charge of his stomach."

Kook, Rabbi Abraham Isaac. *A Vision of Vegetarianism and Peace* (Hebrew). Rav Kook is considered the pre-eminent thinker on Vegetarian Judaism.

--------------------------- "Fragments of Light: A View as to the Reasons for the Commandments," Collection of Rabbi Kook's works, edited and translated by Ben Zion Bokser. Paulist Press, 1978. Summarizes Rav Kook's thoughts on vegetarianism.

Pick, Philip, ed.*Tree of Life*:. A.S. Barnes, 1977. Anthology of articles which appeared in *The Jewish Vegetarian,* 1966-1974.

Raisin, Jacob A. *Humanitarianism of the Laws of Israel: Kindness to Animals.* Jewish Tract 06. Union of American Hebrew Congregations. Summary of laws in the Jewish tradition relating to kindness to animals.

Schochet, Rabbi Elijah J. *Animal Life in Jewish Tradition.* K'tav, 1984. Well-documented, but conservative interpretation of tsa'ar ba'alei chaim.

Schwartz, Richard,*Judaism and Vegetarianism.* Micah Publications, 1988. Thorough analysis of the Jewish case for vegetarianism. Officially out of print, but copies may be available from author and New Leaf Distributors.

-----------------*Judaism and Animal Issues.* Micah Publications, 1993. Green Mitzvah Booklet. Summary of issues in question and answer format.

------------------*Judaism, Health, Nutrition, and Vegetarianism.* Micah Publications, 1993. Green Mitzvah Booklet. Summary of issues in question and answer format.

Shoshan, A. *Man and Animal* . Shoshanim, 1963. Hebrew. Thorough treatment of Jewish literature on animals from ancient to modern times

Vegetarianism, Food, and Meat Production

Akers, Keith. *A Vegetarian Sourcebook.* Vegetarian Press, 1985.

Altman, Nathaniel, *Eating for Life*. Theosophical Publishing House, 1977.

Coats, David, C. *Old MacDonald's Factory Farm.* Continuum, 1989. Surveys all aspects of factory farming. Foreword by Dr. Michael W. Fox.

Davis, Karen. *Prisoned Chickens, Poisoned Eggs.* Book Publishing Co., 1997. A definitive book on the chicken and egg industry.

Diamond, Harvey,*Your Heart, Your Planet* . Hay House,1990.

Eisman, George L.,*The Most Noble Diet* . Diet-Ethics, 1984.

Eisnitz, Gail A., *Slaughterhouse*, Prometheus Books, 1997. Muckraking exposé of conditions in slaughterhouses.

Fox, Nicols, *Spoiled: The Dangerous Truth About A Food Chain Gone Haywire*, Basic Books, 1997. Concise, readable account of pathogens in meat and chicken, by a journalist.

Harrison, Ruth. *Animal Machines*. London. Vincent Stuart, 1964. A classic, one of the first books to research the evils of factory farming. Foreword by Rachel Carson.

Hur, Robin, *Food Reform: Our Desperate Need.* Heidelberg, 1975.

Lappé, Frances Moore, *Diet for a Small Planet.* Ballantine Books, Revised edition, 1982. A pioneer work.

Lacey, Richard, *Hard to Swallow,* Cambridge University Press, 1994. Account of the rise of mad cow disease in England by a famous biologist.

Mason, Jim and Peter Singer, *Animal Factories*. Harmony Books, 1990.

Melina, Vesanto, R.D., Davis, Brenda, R.D. Harrison, Victoria, R.D. *Becoming Vegetarian.* Book Publishing Co., 1995. Written by dieticians, gives nutritional values in non-meat diet. Charts, statistics and references to different stages of life.

Moran,Victoria,*Compassion, The Ultimate Ethic.* England. Thorsons, 1985.

Nearing, Helen & Scott. *Living The Good Life.* Schocken Books, 1970. In the Thoreau tradition by philosophical homesteaders in Maine.

Rifkin, Jeremy, *Beyond Beef--The Rise and Fall of the Cattle Culture.* Dutton, 1992. Survey of the rise of cattle culture over millennium, and analysis of its negative effects.

Rhodes, Richard, *Deadly Feasts: Tracking the Secrets Of A Terrifying New Plague*, Simon & Schuster, 1997. Readable account of the emergence of mad cow disease.

Robbins, John, *Diet For a New America.* Stillpoint Publishing, 1987. Documents health, animal-rights, and ecological reasons for not eating flesh, eggs, and dairy foods.

Schell, Orville, *Modern Meat* . Vintage Books, 1985. Detailed discussion of problems related to modern meat production. Author is a cattleman, journalist and non-vegetarian.

Singer, Peter, *Animal Liberation.* New York Review of Books Publishers, 1990. Important survey of cruelty to animals in factory farming and scientific experimentation.

Health and Nutrition Issues

Barnard, Neal D., M. D. *The Power of Your Plate--A Plan for Better Living.* Book Publishing Company. 1990. Seventeen experts write about how to eat better for health reasons.

Diamond, Harvey and Marilyn Diamond. *Fit For Life.* Warner Books, 1985. Introduction to natural hygiene. Recipes.

-----------------------------*Fit For Life. II--Living Health..* Warner Books, 1987.

Esser, William, M.D. *Dictionary of Natural Foods.* Natural Hygiene Press, 1983. Beautifully illustrated.

Harris, William, M. D. *The Scientific Basis of Vegetarianism.* Hawaii Health Publishers, 1995. Graphs and charts.

Klaper, Michael, M. D. *Vegan Nutrition: Pure and Simple.* Gentle World, 1995.

---------------------*Pregnancy, Children, and the Vegan Diet.* Gentle World, 1988. Common sense discussion by a doctor on the vegan benefits to pregnant women and infants.

McDougall, John A., M. D and Mary A McDougall. *The McDougall Plan..* New Century Publishers, 1983. Information on all aspects of nutrition. Recipes.

-----------------------------*McDougall's Medicine--A Challenging Second Opinion.* New Century Publishers, 1985. Challenges currently accepted treatments for chronic diseases.

Nussbaum, Elaine. *Recovery From Cancer.* Avery Pub. Group. 1992. Autobiographical account of author's recovery from advanced cancer through a strict macrobiotic diet.

Ornish Dean, M. D. *Dr. Dean Ornish`s Program for Reversing Heart Disease*. Ballantine, 1990. Description of important breakthrough in the treatment of heart disease with low-fat diet, exercise, meditation, and stress reduction. Recipes.

Rampton, Sheldon & Stauber, John, *Mad Cow, U.S.A.*, Common Courage Press, 1997. Journalistic investigation of the subject.

Sorensen, Marc, Ed. D. *Mega Health.* National Institute of Health, 1993. Documented discussion of relationship between diet and health.

Vegetarian Cookbooks

Cookbooks are personal. You should choose them to suit your lifestyle and pocketbook, like your clothes. The following list is a good basic one.

Benjamin, Alice and Corrigan, Harriet. *Cooking With Conscience: A Book for People Concerned About World Hunger* . Seabury, 1978.

Brown, Lena. *Cookbook for Health* (Yiddish). Jankovitz, 1931. Early collection of Jewish vegetarian recipes

Chelf, Vicki Rae & Biscotti, Dominique.*The Sensuous Vegetarian Barbecue*. Avery Publishing, 1994. Funky. Good recipes for barbecuing.

Dinshah, Freya, *The Vegan Kitchen.* American Vegan Society, 1987.

Friedman, Rose. *Jewish Vegetarian Cooking.* Thorsons, 1985. Lacto-ovo recipes.

Hagler, Louise. *Tofu Cookery.* Book Publishing Co., 1991. Simplifies cooking with tofu with appetitizing recipes.

Hunt, Janet. *The Vegetarian In the Family.* Thorsons, 1994. Good for beginners. Adaptations of traditional meals.

Kalechofsky, Roberta & Rosa Rasiel, *The Jewish Vegetarian Year Cookbook*. Micah Publications, 1997. Combines Jewish holiday traditions with 170 vegan recipes. Includes a Tu b'shevat seder, extensive notes on the holidays and food tips.

Katzen, Mollie, *The Moosewood Cookbook.* Ten Speed Press, 1982. Lacto-ovo recipes by one of the pioneers of vegetarian cooking.

----------------------*The Enchanted Broccoli Forest.* Ten Speed Press, 1982. Lacto-ovo recipes.

----------------------------*Still Life With Menu.* Ten Speed Press, 1988. Fifty menus, and beautiful to look at.

Kirchner, Bharti,*The Bold Vegetarian.* Harper, 1995. International recipes.

Lerman, Andrea Bliss. *The Macrobiotic Community Cookbook.* Avery Publishing, 1989. An easy way to learn how to use Eastern ingredients.

McDougall, Mary, *McDougall 's Health-Supporting Cookbook.* (Volumes I and II).New Century Publishers, 1985 (Vol. 1), 1986 (Vol.2).

Ornish, Dean. M.D. *Eat More, Weigh Less.* Harper, 1987. Healthy gourmet recipes by the prominent doctor.

Robertson, Laurel, et al. *The New Laurel`s Kitchen: A Handbook for Vegetarian Cookery and Nutrition.* Ten Speed Press, 1986.

Sass, Lorna. *Complete Vegetarian Kitchen.* Hearst Books, 1992. Good all-around vegan cookbook. Useful information on how to shop for and store foods, with a specialty on pressure cooking.

Shulman, Martha, Rose.*The Vegetarian Feast.* Harper, 1995.

-----------------------------*Gourmet Vegetarian Feasts.* Thorsons, 1987. International selection.

Shurtleff, William & Aoyagi, Akiko. *The Book of Miso.* Ballantine Books, 1976. Good introduction to this "mysterious" food from the East.

Wasserman, Debra & Reed Mangels, *Simply Vegan.* Vegetarian Resource Group, 1990.

-------------------- *Meatless Meals for Working People--Quick and Easy Vegetarian Recipes.* Vegetarian Resource Group, 1990.

Wasserman, Debra, *Conveniently Vegan..* Vegetarian Resource Group, 1997.

General Related Books on Vegetarianism

Wheatley, Georgia. *Vegetarian Resource Directory: Guide To Information for a Vegetarian Lifestyle.* Book Publishing Co. 1996. Excellent resource book.

Wynne-Tyson, Jon. *Food For a Future: How World Hunger Could Be Ended By the 21st Century.* Thorsons, 1988.

Philosophical/Spiritual Books About Food

Kass, Leon, *The Hungry Soul*, The Free Press, 1994.
Philosophical inquiry into food, with emphasis on Jewish dietary laws.

Kesten, Deborah. *Feeding the Body, Nourishing the Soul.* Conari Press, 1997. Discusses spiritual values concerning food from traditions and religions around the world. Foreword by Herbert Benson, M.D.

Rosen, Steven, *Food For the Spirit: Vegetarianism and the World Religions*. Bala Books, 1986. Preface by Isaac Bashevis Singer.

Books for The Vegetarian Traveler

Civic, Jed and Susan, *The Vegetarian Traveler,* Larson Publications, 1998. Comprehensive. Lists over 300 places in Central America, Canada, the USA, Israel, and Europe. Many photos. Updates every two years.

Vegetarian Resource Group,*Guide to Natural foods and Restaurants in the U.S. and Canada*, Avery Publishing, 1993.

Weintraub, Mark. *Guide to Vegetarian Restaurants in Israel.* The Vegetarian Resource Group, 1996. Vegetarian-friendly restaurants & health food stores.

Books Related to Food and Farming

Berry, Wendell, *The Unsettling of America,* Yolla Bolly Press, 1977.

Fox, Michael W., Dr., *Agricide, The Hidden Crisis That Affects Us All*, Schocken Books, 1986.

Steinman, David, *Diet For A Poisoned Planet: How to Choose Safe Food For You and Your Family*, Ballantine Books, 1990. Includes lists of organizations, statistics, etc.

Footnotes

Introduction

[1] Diane Ackerman, *A Natural History of the Senses* (Random House, 1990), 147.
[2] Louis Berman, *Vegetarianism and the Jewish Tradition* (KTAV, 1982).
[3] There have been improvements: About 80% of kosher slaughtering plants of large animals have replaced shackling and hoisting with a more benign system, but slaughtering of small animals have not changed.
[4] Captive bolt is a gun that shoots a bolt of iron into the animal's brain.
[5] Gail Eisnitz, *Slaughterhouse* (Prometheus Books, 1997).
[6] Allan Brandt & Paul Rozin, *Morality and Health* (Routledge, 1997), 2.
[7] Nicols Fox, *Spoiled: The Dangerous Truth About A Food Chain Gone Haywire* (Basic Books, 1997), 235.
[8] David Ehrenfeld, "A Techno-Pox Upon the Land," *Harper's*, Oct. 1997.
[9] Jim Mason and Peter Singer, *Animal Factories: What Agribusiness Is Doing To the Family Farm, The Environment And Your Health* (Harmony Books, 1990), xiii.
[10] Dallas Pratt, M.D., *Alternatives to Pain in Experiments on Animals* (Argus Archives, 1980), Introduction.
[11] Quoted in Richard Schwartz, *Judaism and Vegetarianism* (Micah Publications, 1988), 1.
[12] Ehrenfeld, "A Techno-Pox Upon the Land."
[13] Rabbi Samuel H. Weintraub, "The Spiritual Ecology of Kashrut," *To Till and to Tend: A Guide to Jewish Environmental Study and Action* (COEJL), 21. (Reprinted from *Reconstructionist*, Winter 1991/1992).
[14] *Antislavery Reporter* (AntiSlavery International), Dec. 1997.
[15] Rabbi Samuel H. Dresner, *The Jewish Dietary Laws : Their Meaning For Our Time* (The Rabbinic Assembly of America, 1982).

Chapter 1: Kashrut and Modernity

[16] Rabbi Samuel Dresner,*The Jewish Dietary Laws: Their Meaning For Our Time* (The Rabbinical Assembly of America, 1982), 27. It should also be stated that explanations of the dietary laws as either "hygienic" or

"ethical" have been challenged by anthropologists such as Mary Douglas, who regards the dietary laws as part of an intricate system related to a "cognitive ordering of the universe," involving other rituals, such as the purity rituals, etc. A good short view of this matter is in Everett Fox's translation, *The Five Books of Moses* (Schocken, 1995), vol. 1, 554-555. What is given in our introduction is the traditional rabbinic explanation of the dietary laws.

[17] Louis Berman, *Vegetarianism & The Jewish Tradition* (KTAV, 1982), xiii.

[18] Ironically, the process of converting creatures who were once defined as "living" into machines is taking place at the same time that the nature of machines, i.e. the computer, is being debated. Obviously, the definition of "life" is undergoing an historic change.

[19] Jeremy Rifkin, *Beyond Beef: The Rise and Fall of the Cattle Culture* (Dutton, 1992), 283-284.

[20] Rabbi David Rosen, "An Orthodox Jewish Perspective," in *Rabbis and Vegetarianism: An Evolving Tradition* , ed. Roberta Kalechofsky (Micah Publications, 1995), 54.

[21] Dresner, 11.

[22] *Rabbis and Vegetarianism*, 53-55.

[23] Most recently in the introduction to *The Jewish Vegetarian Year Cookbook* by Roberta Kalechofsky and Rosa Rasiel (Micah Publications, 1997).

[24] Walter Burkert, *Homo Necans,* Trans. by P.Bing (University of California Press, 1983)

[25] Ibid., 25.

[26] Everett Fox's translation is "Burial-Places of the Craving." The episode is rendered in his translation with great drama, 713-718.

[27] Dresner, 24-25.

[28] See Rabbi Arthur Green's articles, "To Work It and Guard It: Preserving God's World," and "Vegetarianism, A Kashrut For our Age," in *Seek My Face, Speak My Name* (Jason Aronson, 1992) or *Rabbis and Vegetarianism: An Evolving Tradition.*

[29] Rabbi Alfred A. Cohen, "Vegetarianism From A Jewish Perspective," *Journal of Halacha and Contemporary Society,* Fall, 1981 vol. 1, no. ll. Also in *Judaism and Animal Rights*, ed. by Roberta Kalechofsky (Micah Publications), 1992, 176-195.

[30] Dresner, 40.

[31] Deborah Kesten, *Feeding the Body, Nourishing the Soul* (Conari Press, 1997), 11-27.

[32] Robert Eisenmann, *James the Brother of Jesus* (Viking, 1996), examines the twin advocacy of celibacy and vegetarianism in James and first century "Jewish Christians."
[33] John Cooper, *Eat and Be Satisfied: A Social History of Jewish Food* (Jason Aronson, 1993), 19, 21.
[34] *Rabbis and Vegetarianism,* 27.
[35] Elijah Judah Schochet, *Animal Life in Jewish Tradition: Attitudes and Relationships* (Ktav, 1984), 47.
[36] However, note that Deut. 12: 21 states that if there is no Temple available for proper sacrifice "...you may slaughter animals from among your herds and your flocks." Nevertheless, this would not affect most Diaspora Jews who lived in cities and did not have access to herds and flocks.
[37] We know of only one other place in the Diaspora in which a temple for animal sacrifice was built. This was by a Jewish garrison on the island of Elephantis in Egypt.
[38] Cooper, 4.
[39] On the occasion of the 25th anniversary of the World Wildlife fund.
[40] For texts by other rabbis, see *Rabbis and Vegetarianism: An Evolving Tradition.*
[41] Much of the section on Rav Kook was prepared by Richard Schwartz.
[42] Rabbi Samuel Weintraub, "The Spiritual Ecology of Kashrut," *To Till and to Tend: A Guide to Jewish Environmental Study and Action* (COEJL).
[43] Ibid.

Chapter 2: From Living Soul to Animal Machine

[44] Much of this discussion is based on Leonore Cohen Rosenfield's book, *From Beast Machine to Man-machine* (Oxford, 1941). For other material on this and related subjects, see T.H. Huxley, "On The Hypothesis: The Animals Are Automata and Its History," 1874; Joseph Needham, *Man A Machine,* (Norton, 1928), and Hans Jonas, *The Phenomenon of Life* (University of Chicago Press, 1966).
[45] Developments in quantum mechanics in the last half century have diminished the importance of "extension" as the basis for reality and science. But these new views pertain, so far, only to the atomic level.
[46] Leon Kass, *The Hungry Soul* (The Free Press, 1994) 4.
[47] T.H. Huxley, who was sympathetic to Descartes' notion of animals as automata, was constrained to reconcile it with the Darwinian view of the continuity of animal and human life. Since Huxley believed that conscious-

ness was part of the evolutionary process, he developed the theory that animals are "conscious automata." T.H. Huxley, "On the Hypothesis that Animals are Automata, and Its History, 1874," *Method and Results: Essays* (D. Appleton, 1915), 199.

[48] Fox reports that two maternity hospitals in Zurich, Switzerland had disposed of human placenta by selling them to a supplier of offal, which offal then made its way into animal feed. 324-325.

[49] Kass, 222. "To mark his self-conscious separation from the animals, man undertakes to eat them...."

[50] Ibid., 61.

[51] Ibid., 60.

[52] Descartes was not without precedents. Heraclitus had already argued that only man possessed a soul. He and the Stoics also believed that the animals behaved automatically. Aristotle believed that human beings were in the first rank of creatures, but in other ways were similar to animals.

[53] Rosenfield, 7-8.

[54] Ibid, 3.

[55] Ibid., 205.

[56] See "Sherira Gaon Defends The Rights of Animals," Jacob S. Raisin, "Humanitarianism of the Laws of Israel," Roberta Kalechofsky, "Jewish Law and Tradition on Animal Rights," *Judaism and Animal Rights,* ed. Roberta Kalechofsky (Micah Publications, 1992.)

[57] Ibid., 163.

[58] The British philosopher, Mary Midgley, recounts a television program in 1974 in which Robert Nozick asked several scientists, "Whether the fact that an experiment will kill hundreds of animals is ever regarded by scientists as a reason for not performing it?" One of the scientists answered, "Not that I know of." Nozick pressed his question; "Don't the animals count at all?" Dr. A. Perachio, of the Yerkes Centre, replied, "Why should they?" while Dr. D. Baltimore, of the Massachusetts Institute of Technology, added that he did not think that experimenting on animals raised a moral issue at all." Mary Midgley, *Animals and Why they Matter* (University of Georgia Press, 1984), 10.

[59] Rosenfield, 54.

[60] *Harper's Magazine,* August, 1997, p. 61.

[61] For a recent history of this process, Rifkin, *Beyond Beef*.

[62] For an interesting comparison between slaughter in the era of sacrifice and modern slaughter, see Richard Selzer, "How to Build A Slaughter-house," *Taking the World in for Repairs* (William Morrow, 1986).

[63] Kass, footnote, p. 216.

---

[64] Ibid.
[65] They accepted Jesus as messiah, but not as the son of God; they accepted only the Gospel of Matthew, and the Torah as their Bible and insisted that it be read in Hebrew; they practised circumcision, embraced poverty and vegetarianism. They survived at least into the fifth century, probably later. Manuscripts of theirs have come to light, dating from the 10th century.
[66] Eisenman, 258 ff.
[67] Noah J. Cohen, *Tsa'ar Ba'ale Hayim: The Prevention of Cruelty to Animals: Its Bases, Development and Legislation in Hebrew Literature* (Feldheim, 1976), 1.
[68] James Gaffney, "The Relevance of Animal Experimentation to Roman Catholic Methodology," *Temple Sacrifices: Religious Perspectives on the Use of Animals in Science*, ed. Tom Regan (Temple University Press, 1986), 151.
[69] See E.R. Dodds, *The Greeks and the Fear of The Irrational* (University of California Press, 1959).
[70] See "Animals: An Historical Perspective," Roberta Kalechofsky, *Autobiography of A Revolutionary* (Micah Publications, inc., 1991). For a Christian perspective, see Andrew Linzey, *Christianity and the Rights of Animals* (Crossroad, 1987).
[71] A good summary chapter of the Medieval era and Jewish philosophers can be found in Schochet, *Animal Life in Jewish Tradition* , p.195 ff.
[72] An effort to come to terms with this problem within the modern Darwinian framework is by Jay B. McDaniel, *Of God and Pelicans* (John Knox Press, 1989).
[73] Rabbi Joseph B. Soloveitchik, *The Halakhic Mind: An Essay on Jewish Tradition and Modern Thought* (Seth Press, 1986), 100.
[74] See Kenneth H. Simonsen, "The Monstrous and The Bestial: Animals in Greek Myths," *Between the Species*, Spring, 1986, p.59.
[75] Karen Davis, *Prisoned Chickens, Poisoned Eggs: An Inside Look At the Modern Poultry Industry* (Book Publishing Co., 1996), 142.
[76] Luddites were workers in England in the early part of the industrial revolution who smashed machines because they believed the machine would take work away, often ridiculed as people "who tried to stop progress."

Chapter Three: Pikuach Nefesh

[77] 1997, Vol 26, no. 4
[78] Ibid., 21. (Several of Judaism's prominent enemies, such as the Nazi, Alfred Rosenberg, identified their hatred of the "Jewish spirit" with the

---

affirmation of life. In his article, "The Earth-Centered Jew Lacks A Soul," Rosenberg wrote: "The world is preserved...only by a positive yea-saying to the world. Among the Jewish people this world-affirmation is totally pure, without any admixture of world-denial. All other nations that have ever existed, and exist today, had, or have, such an admixture, characterized by the idea of a Hereafter....If...the Jewish people were to perish, no nation would be left which would hold world-affirmation in high esteem--the end of all time would be here." For these reasons, Rosenberg argued, the Jew lacks spirituality and has to be destroyed. (quoted in George L. Mosse, *Nazi Culture: Intellectual, Cultural and Social Life In The Third Reich,* Grosset & Dunlap, 1966), 75. In his eccentric book, *The Silence of the Body* (Farrar, Strauss and Giroux, 1993), Guido Ceronetti expresses a similar idea without, however, the implication that the Jew must be destroyed. "The Jewish mistake and miracle is the refusal to mix with death; this prevents the Jews from experiencing a true spiritual transcendance and instead roots them in human time *dor-va-dor*, until the end of the world." (p. 13) Ceronetti identifies matza with the principle of life and yeast with the principle of death.

[79] A summary of these prohibitions is in *Judaism, Health, Nutrition & Vegetarianism*, by Richard Schwartz (Micah Publications, 1993).

[80] *Self*, Dec., 1995.

[81] Dr. James W. Anderson, *High-Fiber Fitness Plan* (University Press of Kentucky, 1994) 5-6.

[82] Lane HW, Carpenter JT. "Breast Cancer: incidence, nutritional concerns, and treatment approaches," *J. Am. Diet Assoc.* 1987; 87:765-769.

[83] Minowa M. et al. "Dietary Fiber Intake in Japan," *Human Nutr Appl Nutr.* 1983:37A:113-119.

[84] Wynder E.L., et al. "Diet and Breast Cancer in Causation and Therapy," *Cancer* 1986:58:1804-1813.

[85] *The Newsletter of Nutrition, Fitness and Stress Management,* June, 1997, vol 13, issue 9.

[86]Melina, Davis & Harrison, *Becoming Vegetarian: The Complete Guide to Adopting A Healthy Vegetarian Diet* (Book Publishing Co., 1995) 21-22.

[87] Elaine Nussbaum, *Recovery From Cancer* (Avery Pubishing, 1992).

[88] Alexander Todd, *Double Vision* (University Press of New England, 1994).

[89] T. Colin Campbell and Christine Cox, *The China Project* (New Century Nutrition, 1996) 9.

[90] Ibid., 17.

[91] Ibid., 18.

[92] Ibid., 17.

[93] Dean Ornish, M.D., *Eat More, Weigh Less* (Harper Perennial, 1994).
[94] Colin Tudge, *The Engineer in the Garden* (Hill and Wang, 1993), 190.
[95] Ibid., 190-191.
[96] C. David Coats, *Old MacDonald's Factory Farm* (Continuum, 1989), 65.
[97] Excerpted from Roberta Kalechofsky, "Factory Farming," *Lynn Magazine*, June-July, 1986, 21.
[98] Coats, 65-66.
[99] Ruth Harrison, *Animal Machines* (London, 1964).
[100] *Rabbis and Vegetarianism*, 54.
[101] See chapter by Hans Jonas, "To Move and To Feel: On the Animal Soul," *The Phenomenon of Life: Toward a Philosophical Biology* (University of Chicago Press, 1966).
[102] Ornish. (See also *Dr. Dean Ornish's Program For Reversing Heart Disease.)*
[103] Ibid., ix.
[104] Robert Proctor, *Cancer Wars (Basic Books, 1995)* 1.
[105] Ibid., 230.
[106] Sandra Blakeslee, "Some Biologists Ask 'Are Genes Everything?'"*The New York Times* , Sept. 2, 1997, C1.
[107] Richard Lewontin, "Cloning Human Beings: Report and Recommendations of the National Bioethics Advisory Commission, June, 1997), *The New York Review of Books*, vol XLIV, number 16, October 23, 1997, 18.
[108] Patricia Hausman, *Jack Spratt's Legacy: The Science and Politics of Fat and Cholesterol* (Richard Marek Pub., 1981), 26.
[109] Richard Lacey, *Hard To Swallow* (Cambidge University Press).
[110] Ibid., 172.
[111] See Richard Rhodes, "Pathological Science," *The New Yorker,* Dec. 1, 1997, p.54.
[112] Lacey, 173.
[113] Ibid.
[114] Richard Rhodes, *Deadly Feasts: Tracking The Secrets of A Terrifying New Plague* (Simon & Schuster, 1997), 15.
[115] See Sheldon Rampton and John Stauber, *Mad Cow U.S.A.: Could the Nightmare Happen Here* (Common Courage Press, 1970).
[116] For the full story of the problem in the U.S., see above book and the chapter, "The Madness Behind Mad Cows," in Nicols Fox, *Spoiled.*
[117] See issue of *Vegetarian Voice,* 1996, vol 21, number 4.
[118] Fox, 305.

---

[119] Ibid., 311-312.
[120] See chapter in Fox, "The Madness Behind Mad Cows."
[121] Rhodes, *Deadly Feasts*, 233.
[122] The phrase is used in Eisnitz and Fox.
[123] Eisnitz, 159.
[124] Ibid., 37
[125] Ibid.
[126] MacDonald's fast-food chain targets children as part of its marketing strategy.
[127] Damion's story is told in detail in Fox, 211 ff.
[128] Ibid., 180-181.
[129] Ibid, 49.
[130] Ibid, 13.
[131] Ibid., 211-264.
[132] Ibid., 219.
[133] Ibid, 178.
[134] "Health Concerns Mounting Over Bacteria in Chickens," *The New York Times*, October 20, 1997.
[135] Fox,191.
[136] *The Washington Post*, Health Section, Dec. 9, 1997. Cites nine million cases a year of campylobacter.
[137] Ibid.
[138] Fox, 155-156.
[139] Eisnitz, 172.
[140] Fox, 251.
[141] William H. McNeill, *Plagues and Peoples* (Anchor Press)Doubleday, 1976).
[142] Harrison, 5.
[143] McNeill, 7.
[144] Ibid.
[145] Ibid., 257.
[146] Lacey, 55.
[147] Ibid, 56.
[148] Jim Mason and Peter Singer, *Animal Factories (*Harmony Books, 1990), 52-53.
[149] Ibid., 67.
[150] quoted in *Animal Factories*, 79.
[151] Ibid.
[152] Rifkin, 144.

---

[153] Tudge, 235.
[154] See Orville Schell, *Modern Meat*, for a discussion of DES.
[155] C. David Coats, *Old MacDonald's Factory Farm* (Continuum, 1989) 51.
[156] Tudge, 235.
[157] Ehrenfeld, "A Techno-Pox Upon the Land," 16.
[158] *Good Medicine*, Autumn, 1992, vol 1, number 1.
[159] Ibid.
[160] Tudge, 191.
[161] Ibid.
[162] Ibid., 242.
[163] Erwin Chargoff, *Heraclitean Fire* (Rockefeller University Press, 1978), 189-190.
[164] Lacey, 125-127.
[165] Rhodes, 15-16.
[166] Joy Williams, 61.
[167] Harrison, vii.
[168] "Antibiotics and Livestock: *Feeding A Controversy," The Harvard Medical School Letter*, August, 1985, vol X, number 9.
[169] Jim Mason and Peter Singer, *Animal Factories* (Harmony Books, 1990).
[170] Schell, op cit.
[171] Sylvia Tesh, *Hidden Arguments: Political Ideology and Disease Prevention Policy (Rutgers University Press, 1988)* 184.
[172] John H. Knowles, M.D., "The Responsibility of the Individual," *Doing Better and Feeling Worse: Health In The United States* (W.W. Norton, 1977), 58.
[173] *Rabbis and Vegetarianism*, 54.
[174] The following material is taken from an unpublished article, "Prevention: Jewish Perspectives on Preserving Health," by Yoseph Ben Shlomo Hakoen and Richard Schwartz.
[175] Yalkut Lekach Tov, Shmos, B'shalach
[176] Mishneh Torah Hilchot Deot 4:1
[177] Chulin 9a; Choshen Mishpat 427; Yoreh De'ah 116.
[178] Pesachim 25a; Maimonides, Yad, Yesode ha Torah, p. 7.
[179] Yoma 85b: Sanhedrin 74a
[180] Rabbi J. H. Hertz, The *Pentateuch and Haftorahs* (London: Soncino Press, 1958), p. 843.

[181] Quoted in Fred Rosner, *Modern Medicine and Jewish Law* (Bloch, 1972), p. 28.
[182] Ibid.
[183] Sanhedrin 4:5
[184] Shabbat 151b
[185] Sefer Hasidim 724
[186] Ta'anit 11 a,b
[187] Shabbat 140b
[188] Chulin 84a; Avodah Zarah 11a
[189] Shabbat 50b
[190] Leviticus Rabbah 34:3

Chapter 4: Frequently Asked Questions

[191] The questions were prepared by Richard Schwartz. A fuller version is available in his booklet, *Judaism, Health, Nutrition, & Vegetarianism* (Micah Publications, 1993).
[192] When Jane Brody, the nutritional columnist for *The New York Times*, was once asked what defined a "moderate" amount of meat, her answer was 5 ounces a week.
[193] Melina, Davis and Harrison, 95.
[194] Ibid., 93.
[195] This brand is recommended by Dr. Jay Lavine and Melina, Davis and Harrison for its reliability. It can be found in health food stores, or ordered from the Mail Order Cataologue, P.O. Box 180, Summertown, TN 38483 (800-695-2241; fax: 615-964-3518).
[196] Jean Pennington, *Food Values*, 15th edition (Perennial Library Press, 1989), quoted in Earthsave Newsletter.
[197] "Is Our Fish Fit to Eat?", *Consumer Reports,* Feb., 1992.
[198] Ibid.
[199] Michael Jacobson et al., *Safe Food: Eating Wisely in a Risky World* (Living Planet Press, 1991) 118.

Chapter 5: Tsa'ar Ba'alei Chaim

[200] Al-Hafiz B.A. Masri, *Islamic Concern for Animals* (The Athene Trust, 1987), 2-4.
[201] Mary Midgley, *Animals and Why They Matter* (University of Georgia Press, 1984).

---

[202] Ibid., see Chapter 7, "Women, Animals and Other Awkward Cases."
[203] Christopher Chapple, "Noninjury to Animals: Jain and Buddhist Perspectives," *Animal Sacrifices: Religious Perspectives on the Use of Animals in Science,* ed. by Tom Regan (Temple University Press, 1986), 219.
[204] Henry Beston, *The Outermost House* (Penguin,1976), 25.
[205] Mary Midgley, *Beast and Man: The Roots of Human Nature* (Cornell University Press, 1978) 39.
[206] Ibid., 37.
[207] Unfortunately, many so-called "nature" documentaries are "canned" or arranged videos, particularly those that persistently offer views of violent animal behavior for audience thrills.
[208] Leon Kass, *The Hungry Soul* (The Free Press, 1994), 45.
[209] Ibid.
[210] Ibid., 48.
[211] Phyllis Trible, 'Eve and Adam: Genesis 2-3 Reread," Carol Christ and Judith Plaskow, *Womanspirit Rising* (Harper & Row, 1979), 76.
[212] Kass, 60.
[213] Midgley, 112.
[214] Ibid.
[215] Ibid., 21
[216] Ibid., 27.
[217] FARM (Farm Animal Reform Movement) Newsletter, Summer/Fall 1997
[218] Andrew Linzey, *Christianity and The Rights of Animals* (Crossroad, 1987) 8. Oxford University supports a chair sponsored by IFAW, the International Fund for Animal Welfare.
[219] Kass, 206.
[220] Rabbi A. Kook, "A Vision of Vegetarianism and Peace," *Rabbis and Vegetarianism,* 2.
[221] Karen Davis, *Prisoned Chickens, Poisoned Eggs* (Book Publishing Co., 1996), 54.
[222] Rabbi Everett Gendler, "The Life of His Beast," *Tree of Life* (A.S. Barnes & Co., 1977) 42.
[223] Davis, 48.
[224] Colin Tudge, *The Engineer in the Garden* (Hill & Wang, 1993), 236.
[225] Davis, 57.
[226] Ibid., 77.
[227] Ibid., 76-77.

[228] Ibid., 62-64.
[229] Ibid., 60-61.
[230] Rabbi Everett Gendler, "The Life of His Beast," 46.
[231] Hans Jonas, "Philosophical Reflections on Human Experimentation," *Experimentation With Human Subjects*, ed. by Paul A. Freund, (Braziller, 1969) 28.
[232] Davis, 114.
[233] Ibid.
[234] Ibid., 115-120.
[235] Ibid., 118.
[236] Judy Oppenheimer, "A Cutthroat Business," *The Baltimore Jewish Times*, June 2, 1995, 46. The article describes the working day of a shochet at Empire, where as many as 8,000 chickens arrive each day and are transformed into packages of food three hours later. Automation, speed and the mass numbers of daily slaughtering prompts her to ask,"What does it do to a person to kill like that?"
[237] Andrew Nicholson, M.D. "Chicken Is Not a Health Food," *Good Medicine*, Autumun, 1994, p. 14.
[238] *Consumer Reports*, March, 1998, 13-18.
[239] Elijah Judah Schochet, *Animal Life In the Jewish Tradition* (KTAV, 1984), 254-256.
[240] Jonas, 99-107.
[241] Kass, 35.
[242] Ibid., 38.
[243] Ibid.,41.
[244] For a review of Jonas' book, see Roberta Kalechofsky, *Autobiography of A Revolutionary* (Micah Publications, 1991), 160-170.
[245] Kass, 34.
[246] Linzey, 9.
[247] W.E.H. Lecky wrote of this commandment, "That tenderness to animals which is one of the most beautiful features in the Old Testament (sic) writings, shows itself, among other ways, in the command not to muzzle the ox that treads out the corn, nor to yoke together the ox and the ass." (Because of the unequal strength of the ox and the ass, the ass would be at a great disadvantage.) W.E.H. Lecky, *A History of European Morals* (Arno Press, 1975).
[248] Noah J. Cohen, *Tsa'ar Ba'ale Hayim: The Prevention of Cruelty to Animals: Its Bases, Development and Legislation in Hebrew Literature* (Feldheim, 1976), 1.

[249] James Gaffney, "The Relevance of Animal Experimentation to Roman Catholic Methodology," Temple Sacrifices: *Religious Perspectives on the Use of Animals in Science*, ed. Tom Regan (Temple University Press, 1986), 151.
[250] *Guide for the Perplexed*, 456.
[251] Gendler, 44.
[252] Ibid., 45.
[253]William E.H. Lecky, *History of European Morals* (Arno Press, 1975), vol. 2, 167.
[254] See Roberta Kalechofsky, "Jewish Law and Tradition on Animal Rights," *Judaism and Animal Rights* (Micah Publications, 1992), 46-55.
[255] *Yerushalmi Ketuvot* 4:8; *Yevamot* 15:3.
[256] *Shulchan Aruch, Orach Chayim* 167:6; *Berachot* 40a.
[257] Much of this material is based on Richard Schwartz, *Judaism and Animal Issues*, A Green Mitzvah Booklet (Micah Publications, 1993).
[258] Rabbi Solomon Ganzfried, *Code of Jewish Law* (Hebrew Publishing Co., 1961), Book 4, chapt. 191, 84.
[259] Rabbi Samson Raphael Hirsch, *Horeb*, Dayan Dr. I. Grunfeld, trans. (Soncino Press, 1962) vol 2., 293.
[260] Ibid., 293.
[261] Masri, 28.
[262] Kilayim 8:2,3; Baba Metzia 90b.
[263] *Shulchan Aruch*, Yorah De'ah 297:2
[264] Maimonides, *Guide for the Perplexed*, 3:48.
[265] Schochet, 216.
[266] Lewis Mumford, *The Myth of the Machine* (Harcourt, Brace & Jovanovich, 1960) 61.
[267] John Vyvyan, *The Dark Face of Science* (Micah Publications, 1989) 159.
[268] Dr. Robert White has already performed the experiment of keeping a primate's head alive on top of a computer. For a description of his work and that of similar experiments, see Chet Fleming, *If We Can Keep A Severed Head Alive...* (Polinym Press, 1987).
[269] John Robbins, *Diet For A New America* (Stillpoint, 1987), 44.
[270] Rabbi Everett Gendler, "The Universal Chorus," *Rabbis and Vegetarianism--An Evolving Tradition* (Micah Publications, 1995), 18-22.

Chapter 6: Bal Tashchit

[271] Quotations are from *To Till and To Tend:: A Guide to Jewish Environmental Study and Action* (The Coalition on The Environment and Jewish Life, or COEJL), 13.
[272] *Avot de Rabbi Nathan,* 31b.
[273] Wendell Berry, *The Gift Of the Good Land* (North Point Press, 1981).
[274] Rabbi Ismar Schorsch, "Tending to Our Cosmic Oasis," *To Till and To Tend:* 21.
[275] *To Till and To Tend: A Guide to Jewish Environmental Study and Action* (COEJL), 9.
[276] C. David Coats, *Old MacDonald's Factory Farm* (Continuum, 1989), 137.
[277] Ibid.
[278] Ibid.
[279] Ibid., 137-138.
[280] Ibid., 138.
[281] David Stipp, "Science Says the Heat Is On," *Fortune*, Dec. 8, 1997, p. 128.
[282] AntiSlavery Reporter, Dec., 1997.
[283] Marybeth Abrams-McHenry, "E-Coli:New Concerns," *Vegetarian Voice*, vol 22, number 2, Summer, 1997.
[284] Coats, 139.
[285] John Robbins, *Diet For A New America* (Stillpoint, 1987).
[286] Coats, 129.
[287] Ibid, 129-130.
[288] Jeremy Rifkin, *Beyond Beef: The Rise and Fall of Cattle Culture* (Dutton, 1992), 201.
[289] Robert Kaplan, "The Coming Anarchy," *The Atlantic Monthly*, February, 1994, p. 44-76.
[290] Ibid., 185-186.
[291] Susan Steingraber, *Living Downstream An Ecologist Looks at Cancer and The Environmen*t (Addison-Wesley, 1997)168.
[292] Ibid., 168-169.
[293] Ibid., 168.
[294] For a more detailed analysis of how xenoestrogens work, see Steingraber, 248-250.
[295] Ibid., 109-110.
[296] From a report by Richard Schwartz, based on information from the Environmental Research Foundations' Rachels' Environmental and Health Weekly Issues.

---

[297] Richard Schwartz, "Global Warming," (Internet article)
[298] For a longer analysis, see Roberta Kalechofsky, "The Seed of Peace: Vegetarianism in Prophetic Writing," *Autobiography of A Revolutionary* (Micah Publications,1991) 171.

Chapter 7: Tzeddakah

[299] Paul Starr, *The Social Transformation of American Medicine* (Basic Books, 1982), 371.
[300] Jeremy Rifkin, *Beyond Beef* (Dutton, 1992), 55-56.
[301] Patricia Hausman, *Jack Spratt's Legacy: The Science and Politics of Fat and Cholesterol* (Richard Marek Pub. Co., 1981).
[302] John Robbins, *Diet For A New America* (Stillpoint, 1987), 171.
[303] Ibid., 173.
[304] Harriet Schliefer, "Images of Death and Life: Food Animal Production and The Vegetarian Option," Singer, ed. *In Defense of Animals* (Perrenial Library, 1986) 68.
[305] Rifkin, 201.
[306] Steingraber, 150.
[307] Ibid., 3.
[308] William Shurtleff and Akiko Aoyagi, *The Book of Miso: Food For Mankind,* (Ballantine Books, 1976), 3.
[309] W.W. Norton, 1996.
[310] Shurtleff and Aoyagi, 5-6.
[311] Ibid., 6.
[312] Ibid.
[313] Ibid., 7-9.
[314] Louise Hagler, *Soyfoods Cookery* (Book Publishing Company, 1996), 14.
[315] Shurtleff and Aoyagi, 11.
[316] Yehuda Feliks, *Nature and Man In the Bible: Chapters in Biblical Ecology* (Soncino Press, 1981), 170.

Chapter 8: Klal Israel

[317] Louis A. Berman, *Vegetarianism & the Jewish Tradition* (Ktav, 1982), 70.
[318] A Christian "heretical" sect which occupied much of what is now called southern France, and the territory from the Pyrennees to the Balkans. They were powerful for about two hundred years, and were destroyed in a crusade

preached against them in 1215. The Inquisition was created for the purpose of destroying them, and obviously outlived them. Everyone knows the subsequent history of the Inquisition. Few know the history of the Cathars, or the origin of the Inquisition in its struggle with the Cathars.

[319] Rabbi Arthur Hertzberg, "The Jewish Declaration on Nature," Address on the 25th anniversary of World Wildlife Fund.

[320] *The Jerusalem Report,* Feb. 19, 1998, p.52

[321] *A Facsimile of The First Jewish Cookbook in English Published in 1846: The Jewish Manual, or Practical Information in Jewish and Modern Cookery with a Collection of Valuable Recipes & Hints Relating to the Toilette, edited By A Lady* (Nightingale Books, 1983) 8.

[322] For a vegetarian cookbook adapted to the Jewish holidays, see *The Jewish Vegetarian Year Cookbook* by Roberta Kalechofsky and Rosa Rasiel (Micah Publications, 1997). Also *Vegetarianism and The Jewish Holidays,* by Roberta Kalechofsky (Micah Publications, 1993).

[323] Adapted from "Mixed Marriages: When Only One of You Is A Vegetarian," by Richard Schwartz.

[324] It is difficult to find scientific evaluation of the relationship between diet and the *cure* of disease. One reason for this is that the study of the relationship between diet and the cure of specific diseases is in its infancy. Another reason is that there has been little interest in the subject by traditional doctors. For one discussion of this problem, see Michael Lerner, *Choices in Healing.*

[325] Melina, Davis & Harrison, *Becoming a Vegetarian: The Complete Guide to Adopting a Healthy Vegetarian Diet* (Book Publishing Co.,1995) 3.

[326] Ibid.

[327] Kalechofsky & Rasiel, *The Jewish Vegetarian Year Cookbook* (Micah Publications, 1997).

Index

Index

Index

Index

Index